Accounting and Financial Analysis in the Hospitality Industry

Accounting and Financial Analysis in the Hospitality Industry

JONATHAN A. HALES

ELSEVIER
BUTTERWORTH
HEINEMANN

AMSTERDAM • BOSTON • HEIDELBERG • LONDON
NEW YORK • OXFORD • PARIS • SAN DIEGO
SAN FRANCISCO • SINGAPORE • SYDNEY • TOKYO

Elsevier Butterworth–Heinemann
30 Corporate Drive, Suite 400, Burlington, MA 01803, USA
Linacre House, Jordan Hill, Oxford OX2 8DP, UK

Front Cover Photo Credits L–R
Four Seasons Resort, Scottsdale, AZ
Orlando World Center Marriott Resort and Conference Center, Orlando, FL
Otesaga Hotel, Cooperstown, NY
Back Cover Photo Credit
WeKoPa Golf Club in Fort McDowell, Fountain Hills, AZ

 Recognizing the importance of preserving what has been written, Elsevier prints its books on acid-free paper whenever possible.

Library of Congress Cataloging-in-Publication Data
Hales, Jon.
    Accounting and financial analysis in the accounting industry / Jon Hales.
        p. cm.
    Includes index.
    ISBN 0-7506-7896-8
    1. Hospitality industry—Accounting.   I. Title.
    HF5686.H75H33 2005
    657'.837—dc22

                                                    2005009790

British Library Cataloguing-in-Publication Data
A catalogue record for this book is available from the British Library.

ISBN: 0-7506-7896-8

For information on all Elsevier Butterworth–Heinemann publications
visit our Web site at www.books.elsevier.com

Printed in the United States of America
05 06 07 08 09 10   10 9 8 7 6 5 4 3 2 1

Contents

Preface ix

Foreword xiii

Chapter 1

Introduction to Numbers, Accounting, and Financial Analysis   1

Numbers: The Lifeblood of Business   3

Career Success Model   6

The Three Main Financial Statements   9

Revenues: The Beginning of Financial Performance   15

Profit: The Ultimate Measure of Financial Performance   20

Summary   23

Hospitality Manager Takeaways   24

Key Terms   24

Formulas   25

Review Questions   26

Chapter 2

Foundations of Financial Analysis   27

Fundamental Methods of Financial Analysis   28

Comparing Numbers to Give Them Meaning   30

Measuring Change to Explain Performance   32

Using Percentages in Financial Analysis   34

Four Types of Percentages Used in Financial Analysis   35

Trends in Financial Analysis   39

Summary   41

Hospitality Manager Takeaways   42

Key Terms   42

Formulas   43

Review Questions   43

Problems   43

Chapter 3

Accounting Department Organization and Operations 47

Organization Charts 48

Accounting Operations in Full-Service Hotels 57

Accounting Operations in Restaurants and Smaller Hotels 62

Summary 64

Hospitality Manager Takeaways 65

Key Terms 65

Review Questions 66

Chapter 4

The Profit and Loss (P&L) Statement 67

Hotel Consolidated P&L Statements 69

Formats for a Consolidated P&L 75

Department P&L Statements 82

Summary 84

Hospitality Manager Takeaways 85

Key Terms 86

Review Questions 87

Chapter 5

The Balance Sheet (A&L) and Statement of Cash Flow 89

The Balance Sheet or Asset and Liability (A&L) Statement 90

Working Relationships between the Balance Sheet and the P&L Statement . . 99

The Statement of Cash Flow 101

Summary 107

Hospitality Manager Takeaways 108

Key Terms 108

Review Questions 109

Chapter 6

Hotel Management Reports 111

Internal Hotel Management Reports 112

Daily Reports 113

Weekly Internal Management Reports 125

Monthly Internal Management Reports 127

Summary 131

Hospitality Manager Takeaways   132

Key Terms   132

Review Questions   133

Chapter 7

Revenue Management   135

REVPAR: Revenue per Available Room   136

Rate Structures and Market Segments   141

Revenue Management Systems   143

Selling Strategies   147

Summary   149

Hospitality Manager Takeaways   150

Key Terms   150

Review Questions   151

Chapter 8

Comparison Reports and Financial Analysis   153

Profitability: The Best Measure of Financial Performance   154

Review of Chapter 2: Foundations of Financial Analysis   159

Variation Analysis   161

STAR Market Report   167

Summary   170

Hospitality Manager Takeaways   170

Key Terms   171

Review Questions   171

Chapter 9

Forecasting: A Very Important Management Tool   173

Forecasting Fundamentals   175

Types and Uses of Forecasts   176

Revenue Forecasting   182

Wage Forecasting and Scheduling   184

Summary   185

Hospitality Manager Takeaways   186

Key Terms   186

Review Questions   187

Problems   187

Chapter 10

Budgets **229**

The Use of Budgets in Business Operations 231

Annual Operating Budgets 234

Formulas and Steps in Preparing a Budget 236

Capital Expenditure Budgets 240

Summary 243

Hospitality Manager Takeaways 243

Key Terms 244

Review Questions 244

Problems 245

Chapter 11

Corporate Annual Reports **249**

The Purpose of Corporate Annual Reports 251

The Message to Shareholders 254

The Content of the Corporate Annual Report 257

Financial Results for the Year 261

Summary 262

Hospitality Manager Takeaways 263

Key Terms 263

Review Questions 264

Chapter 12

Personal Financial Literacy **265**

Personal Financial Literacy 266

Managing Personal Finances 271

Evaluating Assets and Sources of Income 274

Summary 276

Hospitality Manager Takeaways 277

Key Terms 277

Review Questions 278

Glossary 279

Index 287

Preface

Most hospitality programs in the United States require several accounting classes as part of their curriculum. Although these accounting classes are important and provide the knowledge and skills that every hospitality manager will need, students are generally afraid of, do not like, have high anxiety levels about, and do not do well in these classes. Often the result is that they just try to survive the class and do not try to understand and learn the accounting and finance concepts presented in the class that will help them in their hospitality careers.

This textbook seeks to reduce students' fears and anxieties by focusing on the fundamentals of using numbers in operating a business. This means focusing on the essential fundamentals that are easier to understand and apply. It means teaching students to use numbers in hospitality operations. It does not include the accounting details and complexity that are used by Directors of Finance and CPAs. The focus is on using financial reports in operating the departments, not on preparing accounting reports.

Fundamental accounting concepts and methods of financial analysis are important skills for graduating students to understand and possess as they begin their hospitality careers. They should have a solid foundation of accounting knowledge and fundamentals that will enable them to quickly learn, understand, and apply the accounting policies and procedures of the hospitality company that they work for. This understanding often means the difference between steady career advancement and no advancement at all.

Hospitality students need to have a fundamental understanding of using numbers in operating their departments and analyzing their financial statements. This textbook is written to present and focus on the following important goals in teaching hospitality accounting:

1. Presenting students with accounting information that will provide a solid foundation of fundamental accounting concepts and methods of financial analysis.

2. Teaching students to understand numbers and be able to use numbers to help them perform their managerial responsibilities more effectively.

3. Assisting students in understanding that using financial analysis to evaluate business operations involves basic arithmetic and fundamental formulas and need not be complicated and overwhelming.

4. Teaching students to understand that numbers resulting from operations are used as a management tool and a means to measure financial performance.

5. Enabling students to apply accounting concepts and methods of financial analysis in managing their operations and evaluating financial statements.

This textbook was written to provide hospitality students and hospitality managers with a solid foundation of accounting concepts and methods of financial analysis that they will need to use in their jobs in the hospitality industry. The Directors of Finance for several major hotel companies have reviewed a major portion of the material. Their input was instrumental in enabling the material presented in this textbook to be consistent with the actual accounting processes and procedures used in the hospitality industry.

This textbook is written for students who desire to become hospitality operations managers and not Assistant Controllers, Controllers, or Directors of Finance. It is critical that hospitality managers be able to understand numbers and use them in the daily operations of their departments. Accounting fundamentals and accounting applications to operations are the main themes of this book.

Chapters 1 and 2 provide an introduction to accounting and a solid foundation of accounting concepts and methods of financial analysis. The focus is on the fundamentals of using numbers in hospitality operations. Chapter 3 explains the organization and operation of the accounting department in a hotel. This is intended to help hospitality students understand how accounting department operations fit into hotel operations and how they can help hospitality managers operate their departments.

Chapters 4 through 8 discuss the three main financial statements used in financial analysis and hotel management reports that are used as management tools and to measure financial performance. The purpose is to introduce students to the actual use and application of financial reports in the operations of departments within a hotel or restaurant. The focus is to present accounting and financial information that students will need to know and be able to use in managing their departments.

Chapters 9 and 10 emphasize the importance of forecasting and budgeting as a management tool and as a way to measure financial performance. Forecasting revenues and scheduling wages are two important responsibilities of hospitality managers. These chapters focus on the importance of a manger's ability to review current operations and to prepare weekly forecasts that update the budget and reflect current market conditions.

Chapters 11 and 12 are intended to provide students with additional knowledge to broaden their financial skills and understanding. Chapter 12 is intended to encourage students to apply fundamental financial skills to their personal management of money.

The glossary summarizes key terms presented in the text that students should know.

As students read this text and progress through a hospitality accounting course, it is the author's hope and intent that they will be able to learn fundamental accounting concepts and use methods of financial analysis in operating their departments when they start their hospitality careers. By focusing on accounting fundamentals and building on accounting concepts, student fears and anxieties of accounting will be replaced with a solid and useful understanding of accounting that they will be able to use and apply in their hospitality careers.

Jonathan A. Hales

Foreword

The Butterworth-Heinemann Hospitality Management Series covers all aspects of the management of hospitality enterprises from an *applied perspective*. Each book in the series provides an introduction to a separate managerial function such as human resources or accounting, to a distinct management segment in the hospitality industry such as club management, resort management, or casino management, as well as to other topic areas closely related to hospitality management, such as information technology, ethics, or services management.

The books in the series are written for students in two- and four-year hospitality management programs, as well as entry- and mid-level managers in the hospitality industry. They present readers with three essential features they are looking for in textbooks nowadays: these books are affordable, they are high quality, and their applied and to-the-point approach to hospitality management issues appeals to students and instructors alike. The authors in the series are selected because of their expertise and their ability to make complex materials easy to understand.

Accounting and Financial Analysis in the Hospitality Industry by Dr. Jon Hales is the first text in this series. Because of his industry experience (Dr. Hales served as a Controller, Resident Manager, and General Manager at six properties for the Marriott Corporation for 25 years) and his educational experience as a college-level instructor, Dr. Hales knows exactly what students and entry-level managers need to be aware of when it comes to managerial accounting. He also has the educational expertise to convey this knowledge in a very applied and easy-to-understand format, as he teaches this subject every day. This is what you need to know about managerial accounting and what the numbers tell you when you leave school and become a manager!

Students and educators alike will find affordability, relevance and high quality in this and all other texts in the series. As we say in the hospitality industry: welcome and enjoy!

Hubert B. Van Hoof, Ph.D.
Series Editor

Introduction to Numbers, Accounting, and Financial Analysis

Learning Objectives

1. To understand the three most common measurements of a company's success.

2. To recognize how important understanding accounting and finance is to the career of any hospitality manager.

3. To learn about and describe the three fundamental financial statements.

4. To become familiar with fundamental revenue accounting concepts.

5. To understand fundamental profit accounting concepts.

6. To learn the revenue and profit formulas.

Chapter Outline

Numbers: The Lifeblood of Business

Accounting Concept
Customers, Associates, and Profitability

Career Success Model

Technical Skills
Management/Leadership Skills
Financial Skills
Marketing Skills
High-Performance Organizations

The Three Main Financial Statements

Profit and Loss Statement
Balance Sheet
Statement of Cash Flows

Revenues: The Beginning of Financial Performance

    Formulas

    Market Segments

    The Customer

Profit: The Ultimate Measure of Financial Performance

    Department Profit

    House Profit (Marriott) or Gross Operating Profit (Hyatt and Four Seasons)

    Net House Profit or Adjusted Gross Operating Profit

    Profit Before and After Taxes

Summary

Hospitality Manager Takeaways

Key Terms

Formulas

Review Questions

Accounting concepts and methods of financial analysis generally sound intimidating and complicated. Visions of CPAs, financial advisors, tax laws, attorneys, big ugly books, spreadsheets, paperwork nightmares, and migraine headaches regularly accompany any mention of accounting and finance. And this is often the case. However, entry-level hospitality managers need to be able to use accounting concepts and methods of financial analysis to conduct the daily operations of their departments. They need to understand them and be able to effectively apply them to their department operations.

Numbers are also used to measure a company's performance in meeting expected strategies, goals, and objectives. Typically, there are three commonly used measurements of success:

    Customer satisfaction

    Employee satisfaction

    Profitability and cash flow

Performance is measured and defined against these goals with the use of numbers.

This chapter introduces fundamental accounting concepts and explains how numbers are used to apply these accounting concepts to daily operations. It likewise introduces fundamental methods of financial analysis and explains how numbers are used to perform financial analysis. The objective is, first, to understand these fundamental concepts; second, to be comfortable working with them; and, third, to be able to apply them. Subsequent chapters will go into more detail and build on the foundation developed in this chapter.

Numbers: The Lifeblood of Business

Numbers—understanding them and working with them—form the foundation of both accounting concepts and methods of financial analysis. Numbers provide descriptions and measurements that relate to the operations of a business. Let's define a few terms.

Accounting Concept

Accounting refers to the bookkeeping methods involved in making a financial record of business transactions and in the preparation of statements concerning the assets, liabilities, and operating results of a business. A concept is a general understanding, especially one derived from a particular instance or occurrence. These definitions are from Webster's dictionary and not from an accounting book. We combine the two definitions and the resulting definition of accounting concepts is *a general understanding of the bookkeeping methods and financial transactions of a business*.

Financial Analysis: Finance is the management of monetary affairs. Analysis is the separation of an intellectual or substantial whole into its parts for individual study. These definitions are also from Webster's dictionary. We combine the two definitions, and our definition of financial analysis is *the separation of the management of monetary affairs of a business into parts for individual study*.

Fundamental arithmetic is all that is required to use and apply numbers to understand business operations. Two of the most important formulas in financial analysis only require multiplication and subtraction:

$$Revenue = Rate \times Volume$$
$$Profit = Revenues - Expenses$$

Although these two formulas can be applied to many market segments, departments, and volume levels and can become rather detailed, the fact remains they are each calculated with arithmetic and not calculus, trigonometry, or college algebra.

There is a common theme in today's business world about how to measure the success of a company or business. It involves satisfied customers, satisfied employees, and satisfactory profitability. As an example, we can look at one of the largest and most successful companies in the world to examine these concepts.

By two important measurements—market capitalization and recognition—General Electric (GE) is a company we can learn from. In 2003, GE was the largest company in the world in terms of **market capitalization**. The formula for market capitalization is the stock price times the number of shares of stock outstanding. To be the largest capitalized company in the world means that more individuals and institutions are investing in GE than in any other company, which is quite an accomplishment. GE was also the Most Admired Company in the United States from 1997 to 2001 and in 2005 was #2 on the Most Admired Company List according to *Fortune* magazine. Former CEO Jack Welch, in discussing the GE management philosophy in *Jack Welch and the GE Way* by Robert Slater (1999), is quoted as saying:

> We always say that if you had three measurements to live by, they'd be employee satisfaction, customer satisfaction and cash flow. If you've got cash in the till at the end, the rest is all going to work, because if you've got high customer satisfaction, you're going to get a share. If you've got high employee satisfaction you're going to get productivity. And if you've got cash, you know it's all working. (p. 90)

This statement highlights the relationship or balance between three essential ingredients of a successful business: customers, employees, and profitability. These three measurements are interrelated, and problems with one will lead to problems with the others. Numbers are involved in measuring the success of each of these measurements.

Customers, Employees, and Profitability

Customer satisfaction can be measured by percentage of market share, percentage of revenue growth, or the successful introduction of new products and services. All of these measurements use numbers. For example, market share can increase from 7% to 8%. This tells us that customers are buying more of our products, and our sales have now increased from 7% to 8% of the total market. If a company's market share is growing, it means that customers choose to buy its products over those of the competitors because of quality, value, or both. That is obviously a good thing. If our market share is declining, that means customers are not buying as many of our products and services, and that is a bad thing. Numbers tell us to what degree our business is improving or declining.

Another way to measure customer satisfaction is with customer satisfaction surveys. This process provides direct customer feedback based on questions asked in a survey. A typical question is "Are you willing to return?" The hotel will have a historical score that shows the performance for the previous year and will set a new goal for the next year of operations. Each time the current score is reported—generally monthly—it is compared with the actual score from the previous year to see if the hotel is improving. It is also compared to the goal for the current year to see if the goal will be missed, met, or exceeded.

Employee satisfaction is measured in the same way. Each hotel will have its score from the previous year for the questions asked, as well as a goal for the year. The current score on the survey is compared to these benchmark scores, and then evaluations are made if there has been progress toward reaching the goal. For example, the most recent employee satisfaction score of 85% favorable would be compared to last year's 83% and this year's goal of 84%. The 85% current score is a 2-point improvement over last year and is 1 point above this year's goal. In this example, the actual score of 85% beat both last year's actual and this year's goal. Numbers define the relationship between the scores and determine if performance is declining, staying the same, or improving.

Profit or profitability is the third measure. Is a company making or losing money? **The equation for profitability is revenues minus expenses**. For example, $1,000,000 in revenues minus $750,000 in expenses would result in a $250,000 profit. In addition to being expressed in dollars, profit can also be expressed in terms of percentages. **The equation for profit percentage is profit dollars divided by revenue dollars**. In our example, the profit percentage is 25% ($250,000 profit divided by $1,000,000 in revenues).

Each of these numbers or measures tells us something about the operations of the business. The $250,000 in profit dollars tells us that we have that much money in the bank after recording all the revenues and paying all the expenses. It is a tangible amount. In other words, there is a $250,000 balance in the cash account of the business. The 25% profit percentage tells us the amount of every revenue dollar that is left over as profit. It is a relationship measure. In other words, 25 cents out of every sales dollar represents profits, and 75 cents out of every sales dollar represents expenses. Add the two and you get $1, or 100%.

The best-selling book, *Built to Last, Successful Habits of Visionary Companies* by James E. Collins and Jerry I. Porras (1994), talks about the role of profits in some of the most well-respected companies in the world. Consider this comment:

> Profitability is a necessary condition for existence and a means to more important ends, but it is not the end in itself for many of the visionary companies. Profit is like oxygen, food, water and blood for the body; they are not the point of life, but without them, there is no life. (p. 55)

The authors point out that the visionary companies focus on other elements of their business that reflect their core values, not profits. This focus can be on new product development, risk taking customers, employees, or stretch goals. Because they do this so well, products and services are well received in the marketplace, and sufficient profits result.

These discussions of customer satisfaction, employee satisfaction, and profitability illustrate the role that numbers play in measuring or defining results and achievements. Numbers assign a tangible value to performance and results. Instead of simply saying that revenues are up, numbers enable us to say, for example, revenues are up $100,000 or 8.5%.

This is more specific and helps a business identify and compare its performance from month to month or year to year. These concepts will be discussed in more detail in later chapters.

Career Success Model

Certain skills and abilities are required for any manager to have a successful business career. Stephen R. Covey talks about three of these in his book *The Seven Habits of Highly Effective People* (1989). Covey defines skill as "how to do," knowledge as "what to do," and attitude as "want to do" (p. 47). The use of these three abilities determines how successful a manager can be.

The Career Success Model Figure 1.1 identifies four individual skills and one organizational skill that are helpful in enabling managers to grow and advance with a company. It is important that managers continue to grow and learn, and this includes new areas that will broaden their knowledge and skills.

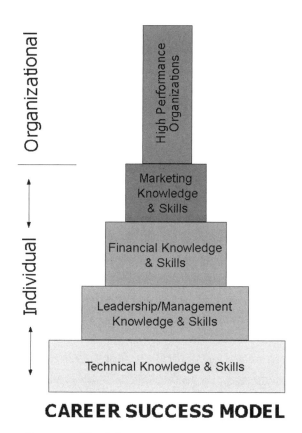

CAREER SUCCESS MODEL

FIGURE 1.1   Career Success Model.

Technical Skills

These are the day-to-day operational knowledge and skills required to get the job done. Entry-level managers in the hospitality industry start out, for example, as Assistant Desk Managers, Assistant Housekeeping Managers, Assistant Restaurant Managers, and so forth. The job title defines what they are expected to know and be able to do to perform all the tasks and responsibilities for operating their department. So they spend the first year learning and doing. That should be their focus—to learn all the technical and operational aspects of their job. This includes knowing and being able to perform the job responsibilities of all the employees that report to them. Assistant Desk Managers will be checking guests in and out, managing room inventories, handling group business, staffing the concierge level, running fronts for the bellman, and so on. Assistant Restaurant Managers will be seating customers, busing tables, and expediting food orders. Understanding these technical aspects of a department's operations is essential to its success and to establishing a solid foundation for personal career growth.

Management/Leadership Skills

The first promotion provides a manager with the opportunity to manage others in getting the job done. The knowledge and skills needed include working with other managers as well as hourly employees. This step involves the progression from managing (we manage things) to leading (we lead people) (Covey). A manager is now paid to get other people to do the job. This includes the typical management responsibilities of planning, organizing, and control, but has now progressed to the leadership responsibilities of motivating, challenging, engaging, supporting, and recognizing employees. The real definition of a leader is the ability to teach and inspire the people he or she works with to do the best job that they are capable of doing.

Leaders also have the responsibility to allocate company resources. This includes allocating time, money, labor, and ideas to the most productive or profitable areas. They do this by listening to employees and customers, then prioritizing projects or job responsibilities, and then supporting them with sufficient resources.

Effective leaders take the time to organize their work and make sure that they are spending as much of their time as possible operating in Covey's Quadrant 2—important but not urgent. Most managers operate in Quadrant 1—important and urgent—which can best be defined as putting out fires and going from one situation to another. By shifting to Quadrant 2, a manager has more time to plan, prioritize, and organize the work to be done. Quadrant 2 is proactive; Quadrant 1 is reactive (Covey, p. 151).

What does this have to do with accounting and finance? Everything! Specifically, the more knowledgeable and comfortable managers are working with numbers and completing the accounting and financial analysis part of their job, the more time they will have to spend with their customers and employees—their top priorities!

Unfortunately, the careers of many managers slow down or stop at this point. They do not have the interest, knowledge, or ability to learn the next skills that will help them to do a better and more complete job, and advance to taking on more and wider levels of responsibility. It is not enough to have technical skills and management/leadership skills when attempting to advance to higher positions within a company. These positions require the knowledge and the ability to understand and use accounting concepts and marketing concepts in the daily operations of the company.

Financial Skills

Financial knowledge and skills begin with understanding numbers, having the ability to communicate or teach what the numbers mean, and finally having the ability to apply what is learned from numbers to improve the operations of the business. Specifically, it is the ability to interpret and discuss the information contained in all types of financial reports with all levels of management. A manager must be comfortable talking about the financial aspects of his or her department with the hotel's Director of Finance and the General Manager. Explaining revenues and expenses, comparing actual results to budgets and forecasts, and making adjustments to improve operations are all important financial skills for any manager to possess.

The rest of this textbook is devoted to developing an understanding of accounting concepts and methods of financial analysis. At this point it is important to understand that any manager must have a fundamental understanding of accounting and finance to grow and advance with a company. Managers do not have to be Certified Public Accountants or Directors of Finance. But they must be able to understand and intelligently discuss their department operations and financial performance with senior management.

Marketing Skills

The next step in the Career Success Model is developing sales and marketing knowledge and skills, which begins by understanding customers and their expectations. What does a hotel or restaurant do to develop and maintain a competitive advantage over its competitors? Why does a customer choose to stay in a particular hotel or eat in a particular restaurant? The marketing department is responsible for identifying customer preferences, expectations, buying patterns, and behavior patterns. These customer descriptions are then classified into different market segments. A hotel or restaurant chooses the market segments where it wants to and can successfully compete.

Examples of major hotel market segments are Transient, Group, and Contract. The transient market segment includes concierge customers at the higher end of room rates, then progressively lower market rate segments of regular, corporate, special corporate, and finally discounts. The discount market segment can further be separated into government and military, American Association of Retired People (AARP), the travel industry, and special promotions like weekend or super saver rates. Examples of the major restaurant market segments are fine dining, casual dining, and fast food.

Each of these market segments is defined by specific customer expectations and behavior patterns. For a manager to continue to advance, she or he must understand the marketing of the hotel or restaurant. What are the strengths and competitive advantages of a property? What are the expectations and preferences of customers? A manager must be able to discuss customers with the Director of Sales or Marketing and understand the marketing plan and positioning of the hotel or restaurant.

High-Performance Organizations

When a manager is knowledgeable and comfortable with these four individual skills—technical, management and leadership, financial, and marketing—then he or she has the potential to be a part of a high-performance organization. A manager with strong individual skills and knowledge and with a positive and proactive attitude can then create or be a part of an organization that not only meets but exceeds the expectations and goals it has established. This should be an important career goal.

The ultimate goal of any department within a hotel or restaurant is to achieve outstanding performance and results. This requires a team effort by all involved in the operation. The greater the degree of knowledge and skill in these four areas, the greater the contribution a manager can make to the performance of his or her team or department. Only when a manager can translate excellence of individual performance into excellence of team performance can the manager truly excel and achieve excellence.

The Career Success Model outlines the knowledge, skills, and abilities that are required to be successful in business and to advance to senior management positions. The goal of this textbook is to provide students with the accounting and financial knowledge, skills, and abilities necessary to be successful in the careers that they choose.

The Three Main Financial Statements

It is important for any business manager to be aware of and understand the financial statements that are used in evaluating the performance of a business. These financial statements are applied in many different ways in describing and evaluating the operations and financial strength of a business. Each of these financial statements or reports measures a specific aspect of the operation of a business. They are introduced here and explained in more detail in a future chapter.

Profit and Loss Statement

The **Profit and Loss (P&L) Statement** measures the operating success and profitability of a business. It is also known as the Income Statement. This is the main financial report that describes and measures the profitability of the daily operations of a business. Key characteristics of the P&L Statement are as follows:

1. It covers a specific time period, for example, monthly, quarterly, or annually.

2. It reports the actual financial results for a business for the specific time period.

3. It compares the actual performance to other measures such as budget, the previous year, previous months, or previous periods.

4. It includes a summary or consolidated P&L statement and supporting department P&L Statements.

   a. Consolidated P&L Statements summarize revenues and expenses by departments.

   b. Department P&L Statements report in detail revenues, expenses, and profits for specific departments.

5. A new P&L Statement is started each month or period and records information for the current month and year-to-date (YTD).

6. Managers are expected to analyze or critique their monthly P&L Statements to explain variations from the budget or from the previous year, both positive and negative.

The P&L Statement is the most important financial report for a manager to understand and work with on a daily basis. This is because managers work with and can affect revenues or they can control most of the costs and expenses. Their daily activities in operating the business produce the numbers reported on the P&L. Consequently, a manager who knows and understands the P&L will provide accurate and timely information that is used in preparing the P&L Statement and that gives it credibility. It will be an accurate report that measures the financial profitability of a business. A manager who does not understand the P&L Statement might omit important information, provide the wrong information, or miss deadlines that prevent information that should be reported from being included in the proper time frame.

This textbook spends most of its content on explaining the P&L Statement and discussing how it is used as a management tool to measure financial performance. It is also important to understand how the information on the P&L Statement relates to the other key financial statements or reports. Exhibit 1.1 is an example of a Consolidated P&L.

EXHIBIT 1.1

CONSOLIDATED P&L STATEMENT

The ABC Company
December 31, 2003

	Current Period			Year to Date		
	Actual	Budget	Last Year	Actual	Budget	Last Year
Rooms Sales						
Restaurant Sales						
Catering Sales						
Total Sales						
Rooms Profit						
Restaurant Profit						
Catering Profit						
Total Department Profits						
General and Administrative (G&A) Expense						
Repairs and Maintenance (R&M) Expense						
Utilities						
Sales and Marketing						
Total Expense Center Costs						
House Profit or Gross Operating Profit						
Fixed Expenses						
Net House Profit or Adjusted Gross Operating Profit						

Balance Sheet

The **Balance Sheet** measures the value or worth of a business. It is also known as the Asset and Liability (A&L) Statement. This is the main financial report that measures what a company is worth. Key characteristics of the Balance Sheet are as follows:

1. It measures the value or worth of a company at a specific point in time. For example, the Balance Sheet for December 31, 2003, is a snapshot of accounts at that specific point in time and identifies what a company owns (assets), what it owes (liabilities), and how it is owned (owner equity).

2. The fundamental account equation describes the A&L:

$$Assets = Liabilities + Owner\ Equity$$

3. It is made up of accounts organized by asset, liability, or owner equity.

4. These accounts are divided into current accounts (under one-year obligations), also referred to as working capital, and long-term accounts (over one-year obligations), which are referred to as capitalization.

5. Each account has a beginning balance, monthly activity, and an ending balance.

6. Unlike the P&L Statement, managers are not expected to provide critiques of monthly balance sheet activity. This is done by the accounting department.

7. Accounting managers balance monthly the accounts of a balance sheet.

It is important for managers to understand the Balance Sheet because (1) they use the current asset and liability accounts (**working capital**) in the daily operations of their business, and (2) it shows how the company is **capitalized**—with long-term debt, paid-in capital, or both. They are expected to efficiently use the assets of a business to operate it profitability. Exhibit 1.2 is an example of a Balance Sheet.

EXHIBIT 1.2

BALANCE SHEET

The ABC Company
December 31, 2003

Assets	Liabilities
Cash	Accounts Payable
Accounts Receivable	Taxes Payable
	Accrued Liabilities
Inventory	Total Current Liabilities
Prepaid Expenses	
Total Current Assets	Bank Loan
Property	Equipment Loan
Plant	Total Long-Term Liabilities
Equipment	
Total Long-Term Assets	TOTAL LIABILITIES
TOTAL ASSETS	Owner Equity
	Paid-In Capital
	Common Stock
	Retained Earnings
	TOTAL OWNER EQUITY

Statement of Cash Flows

The **Statement of Cash Flows** measures the liquidity and the flow of cash of a business. Specifically, it is the activity of the cash account of a business. Sales are recorded as cash inflows through point of sale systems (cash registers) and expenses are recorded as cash outflows through accounts payable or electronic transfers. It is important for a manager to know how much cash is available in the company's cash account to pay expenses and to plan for future operating obligations. If a business does not have sufficient cash in its cash bank account, it will not be able to pay expenses. It is an important responsibility of any manager to understand the business's working capital accounts and to be able to use them efficiently and effectively.

The increases and decreases in account balances of balance sheet accounts also affect cash flow. Referred to as the Source and Use of Funds Statement, this report describes how cash flows in and out of the different accounts in the Balance Sheet. This also reflects the cash strength or liquidity of a business. Liquidity is the ability of a business to pay its short-term obligations and the amount it has in current assets, specifically cash and cash equivalents.

It is important for every manager to understand that a business can be profitable from month to month and still go out of business. This is because these businesses are not effectively managing their cash. They simply do not have enough money in their cash account to pay expenses; therefore, they go out of business even though they show profits on their P&L Statement and have a fairly good balance sheet. If you cannot pay your expenses, you cannot stay in business. Therefore, understanding the basics of managing cash flow is critical to the success of both managers and a business.

Key characteristics of the Statement of Cash Flows are as follows:

1. It involves the cash account of the Balance Sheet.

2. It has beginning and ending balances.

3. It shows how money is used in the daily operations of the business.

4. It measures liquidity.

5. It is a fundamental component of working capital.

6. It reflects the increases and decreases in Balance Sheet accounts.

There are three classifications of cash flow activities:

1. Operating activities of the daily operations of a business that produce sales.

2. Financing activities that involve raising and spending cash. This is also referred to as capitalization.

3. Investing activities that involve investing cash in other financial options.

See Exhibit 1.3.

EXHIBIT 1.3

STATEMENT OF CASH FLOWS

ABC Company
December 31, 2003

Net Income from Operations

Plus Sources of Funds
   Decreases in Assets
   Increases in Liabilities
   Increases in Owner Equity
Minus Uses of Funds
   Increases in Assets
   Decreases in Liabilities
   Decreases in Owner Equity
Total Sources and Uses of Funds from Operations
Total Sources and Uses of Funds from Investments
Total Sources and Uses of Funds from Financing

TOTAL SOURCES AND USES OF FUNDS

JW Marriott Desert Ridge Resort & Spa

This is a view of the resort's pool complex and Wildfire golf course. This 950-room convention/resort hotel includes 200,000 square feet of meeting space, 10 restaurants and lounge outlets, a 28,000-square foot spa, and two 18-hole golf courses. The resort includes 22 departments, 1,200 employees, and 104 managers. There are nine members of the executive committee/leadership team. Consider the complexity of managing this resort with the additional amenities and services that it provides. Financial reports are important to the successful operation of this convention hotel/resort.

The Revive Spa at Desert Ridge is one of the many profit centers of this resort. It includes 41 treatment rooms, group workout rooms, and a food and beverage outlet occupying 28,000 square feet. It is one of the largest resort spas in the United States.

Revenues: The Beginning of Financial Performance

One of the fundamental business concepts is that a company is in business to make money. The company produces products or services and exchanges them with customers for an agreed-upon price. The assumption is that the business will be in operation for many years, continually offering not only the existing products and services but new ones as well. This process generates **revenues** or sales and involves the following actions:

- The company receives money from customers for products or services.

- Money or method of payment can include cash, credit cards, debit cards, electronic transfers, personal checks, traveler's checks, or company checks.

- The sales transaction is recorded through a **point-of-sale (POS)** system previously referred to as cash registers and now referred to as computer terminals and systems. This completes the sales transaction.

- The method of payment is balanced to the amount of product purchased or type of service experienced.

Revenues are the first step of financial analysis because they start the cash flow process of a company. Revenues result in cash increasing or flowing into the company's cash account. The next step is paying all expenses associated with producing the product or service the company offers. Paying expenses result in cash decreasing or flowing out of a cash bank account through accounts payable, payroll disbursements, or other disbursements. Any remaining amount is referred to as profit.

Revenues are also recorded on the period, monthly, quarterly, or annual P&L Statements. The P&L is the financial report that lists revenues, expenses, and profits in a logical and orderly format. Chapter 4 discusses the P&L Statement in more detail.

In the chapter introduction, we discussed two important formulas. We will now add a third important formula. Each involves revenue. The first formula calculates revenue and the formula is **Rate × Volume = Revenue**. The second formula calculates profit and the formula is **Revenue − Expenses = Profit**. The third formula measures revenue performance and is called **REVPAR**. REVPAR can be calculated two ways. The formulas are

Total Room Revenues / Total Available Rooms or **Average Rate × Occupancy Percentage**. Let's learn more about these important formulas.

Formulas

Rate × Volume = Revenue

All revenues for a business are the result of the number of customers buying a product or service. This is combined with how much they pay for that product or service to calculate revenues or sales. For example:

Room Revenues	Rooms Sold × Room Rates
Restaurant Revenues	Customers Served × Menu Prices
Golf Revenues	Player Rounds × Greens Fees
Spa Revenues	Treatments × Treatment Prices
Gift Shop	Merchandise Sold × Price

Volume is defined as the number of units sold, served, received, or bought by customers during a specific time frame. Rooms sold are generally recorded daily. Restaurant customers are generally recorded by meal period: breakfast, lunch, and dinner. Each one of these transactions has a price or rate associated with it. This is called a rate structure, price list, or menu. For example, rooms sold might be divided into the transient market segment and the group market segment. Each would have a room rate associated with it: Transient rate = $99; Group rate = $85. Golf would have a daily price list per player: Greens fees = $50 with cart, $36 without cart; Twilight special rate = $25. Restaurants have menus listing the items available and their price. Customers in a restaurant choose what they want to eat and how much they are willing to pay for it.

To calculate any of the three revenue variables, we just need to know two variables and apply the appropriate formula. The following is an example for calculating room revenue:

Rate × Volume = Room Revenue or $99 × 150 Rooms Sold = $14,850 Room Revenue
Room Revenue / Volume = Rate or $14,850 Room Revenue / 150 Rooms Sold
= $99 Average Rate
Revenue / Rate = Volume or $14,850 Room Revenue / $99 = 150 Rooms Sold

Following is an example for restaurant revenue:

Rate × Volume = Restaurant Revenue or $8 Average Check × 75 Customers
= $600 Restaurant Revenue
Restaurant Revenue / Volume = Rate or $600 / 75 = $8 Average Check
Restaurant Revenue / Rate = Volume or $600 / $8 = 75 Customers

The POS system records all of this information and produces two types of financial reports. First, it reports financial performance in daily revenue reports. Second, it provides management with reports that are used as management tools to operate the business. A hospitality manager will be expected to understand these reports and use them to analyze rates, price lists, or menu prices along with the number of customers served. These managers are expected to understand their daily operations, to identify how successful or profitable they are, and to determine how to solve problems and improve operations.

When analyzing revenues, it is important to identify where increases or decreases are coming from and what caused any changes. Are there increases in the number of guests or increases in the amount they are spending/paying? In identifying causes, any of the following might apply:

Did lower rates or prices produce higher volumes?

Did an advertising campaign produce higher volumes?

Did new competition lower volumes?

Did a rate increase result in lower volumes?

Revenue – Expense = Profit

All profits for a department, restaurant, or hotel can be calculated with this formula. Although this formula appears quite basic, it is broken down into many different categories that reflect different market segments for sales and specific types of costs or expenses. For example, the Rooms Department profit is calculated by adding Transient, Group, and Contract revenues to identify total room revenue. Then all direct expenses are deducted from total revenue to calculate total room profit. The formula is as follows:

Total Room Revenue minus	$500,000
Wage Expense	$60,000
Benefit Expense	$21,000
Other Operating Expenses	$44,000
Equals Total Room Profit	$375,000

REVPAR: Revenue per Available Room

The most important measurement used to evaluate room revenues is REVPAR, or revenue per available room. The reason it is so important is because it considers both rate and volume in identifying the amount of revenues generated by a hotel. It is only used to evaluate room revenue and is expressed as a dollar rate. For example, suppose REVPAR is $88.43. Two formulas can be used to calculate REVPAR. The first formula is the most accurate, but the second formula will also be very close and it is acceptable to use either one.

17

Total Room Revenue / Total Rooms Available

or

Average Rate × Occupancy Percentage

Let's calculate our REVPAR using the information from our previous revenue example. Room revenue was $14,850 with an average rate of $99 and 150 rooms occupied. We need to include the total number of rooms in our hotel to calculate the occupancy percentage. If we have a 200-room hotel, we can calculate our occupancy percentage by dividing rooms sold by total rooms or 150/200 = 75% occupancy. Now we can calculate our REVPAR:

$99 Average Rate × 75% Occupancy = $74.25 REVPAR

or

$14,850 Room Revenue/200 Total Rooms = $74.25 REVPAR

REVPAR is one of the first and most important measurements used to evaluate financial performance for hotels because it is an indication of how well management is able to increase the average rate and also achieve higher volume and occupancy to maximize revenue. If only one of these measurements is used, it will not be able to determine if a hotel is maximizing room revenues.

For example, if we use occupancy as the main measurement of maximizing room revenue, running a hotel with 99% occupancy but with a $25 average rate is not maximizing room revenue. The hotel is probably selling its rooms too cheap. Likewise, if a hotel has a $175 average rate but is only running a 15% occupancy, it also is not maximizing room revenue. It is probably pricing its rooms too high. If we use occupancy as the most important measure, the hotel in our first example is doing an excellent job and our second hotel is doing a terrible job. If we use average rate as the most important measure, the hotel in our first example is doing a terrible job and our second hotel is doing an excellent job. *REVPAR combines rate and occupancy to more effectively measure management's performance in maximizing revenue!* It shows how well management is able to achieve a high occupancy percentage as well as attain a high average room rate and effectively use both to maximize total room revenues.

Market Segments

REVPAR tells us how the total hotel is doing to maximize total room revenue. To provide more specific information on room revenue maximization, the hotel separates its customers into market segments. Market segments define the customer in terms of expectations, preferences, buying patterns, behavior patterns, and why the customer is traveling. Each market segment has distinctive characteristics. Three of the main market segments used in hotel operations are illustrated next.

Weekday/weekend. Most weekday travel is for business and most weekend travel is for pleasure.

Business/pleasure. People traveling on business generally have their expenses paid for by their employer. People traveling for pleasure are generally with family or friends and pay their own expenses.

Transient, group, and contract. These three primary room market segments identify who is traveling and why the person is traveling.

Transient

The transient segment refers to individual business or pleasure travelers. They can be further segmented by the room rate they are willing to pay. Following is an example of a room rate structure that defines specific market segments and ranges from highest to lowest room rates:

Concierge	$149 room rate
Regular or rack rate	129
Corporate	119
Special corporate	75–110, depending on the number of rooms
Discount	
AARP	95
Government	85
Travel industry	75
Weekend super saver	69

Group

Groups are travelers that include two or more people who stay more than one night. They generally get a discounted rate because they provide greater volume. A hotel will specify what qualifies as a group rate—for example, three or more rooms for one night or two or more rooms for two nights or more. The larger the number of rooms in the group, the lower the room rate. Groups can be business or pleasure travelers and generally involve additional catering and meeting room rental revenue. Market segment examples include the following:

Corporate group	Sports and government
Association group	Other group

Contract

The contract market segment includes a fixed number of rooms sold per night at a fixed room rate for a specific company. The company is charged for this number of rooms each night whether they are occupied or not. The best example of contract rooms is airline crew rooms. American or Delta would contract with a hotel for 25 rooms per night at a room rate of $40. This is for weekday and weekend rooms, year round. Hotels agree to a substantially lower room rate because this company will provide a base amount of business each day of the year. Unless a hotel is selling out with 100% occupancy, a $40 contract room sold is a lot better than an empty room and will generate some incremental revenue.

The Customer

A final thought on revenues. The actual event of checking a customer in or out of a hotel, serving a meal in a restaurant, providing a treatment at a spa, or assigning a tee time at the golf course involves employees talking with the guests and providing them with the product or service they are requesting. How this transaction takes place is extremely important to the success of a business. "Next!" "Checking in?" "Name?" These are hardly gracious or friendly greetings. A friendly greeting, eye contact, personal customer recognition, and a smile all go a long way in making customers feel good about the amount they are paying and the service they are receiving. Although it is important to accurately record the transaction with the customer for the accounting records, it is equally important to do so in a friendly and efficient manner. The POS system will generally take care of all the financial information, leaving the employee more time to talk with the customer and maximize his or her experience. The end result is that the customer wants to come back!

This goes back to our three measurements of a successful business: satisfied customers, satisfied employees, and sufficient cash flow or profitability. Although this textbook focuses on accounting and financial transactions and reports, it is always important to remember that employees and guests are the ones who make the whole cycle work.

Profit: The Ultimate Measure of Financial Performance

Just as revenues provide the starting point for measuring financial performance, profits provide the end result of all the effort and activities in operating a business. This section discusses the different aspects of profits. We will review once again the formula for profits: **Revenue minus expenses equals profits**.

Calculating profits is a simple formula, but it gets more detailed as you apply it to the different departments involved in operating a large business such as a hotel. Profits are what are left over after recording all revenues and then paying all expenses associated with generating those revenues. Just as there are different types of revenues, there are different types of expenses and different levels of profits. We will discuss several of the important profits next.

Department Profit

Department operations are the foundation to operating any business. Each department separates the business into different and distinct operations, and the revenues and expenses involved in operating those departments are shown on the Department P&L Statement. These departments are called revenue centers or profits centers. The largest profit departments in a hotel are rooms, restaurants, beverages, and banquets. The basic profit formula—revenue minus expenses—can be applied, but with more detail:

Rooms Department
  Transient, Group, and Contract Revenues
  Less Expenses
    Wages
    Benefits
    Other Operating Expenses
  Equals Rooms Department Profit
Restaurant Department
  Breakfast, Lunch, and Dinner Revenues
  Less Expenses
    Cost of Sales
    Wages
    Benefits
    Other Operating Expenses
  Equals Restaurant Department Profit

All the department profits are added up to total hotel profit.

House Profit (Marriott) or Gross Operating Profit (Hyatt and Four Seasons)

These two profit terms are interchangeable and reflect basically the same profit measurements. Whereas Marriott identifies these profits as House Profit, Hyatt and Four Seasons prefer to call them Gross Operating Profit. They are the next level of profitability after Total Department Profits.

After Total Department Profits have been calculated, other indirect expenses are involved in operating a hotel that also must be paid as part of the daily operations. These departments are called expense centers or overhead because they generate no revenues but incur expenses in support of those departments that do generate revenues. Examples of expense centers are general and administrative (G&A), repairs and maintenance (R&M), utilities or heat, light, and power (HLP), and sales and marketing (S&M). These departments have total department expenses instead of total department revenues.

An example of these department statements follows:

Expenses
   Wages
   Benefits
   Other operating expenses
Total department expense

All of the expenses centers are added up, and this Total Expense Center cost is sub-tracted from Total Department Profits to produce the House Profit or Gross Operating Profit. Our equation for House Profit or Gross Operating Profit becomes

House Profit or Gross Operating Profit =
Total Department Profit – Total Expense Center Costs
or
Total Department Profit – Deductions from Income

House Profit or Gross Operating Profit is used primarily as a measurement of management's ability to maximize revenues, control expenses, and maximize profits. The hotel management team is organized to have influence and control over all the revenues and expenses recognized at the house profit level. Therefore, it is the profit level used to calculate management bonuses.

Net House Profit or Adjusted Gross Operating Profit

There are still expenses associated with operating a hotel that have not been recognized and recorded at the House Profit level. These expenses are generally referred to as fixed expenses, overhead expenses, or investment factors. What distinguishes these types of expenses is that they are fixed and generally have no relationship to the business levels of the hotel. The hotel could be closed or running a low or a high occupancy level, and, regardless, these expenses will involve the same amount and will have to be paid. Because management has no control of or say over these expenses, they are not included in bonus calculations. Examples of these fixed expenses are bank loans, mortgage payments, insurance costs, licenses, permits and fees, and depreciation.

The equation for Net House Profit or Adjusted Gross Operating Profit is as follows:

House Profit or Gross Operating Profit – Fixed Expenses

Net House Profit or Adjusted Gross Operating Profit is a true or accurate measure of the overall profitability of the hotel. It is the amount of profit or money that goes to the bank. All direct and indirect costs and fixed or variable costs have been recognized and paid.

Think of this profit as the profits that are available to be split among the owner, the management company, the franchisee, or any other entity that has an operating stake in the hotel.

Profit before and after Taxes

The final expenses to be recognized and paid are any taxes associated with operating the hotel. It is important to determine who will pay these taxes. It could be the owner or the management company depending on the management contract. This will have an impact on Net House Profit or Adjusted Gross Operating Profit depending on how the payment of taxes is defined. Generally, Profit before Taxes is the same as Net House Profit or Adjusted Gross Operating Profit. After all applicable taxes are paid, the true bottom line profit or Profit after Taxes is determined. We will not spend much time discussing profit before taxes, as a hospitality manager has little involvement with this profit level.

Summary

The use of accounting concepts and methods of financial analysis all begin with using numbers to measure financial performance. Numbers are a language that provides specific and detailed information that explains and measures company operations. Numbers evaluate operational performance, determine value, measure liquidity, and provide management with a detailed tool to manage the business.

Hospitality managers need to develop business financial literacy, which is the ability to understand numbers and to be comfortable working with numbers and using them to analyze business operations. Numbers are a means to an end; in other words, they help to measure and evaluate business operations. It is equally important for career advancement that a hospitality manager is able to understand and use numbers in business operations *and* is able to discuss and explain the operations in financial terms with senior management, including the General Manager and the Director of Finance for the hotel.

Three financial statements are used in evaluating a company or business. The first and most important is the P&L Statement (also called the Income Statement), which measures financial performance. Second is the A&L Statement (also called the Balance Sheet), which measures the net worth of a company or business. Third is the Statement of Cash Flow, which measures the liquidity and cash balances of a company or business.

Three important formulas for hospitality managers to know and use are revenue, profit, and REVPAR. They also need to understand the main profit levels of a hotel: Total Department Profits, House Profit or Gross Operating Profit, and Net House Profit or Adjusted Gross Operating Profit.

Hospitality Manager Takeaways

1. Hospitality accounting is about using numbers and fundamental arithmetic in evaluating and improving operating performance. It is all about fundamentals!

2. The Profit and Loss (P&L) Statement is the most important financial statement that a hospitality manager needs to completely understand and be able to use in operating his or her departments.

3. Understanding and using numbers (accounting and finance) effectively are essential to the career advancement of every hospitality manager.

4. Numbers contained in financial statements are used to measure financial performance and to provide managers with a valuable management tool.

5. Accounting and financial management is all about maximizing revenues, minimizing expenses, maximizing profits, and using numbers to measure and improve financial performance.

Key Terms

Accounting Concepts—The bookkeeping methods and financial transactions used in daily business operations.

Balance Sheet—Measures the value or net worth of a business.

Capitalization—The source and methods of raising money to invest in and start a business.

Financial Analysis—The separation of a business's management of monetary affairs into parts for individual study.

Liquidity—The amount of cash or cash equivalents that a business has to cover its daily operating expenses.

Market Capitalization—A measure of the value of a company that includes the number of shares outstanding held by individual and institutional investors times the current stock price of the company.

Market Segment—Customer groups defined by expectations, preferences, buying patterns, and behavior patterns.

Point-of-Sale (POS) System—The equipment that records the customer transaction, including identifying the method of payment and reporting the type of transaction.

Profit—The amount of revenues left over after all appropriate expenses have been paid.

Profit and Loss (P&L) Statement—Measures the operating success and profitability of a business.

Property—The term for the physical hotel or restaurant.

Revenue—The monetary amount that customers pay to purchase a product or service. It can be in the form of cash, checks, credit cards, accounts securable, or electronic transfer.

Revenue per Available Room (REVPAR)—An important measure of a hotel's ability to generate room revenue by measuring average rate and occupancy percentage.

Statement of Cash Flows—Measures the liquidity and flow of cash of a business.

Working Capital—The amount of money utilized in the daily operations of a business. It includes using current assets and current liabilities as well as cash in producing a product or service.

 # Formulas

Average Rate	Room Revenue / Rooms Sold
Market Capitalization	Number Shares Outstanding × Stock Price
Occupancy Percentage	Rooms Sold / Total Rooms
Revenue	Rate × Volume
Profit Dollars	Revenue – Expenses
Profit Percentage	Profit $ / Revenue $
REVPAR	Total Room Revenue / Total Available Rooms or Average Rate × Occupancy Percentage
Working Capital	Current Assets – Current Liabilities

Review Questions

1. Name and describe the three main financial statements of a business.

2. List the important characteristics for each of these statements, including the important accounts in each.

3. Define REVPAR and explain why it is so important as a revenue measurement for room revenues as well as total hotel financial performance.

4. Name and describe three profit levels in a hotel.

5. What is the difference between capitalization and working capital? What is each used for in business operations?

6. Why is understanding accounting concepts and methods of financial analysis important to a hospitality manager?

7. What are three key measurements of the performance of a business?

8. Why is the P&L Statement the most important for a hospitality manager to understand?

Foundations of Financial Analysis

Learning Objectives

1. To learn about the fundamental methods of financial analysis.

2. To understand the Financial Management Cycle.

3. To understand the importance of comparing numbers to give them meaning. This involves measuring the actual financial performance of a business to previously established measures or goals.

4. To understand the importance of measuring change and what it tells about the financial performance of a business.

5. To learn how percentages are used in financial analysis to measure financial performance.

6. To be able to identify trends and understand their importance to financial analysis.

Chapter Outline

Fundamental Methods of Financial Analysis

    Two Important Tools

    The Financial Management Cycle

Comparing Numbers to Give Them Meaning

    Last Year

    Budget

    Forecast

    Previous Month or Period

    Pro Forma

    Other Goals

Measuring Change to Explain Performance

Using Percentages in Financial Analysis

Calculating Percentages

What Percentages Measure

Four Types of Percentages Used in Financial Analysis

Cost or Expense Percentages

Profit Percentages

Mix Percentages

Percentage Change

Trends in Financial Analysis

Short- and Long-Term Trends

Revenue, Expense, and Profit Trends

Company and Industry Trends

General Economic Trends—National and International

Summary

Hospitality Manager Takeaways

Key Terms

Formulas

Review Questions

Problems

This chapter presents some of the fundamental accounting concepts and methods of financial analysis that will be used throughout the book and also throughout the career of any hospitality manager. These are not only fundamental accounting concepts but important management tools used to operate a business on a daily basis.

The concepts and terms are explained in a direct and fundamental way. The typical detailed and complicated accounting explanations are missing because they will do no good if they are not understood. The information in this chapter will form a solid financial foundation, one that will enable students to expand in terms of knowledge and application as they work through problems and deal with business situations. It will focus on hospitality industry operations, but the methods of financial analysis presented are useful and applicable to any business operation.

Methods of Financial Analysis

Analyzing financial reports and statements requires a fundamental understanding of where numbers come from, how they are organized and presented, what they mean, what they measure, and how they are used. This section discusses two concepts of working with numbers to analyze financial statements.

Two Important Tools

First, we will talk about two important ways numbers are used in business. They are used to measure financial performance and to provide a management tool to use in operating the business.

To Measure Financial Performance

Numbers provide a way to determine how a business is performing. Measuring financial performance is historical in nature and uses the actual numbers or results from business operations. It tells us what the business has produced, and it compares and evaluates that performance to specific measures. It is looking back through the rearview mirror at operations. The three main financial statements are all used in measuring financial performance.

The Profit and Loss (P&L) Statement shows the revenues, expenses, and profits for a specified time period. Each month, accounting period, quarter, or year, the numbers produced by an operation are recorded in the P&L statement and tell whether the business revenue and profits are improving, declining, or staying the same.

The Balance Sheet shows the assets, liabilities, and owner equity of a business at a specific time. These numbers tell us whether the business is getting financially stronger by increasing assets or owner equity or if it is struggling and increasing liabilities. The numbers also tell us how the business is capitalized or started—with more debt than owner equity or with more owner equity than debt.

The Statement of Cash Flows shows how much cash is generated by a business and how effectively it is used in operating the business over a specified time period. Cash and liquidity are critical to the success of a business, and the numbers included in the Statement of Cash Flows tells us how cash is being acquired and used.

To Provide a Management Tool

Numbers provide a way for managers to plan for varying levels of business volume. This can take the form of forecasting revenues, scheduling wages, implementing cost controls, expanding business operations, or preparing the annual budget. Numbers give managers feedback on their operations and then assist them in making appropriate changes.

This aspect of using numbers is very valuable to a business because it is the process of taking the information numbers provided and applying them back to operating the business.

The Financial Management Cycle

Second is the **Financial Management Cycle**. It is important to understand this process and how numbers are generated and used in business operations. This cycle deals with the flow and use of numbers in business operations.

1. *Operations produce the numbers.* All the activities involved in the daily operations produce the numbers that measure performance. In a hotel, the daily operations

provide products and services to guests, including the rooms department, food and beverage outlets, gift shop, and any other department that produces a sales transaction with a guest. Numbers used in financial analysis have to come from somewhere, and that is the daily operation of the business.

2. *Accounting prepares the numbers and provides financial reports and statements.* At the end of the day, week, or month, the numbers resulting from all operations and activities are collected, summarized, and reported by the accounting department. These reports describe the operations and activities and are distributed to the appropriate managers for their review and use.

3. *Accounting and operations analyze the numbers.* Operations management and accounting management work together to review and analyze the reports. They look for changes, the cause of the change, and the result of the change to understand operations and determine ways to change and improve. Together they have operational experience and financial analysis experience and can identify any changes or improvements that need to be made to ensure that productive operations continue.

4. *Operations applies the numbers back to the business.* After reviews and discussions, the operations managers make any necessary changes to operations to correct or improve them. The ability to analyze quickly and accurately and then make any necessary changes is an important part of any business operation. It enables the business to constantly improve by being more productive or creating more value in the products and services that it provides.

Comparing Numbers to Give Them Meaning

Numbers need to be compared to something to have any meaning. A hotel has monthly sales of $1 million. All this tells us is the sales level. How do we know if this is good or bad, up or down, acceptable or not acceptable? A fundamental concept of financial analysis is to compare a number produced by operations to an established number that will tell us if there was an increase or a decrease. The most common **comparisons** are to (1) last year, (2) budget, (3) forecast, (4) previous month or period, (5) pro forma, or (6) any other established goal.

Last Year

Comparing actual financial results to last year's actual results is a useful comparison. The first evaluation of financial operations is to show if operations are better than the previous year. The best results are if actual operations for the current year are better than last year and the budget. The worst results are if the current year is worse than last year and the budget.

Budget

Actual financial results for a month, quarter, or year are compared to the established budget. The budget is the formal one-year financial operating plan for a company. Budgets include planned increases in revenues and profits, and productivity improvements in costs and expenses. Comparing actual results to the budget shows whether the business is moving in the direction planned and budgeted and how close it is in meeting, exceeding, or missing the budgeted numbers.

Forecast

Forecasts update the budget. Whereas the budget is done once for the entire year, forecasts are done continually to adjust or relate to current business conditions. Forecasts can be weekly, monthly, quarterly, biannually, or can apply to the end of the year. They are important because they are more current and help project business performance compared to the budget.

Previous Month or Period

These comparisons are important because they identify trends in operations. A goal of any business is to continually improve. Examining month-to-month performance tells us the trend and direction of our operations. They can show improvements that we hope are the results of corrective action implemented by management to keep the company moving in the right direction.

Pro Forma

A new business does not have any historical operating information. Therefore, management, developers, and bankers prepare a pro forma based on market conditions and expected financial returns. The pro formas are estimates or projections of how these financial experts think the business will perform in the first year of operations. The pro forma is used for the first year of business operations and is then replaced by the budget, which is prepared based on the first year's actual performance. Pro formas are used to establish and identify initial business revenues and profits that will generate the cash flow necessary to repay loans and investments.

Other Goals

Occasionally a business will establish other goals or benchmarks to compare actual performance. Examples are improving profit margins to meet an established goal, achieving specific revenue levels, or entering new markets.

Let's use our example to give meaning to the $1,000,000 in monthly sales. Suppose that last year we did monthly sales of $950,000; this year we increased that by $50,000 to $1,000,000, which is good—sales are increasing. However, if the budget was $1,100,000, we missed the budget by $100,000, which is not good—our sales did not increase as much as we had budgeted.

Now let's analyze our $1,000,000 monthly sales performance. Was it good or bad? We know we increased sales $50,000 over last year, but we missed budget by $100,000. The answer, then, is that our performance was both good and bad. It was good because we improved $50,000 over last year. It was bad because we missed the budget by $100,000. The next question we have to ask is, "Was the budget set too high?" Comparing the budget of $1,100,000 to last year's actual sales of $950,000 tells us that we expected (or budgeted) sales to increase $150,000. We can also measure this increase in percentages by dividing the $150,000 increase by last year's sales of $950,000 to get a budget percentage increase of 15.8%. That is an aggressive budget increase. If I were the manager of this business, I would be very happy to have the $50,000 increase over last year (a 5.3% increase). I would also review the reasons we thought we could increase by 15.8% and analyze why that didn't happen.

Comparing numbers to something concrete is essential to give any meaning to the numbers. This is particularly important for the P&L Statements. The Balance Sheet and the Statement of Cash Flow are analyzed more to look for changes from previous statements or to goals or benchmarks than to budgets. Typically there is no budget for these two financial statements. That is why they are compared to the previous month or period or to a goal. Remember to compare any financial report to last year, last month, the budget, the forecast, the pro forma, or the goal to give it meaning. Then we can tell whether operations are improving or not.

Measuring Change to Explain Performance

One of the most important elements of financial analysis is to be able to identify where changes occur and what caused the **change**. In a large business with many products and departments, an effective financial analysis of the financial reports must locate the department that is changing and identify the causes of that change. Is it in revenues—volume or rate? Is it in expenses—cost of sales, wages, benefits, or other operating expenses? Is it a direct or indirect, fixed or variable expense? One department or many departments may be affecting operations with positive or negative changes.

Changes are identified by comparing actual performance to previous performance or a specific goal or measure. These changes can be for a month, a quarter, or a year. The more information that is obtained about the changes, the better chance that good decisions can be made to respond to the changes.

Changes, both positive and negative, are measured in terms of units, dollars, and percentages. These three measurements can tell us a lot about the performance of a business. From our $1,000,000 monthly sales example, we have already looked at the dollar *increase*

(+$50,000 over last year) and the percentage *increase* (+5.3% over last year). We know that we have $50,000 more sales dollars, a positive change. We know that we increased sales by 5.3%, also a positive change.

Performing that same financial analysis process, our $1,000,000 is $100,000 *below* the budget of $1,100,000 and 9.1% *below* the budget. We know that we have $100,000 fewer sales dollars than budgeted, a negative result. Our 9.1% is also a negative result from our budget.

The final measurement is units. If the entire $1,000,000 in monthly sales was from room revenue, our unit will be the number of rooms sold. Our accounting reports would tell us how many rooms were sold and what the average room rate was. Let's assume the average room rate was $80. We can then calculate the number of rooms sold by dividing total room sales of $1,000,000 by the average room rate of $80, which gives us 12,500 rooms sold. That should match the number of rooms sold on our accounting report.

So now we have the units or volume—12,500 rooms sold—but we don't know if this is better or worse than last year's monthly sales of $950,000. The answer will come from last year's accounting reports. If the report tells us that the average rate for last year was $78 and 12,180 rooms were sold, we can multiply these together and get the monthly sales of $950,000. Now we can compare our actual rooms sold this year of 12,500 to last year's rooms sold of 12,180. We can also compare this year's average rate of $80 to last year's average rate of $78.

Take a minute to calculate the increases from last year in dollars, units, and percentages for this year's monthly sales of $1,000,000 (Table 2.1).

TABLE 2.1
Comparison Actual to Last Year

	Sales	Rooms Sold	Average Rate
This year	$1,000,000	12,500	$80
Last year	$950,000	12,180	$78
Dollar difference			
Percentage difference			

The Answers to Table 2.1
Comparison Actual to Last Year

	Sales	Rooms Sold	Average Rate
This year	$1,000,000	12,500	$80
Last year	$950,000	12,180	$78
Dollar difference	$50,000	320	$2
Percentage difference	+5.3%	+2.6%	+2.6%

Using Percentages in Financial Analysis

Percentages are one of the three ways numbers are used to measure financial performance. They provide an additional dimension or perspective in financial analysis. Percentages measure relationships and changes and always involve two numbers.

Calculating Percentages

Percentages are the result of combining two numbers that define a relationship. A change in one number changes the resulting percentage. Both numbers can also change. When a percentage changes, it is important to know which number changed and what caused the change. For example:

*Wage cost percentage equals wage expense dollars divided
by the associated revenue dollars*

If our department wage expense is $350 and our department revenue is $1,000, our wage cost percentage is 35% ($350 / $1,000).

Wage cost percentage can go up or down in two ways. An increased wage cost would result from our actual wage expense increasing or our revenues decreasing. Continuing our example:

1. *$400 Wage Expense / $1,000 Department Revenue = 40% Wage Cost Percentage*
2. *$350 Wage Expense / $875 Department Revenue = 40% Wage Cost Percentage*

If our wage cost expense went up, we would analyze the labor numbers to see where the increase was and what caused the increase. In our first example, our wage expense went up $50 to $400, but our department revenue remained the same at $1,000. This is not good because we spent $50 more on wages but did not increase our output or revenues. The business operation was *less productive*.

In our second example, our wage cost remained constant at $350, but our department revenue went down $125 to $875. This is also not good because we spent the same amount on wages, $350, but it resulted in less sales, $875. Again, our business operation was *less productive*.

When you identify where the changes occurred, then you can look for the causes of the changes and make any necessary adjustments to improve operations. Our corrective action will be different in each example. In the first example, we would look at our work schedule to make scheduling changes to get back to 35% wage cost. In our second example, we would look to the sales department to see what caused the drop in sales to $875 and to determine how we can correct it. In either case, it is an important part of financial analysis to make any necessary changes in our work schedule to adjust to the forecasted production volumes and their corresponding sales.

What Percentages Measure

Percentages measure relationships and *changes*. An example of relationships is the previous wage cost example. A 35% wage cost means that 35 cents out of every revenue dollar is used to pay the wage cost associated with producing that revenue dollar. Another example is food cost percentage. An actual food cost percentage of 40% means that 40 cents out of every food revenue dollar is used to pay for the associated food cost to produce that one food revenue dollar.

The food cost percentage will go up or down based on changes in food costs or food revenues. To become more productive and profitable, the actual food expense that results in a sale would have to decline or stay the same, but the food revenue would increase. To become less productive, our food cost would have to remain the same and our food revenues go down or our food cost would have to increase but our food revenues would remain the same. By looking at each number and identifying any changes, we analyze the numbers and identify what changed and how that affects our operational performance.

Let's look at another example of percentages and change. If our revenues increase from $1,000 to $1,200, the resulting dollar change is an increase of $200. To calculate the associated percentage change, divide the $200 increase by the original $1,000 revenue, and the result is a 20% increase in revenues. *The amount of change is always divided by the base, beginning, or original number.* Percentage change can be calculated for changes in revenues, expenses, profits, assets, units, liabilities, owner equity, or any other specific account.

Using percentages in the process of financial analysis includes three steps. First is identifying and measuring the change. Second is identifying the cause of the change. Third is developing and implementing corrective action into daily operations.

Four Types of Percentages Used in Financial Analysis

Cost or Expense Percentages

These percentages tell us what dollar amounts of expenses are associated with corresponding revenues or sales. The previous examples of wage cost and food cost demonstrate cost percentages. Cost percentages can be calculated for any expense account or type that has a specific dollar cost associated with it. The formula for cost percentage is expense dollars divided by corresponding revenue dollars. For example, suppose that the room revenues for January are $40,000, wage costs are $5,000, benefit costs are $2,000, reservation costs are $4,000, and linen costs are $1,500. Our expense formula is dollar cost / department revenue. Our cost percentages for January are as follows:

$$Wage\ Cost = 12.5\%\ (\$5,000\ /\ \$40,000)$$
$$Benefit\ Cost = 5.0\%\ (\$2,000\ /\ \$40,000)$$
$$Reservation\ Cost = 10.0\%\ (\$4,000\ /\ \$40,000)$$
$$Linen\ Cost = 3.8\%\ (\$1,500\ /\ \$40,000)$$

Profit Percentages

Profit percentages tell how much of the revenue dollar is remaining after all expenses are paid. Profits are measured in dollars and percentages. Dollar profit measures the absolute number of dollars remaining as profit, whereas percentage profit measures how much of the sales dollar is remaining as profit. Profit percentages can be applied to different levels of profit: department profits, house profits, or gross operating profits.

Department profit percentages are important because each department that is a profit center has a different profit percentage resulting in different department profitability. For example, the rooms department typically has a department profit range of 65% to 75%, the banquet or catering department profit typically ranges from 30% to 40%, lounge and retail shop profits range from 25% to 35%, and restaurant profits range from 0% to 10%. It is also possible for some restaurants to operate at a loss, therefore having a negative percentage referred to as department loss percentage rather than department profit percentage.

Mix Percentages

Mix percentages tell you how much of your total comes from different departments, or how much each department adds to the total. Mix percentages can be measured in units or dollars. They are useful because they provide a quantified measure of each part to the whole.

The sales mix percentage identifies the portion or amount each department's sales adds to total sales. Following is an example of a hotel sales mix:

Department	Sales Dollars	Sales Mix Percentage
Rooms sales	$1,000	50%
Restaurant sales	300	15%
Beverage sales	200	10%
Banquet sales	500	25%
Total sales	$2,000	100%

If each department has the same profit percentage, the sales mix percentage is not very helpful. In this case, the same amount of profit will result from each revenue dollar regardless of the department. However, the actual department profit percentages are very different as demonstrated in the previous section. Let's add department profit percentages to our example:

Department	Profit Percentage	Sales Dollars	Sales Mix Percentage	Profit Dollars	Profit Mix Percentage
Rooms sales	70%	$1,000	50%	$700	70.7%
Restaurant sales	10%	300	15%	30	3.0%
Beverage sales	30%	200	10%	60	6.1%
Banquet sales	40%	500	25%	200	20.2%
Total sales/profit		$2,000	100%	$990	100.0%

Now we can draw some additional conclusions about the monthly sales and profits:

The Rooms Department generated 50% of sales but 70.7% of total profit dollars.

The Restaurant Department generated 15% of sales but only 3.0% of total profit dollars.

The Beverage Department generated 10% of sales but only 6.1% of total profit dollars.

The Banquet Department generated 25% of sales and 20.2% of total profit dollars.

This information tells us that the Rooms Department is the main contributor of both sales and profits. This department should be our main priority. The Banquet Department is the next highest profit contributor in dollars and percentages. It is still important to focus on Restaurant and Beverage operations, but they do not account for a significant portion of profits—9.1% combined, even though they have a combined 25% of sales.

These mix percentages have given us examples of sales and profit dollar mix percentages. We can also calculate a mix percentage for units sold, market segment, meal periods, or any other unit that we measure and record. Following are examples of the rooms sold market segment mix and the restaurant meal period mix. These are in units, rooms sold, or customer counts.

Rooms Sold Market Segments

	Rooms Sold	Mix Percentage
Transient	1,500	60.0%
Group	700	28.0%
Contract	300	12.0%
Total	2,500	100.0%

Restaurant Meal Periods

Meal Period	Customers	Mix Percentage
Breakfast	325	41.7%
Lunch	190	24.3%
Dinner	265	34.0%
Total	780	100.0%

Percentage Change

This percentage is important because it measures progress or lack of progress. Have our restaurant sales increased or decreased compared to last month? Which meal period showed the most improvement, breakfast, lunch, or dinner? Are the sales up because we had an increase in customers served or because our average check increased? The percentage change gives us this information.

Percentage change is calculated by dividing the amount of the change in dollars (increase or decrease) by the base or original amount. In our example, the change or difference would be calculated by subtracting our actual or current month results from the base or previous month. This change amount would then be divided by the base or, in this example, the previous month's results—for example, this month's sales of $4,800 compared to last month's sales of $4,500. Our percentage change is calculated by subtracting this month's sales of $4,800 from the previous month's sales of $4,500 resulting in a *difference* of $300. This is where it is important to relate the numbers to actual operations. This calculation results in a $300 difference. We then know that this is a positive difference because our current month's sales of $4,800 is larger than the previous month's sales of $4,500.

Photo: Hyatt Hotels & Rentals

The Grand Hyatt Atlanta

This 439-room Hyatt hotel is located in the heart of Buckhead, Atlanta's most prestigious and fashionable area. It has over 18,000 square feet of meeting space including a

9,700-square-foot ballroom, 5,500 square feet of pre-function space, and 10 meeting rooms. Food and beverage facilities include a restaurant, 24-hour room service, pool snack bar, and a lounge.

From an accounting perspective, consider the banquet and catering operations of this hotel. It is located in a very upscale area of Atlanta that provides many opportunities for profitable social banquets in addition to regular group business. It is also able to command high room rates. Do you think that the rooms sales mix will be higher or lower than a typical business hotel? Do you think the banquets and catering sales mix will be higher or lower than a typical business hotel? Do you think the banquet department will be able to generate a higher profit percent than the banquet department in a typical business hotel?

Trends in Financial Analysis

Trends are important because they show the direction or movement of business operations, industry, and national and international economies. Understanding the different types of trends and how they affect the operations of a business is an important part of financial analysis. We will discuss four types of trends that affect a business.

Short- and Long-Term Trends

It is important to look at both short-term and long-term trends. Short-term trends (less than 90 days) often involve seasonality or the expected cycles of a business or industry. A business that is slowing down because of seasonality or an industry cycle should be evaluated differently from a business that is slowing down because of increased competition, product or service quality, or pricing issues. A long-term tend is a better evaluator of products or services, especially when compared to competitors and industry performance.

When looking at the month-to-month performance of a business, it is important to distinguish between one month of poor financial performance and several months of poor financial performance. It is typical for a business to have a problem or one-time event that results in performance below expectations for a month. One month by itself does not make a trend or signal a major or long-term problem. However, it is important to correct any poor performance to prevent it from becoming an ongoing problem.

If a business has several months of poor performance, this is a trend that could signal continuing major long-term problems. Management might have to make major evaluations and analyses to determine what is causing the ongoing poor performance and how it can be corrected. Correcting the cause of several months or years of poor performance is a much larger task than correcting a problem that has affected only one month.

Revenue, Expense, and Profit Trends

These trends are all shown in the P&L Statement. Each individual trend is compared to the other two to determine if financial performance is improving or declining. For example, if revenue is trending up and expenses are staying flat, the profit trend should also be up. These are good trends and good relationships between revenues, expenses, and profits. However, if revenues are trending up but expenses are trending up at a faster rate, that will result in lower profits. That is not a good trend. Most important, are revenues or expenses trending in the direction to increase or decrease profits? Equally important is which of the three trends are increasing or decreasing faster or slower than the other two. For example, if sales are increasing 5% but expenses are increasing 10%, profits will decrease. The best case for increasing profits is if sales are increasing and expenses are decreasing.

Favorable and unfavorable trends that affect productivity and profits are demonstrated here:

Trends That Increase Profits	**Trends That Decrease Profits**
Revenues increasing, expenses decreasing	Revenues decreasing, expenses increasing
Revenues increasing, expenses flat	Revenues flat, expenses increasing
Revenues increasing faster than expenses	Expenses increasing faster than revenues

Company and Industry Trends

It is important to compare the trend of a company with the trends of the industry and general economy. Are the company trends the result of the success or failure of your business operations, the result of conditions that are affecting the entire industry, or the result of the general economic environment? Trends can result from any or all of these conditions, and it is important to identify the causes of trends for the business and the industry. Then appropriate action can be implemented.

For example, if your business profits are down 10% from the previous year and the industry average is down 8% to 12%, then you can safely say that your business profits are down as a result of industry conditions and nothing specific to your business. However, if your profits are down 10% from the previous year and the industry average is up 2%, then you can safely say that the reason your business profits are down is because of problems or the inferior performance of your business and not any industry factors. The causes of the 10% decrease in profitability are different from what is occurring in the industry and should be treated in different ways to correct problems and improve efficiencies of the company so that it gets back to desired profit levels.

General Economic Trends—National and International

The world is indeed shrinking, and problems in other countries or other parts of the United States can affect the performance of an individual business operation. Inflation rates, interest rates, unemployment rates, consumer confidence indexes, budget deficits, exchange rates, and social/political environments are all factors that may have major influences on a business. The most dramatic and tragic example of this is the attack that took place on September 11, 2001, which changed the economic, political, military, and social environment for every country in the world. Each industry and business had to develop new policies, procedures, and strategies to survive in such a turbulent and negative environment.

Another element of national economic influences is the understanding of business cycles. Economic growth, bull markets, bear markets, and stable social and political environments do not go on forever. There are business cycles as short as six months and as long as five to eleven years that occur in normal business and economic activities. Financial analysis can assist a business in identifying business cycles and their causes and determining best practices to permit the best possible operations in any economic environment.

Today's major impact player is China. It is such a large and undeveloped market that major companies throughout the world are planning ways to tap into this new and emerging business environment. Yesterday's major impact player was technology. How it will affect business in the next few years is also a major factor for a company or industry to consider in its plans and strategies for the future.

Summary

This chapter has provided a foundation for accounting concepts and a framework for financial analysis by presenting key components for understanding and working with numbers. Analyzing financial statements provides a way to measure the financial performance of a business and provides information that can be used as a management tool to change or improve the operations of a business.

The four steps of the Financial Management Cycle show the flow of numbers as they are used in financial analysis. Operations produce the numbers, accounting prepares the numbers, both operations management and accounting analyze the numbers, and operations management applies the financial information to daily operations to improve or change them.

Other key elements of financial analysis include (1) comparing actual financial results to other financial information such as the previous year's results, the current year's budget or forecast, or a pro forma; (2) measuring and evaluating changes to other numbers; (3) understanding the importance of percentages in financial analysis; and (4) using trends to interpret financial performance.

Hospitality Manager Takeaways

1. There are four key ways that numbers are used in measuring financial performance and as a management tool:

   a. Numbers must be compared to other numbers or standards to have any meaning.

   b. Numbers are used to identify the cause of change and to measure its impact.

   c. Percentages are used to measure change and describe relationships.

   d. Trends provide an important framework to evaluate financial performance.

2. The Financial Management Cycle describes the flow and use of numbers in a company or business. First, operations produce the numbers; second, accounting prepares the numbers; third, both accounting and operations analyze and evaluate the numbers; and fourth, operations applies the numbers to improve operations or solve problems.

Key Terms

Budget—The formal business and financial plan for a business for one year.

Change—The difference between two numbers.

Comparison—An examination that allows one to note a likeness or difference.

Financial Management Cycle—The process of producing, preparing, analyzing, and applying numbers to business operations.

Forecast—Updates of the budget prepared weekly, monthly, or quarterly.

Last Year—The official financial performance of the previous year.

Percentages —A share or proportion in relation to the whole; part.

   Change—Measures the difference in percentage between two numbers.

   Cost—Measures the dollar cost or expense as a part of total applicable revenue.

   Mix—Measures dollars or units as a part of a whole.

   Profit—Measures the dollar profit as a part of total applicable revenues.

Pro Forma—The projected first year of operations prepared before actual operations begin.

Trend—A general inclination or tendency.

Formulas

Change—Dollars	Actual Results – Previous Results
Change—Percentage	Dollar Change / Previous Results
Cost Percentage	Expense Dollars / Corresponding Revenue Dollars
Mix Percentage	Individual or Department Amount / Total
Profit Percentage	Profit Dollars / Corresponding Revenue Dollars

Review Questions

1. What are the two ways numbers are used in financial analysis? Give examples.
2. Name the four steps in the Financial Management Cycle.
3. Name five reports or financial documents the actual financial performance is compared to.
4. What is the difference between an annual budget and a pro forma?
5. Discuss some of the important components of measuring change in financial analysis.
6. Name the four types of percentages used in financial analysis. Give examples.
7. Name the four types of trends used in financial analysis. Give examples.
8. Discuss, in two paragraphs, why trends are important and how you would use them to analyze the financial operations of a business.

Problems

1. Following are the financial results for January for the Lumberjack Hotel:

	Actual	Budget	Last Year
Room Revenue	$ 695,000	$ 680,000	$ 650,000
Room Profit	$ 500,000	$ 486,000	$ 460,000
Average Room Rate	$ 67.50	$ 68.00	$ 65.66
Rooms Sold	10,300	10,000	9,900
Occupancy Percent	83.1%	80.1%	79.8%

Restaurant Revenue	$ 126,000	$ 125,000	$ 124,000
Beverage Revenue	$ 48,000	$ 50,000	$ 47,000
Catering Revenue	$ 240,000	$ 250,000	$ 245,000
Total Food & Beverage Revenue	$ 414,000	$ 425,000	$ 416,000
Gift Shop Revenue	$ 23,000	$ 22,000	$ 21,000
Total Revenues	$1,132,000	$1,127,000	$1,087,000

Calculate the following:

a. Dollar change for room revenue—actual to budget and last year.

b. Percentage change in room revenue—actual to budget and last year.

c. Dollar and percentage change for rooms sold, occupancy percentage, and average rate—actual to budget and last year.

                                                          Budget   Last Year

d. Sales mix percentages for room revenues, total food & beverage revenue, and gift shop revenue.

                                          Actual   Budget   Last Year

e. Sales mix percentages for restaurant, beverage, and catering revenues.

                                          Actual   Budget   Last Year

2. The following financial information is from the Darden Restaurants 2003 annual report:

	Sales	Mix Percentage	Number of Restaurants	Mix Percentage
Red Lobster	$2,430,000,000		673	
Olive Garden	$1,990,000,000		524	
Bahama Breeze	$ 138,000,000		34	
Smokey Bones	$ 93,000,000		39	
Totals				

a. What was the total annual sales and how many total restaurants did Darden operate in 2003?

b. Calculate the sales mix percentage for 2003.

c. Calculate the restaurant unit mix percentage for 2003.

3. Following is the revenue from continuing operations from the Marriott International 2003 annual report (in millions):

	2003 Mix Percentage	2002 Mix Percentage	2001 Mix Percentage
Full Service	$5,876	$5,508	$5,260
Select Service	$1,000	$ 967	$ 864
Extended Stay	$ 557	$ 600	$ 635
Time Share	$1,279	$1,147	$1,009
Totals	$8,712	$8,222	$7,768

a. Calculate the sales mix percentage for 2003, 2002, and 2001.

b. Calculate the percentage change in revenue for each segment from 2003 to 2002.

c. Calculate the percentage change in revenue for each segment from 2002 to 2001.

d. What is the overall revenue growth (percentage change) from 2002 to 2003 and from 2001 to 2002?

4. Calculate the cost and profit percentages for General Electric for 2003 and 2002.

	2003	2003 Percentage	2002	2002 Percentage
Total Revenues	$134,187		$132,210	
Cost of Goods Sold	37,189		38,833	
Cost of Services Sold	14,017		14,023	
Interest, financial charges	10,432		10,216	
Other Costs and Expenses	52,645		50,247	
Total Costs	$114,283		$113,319	
Earnings before Taxes	$ 19,904		$ 18,891	

5. Problems 1 through 4 represent the second step in the financial management cycle. The following questions represent the third step—analyzing the numbers.

a. For the Lumberjack Hotel, discuss the actual January performance, including dollar and percentage change. Include comparisons of actual with both the budget and last year and identified operating departments that improved or did not improve.

b. For Darden Restaurants, explain what the mix percentages tell about the sales amounts and number of units for each restaurant concept.

c. For Marriott International, which market segment increased its sales mix percentage the most, and which if any had a decrease in its mix percentage? Compare 2003 actual numbers with both 2002 and 2001 for your answers.

d. For General Electric, list the cost areas that resulted in productivity improvements and any that resulted in productivity declines for 2003. Comment on all four cost areas and the total costs. Why did the earnings percentage go up? Is that good or bad?

Accounting Department Organization and Operations

Learning Objectives

1. To understand how hotel accounting departments are organized and operate.

2. To understand how restaurant accounting is organized and operates.

3. To understand the difference between on-property accounting and regional or corporate accounting.

4. To learn how hospitality managers work with accounting departments in the preparation of financial statements.

Chapter Outline

Organization Charts

    Full-Service Hotels

    Accounting Departments

    Smaller Hotels (Fewer Than 100 Rooms)

Accounting Operations in Full-Service Hotels

    Accounting Department Operations

    Hotel Department Operations and Relationships with Accounting

    Monthly Preparation of Financial Reports

Accounting Operations in Restaurants and Smaller Hotels

    Financial Statement Preparation

    Purchasing and Inventories

    Wage and Cost Controls

Summary

Hospitality Manager Takeaways

Key Terms

Review Questions

This chapter discusses accounting structures for large hotels, small hotels, and chain restaurants with a focus on the organization and operation of accounting departments in full-service hotels. Full-service hotels are defined as hotels that have from 250 rooms to more than 2,000 rooms; in addition these establishments provide sleeping rooms, operate food and beverage outlets, provide catering functions and meeting room rentals, and offer gift shops, valet laundry, health workout facilities, bellmen, a concierge, and other services and amenities that are typically included in larger hotels. A wide range of hotels are included in the full-service category, such as corporate hotels, airport hotels, suburban hotels, convention hotels, and resorts. Because of the wide range of activities and the large amounts of revenues and profits generated, full-service hotels have accounting departments in the hotel to take care of all the accounting responsibilities.

Because smaller hotels and select-service hotels do not offer their guests such a wide range of amenities and services, they do not require an onsite accounting department. Their accounting functions are coordinated by a regional or corporate accounting structure, which includes a centralized accounting department that handles the accounting activities of the individual hotels. These hotels provide information daily to the corporate accounting office, which then prepares reports and information and sends them back to the individual hotels for their use and review.

The accounting operations of chain restaurants are similar to the accounting operations of smaller hotels. A regional or corporate accounting office provides the accounting services for each individual restaurant. It is the responsibility of each restaurant to provide the daily operating information to the corporate accounting office, which then prepares the necessary accounting statements and operating information for the restaurant.

Independent operators of small hotels and individually owned restaurants will either do their own accounting or hire an outside accounting company to handle all accounting requirements and to prepare financial reports.

Organization Charts

An **organization chart** is a diagram of the structure and relationships of a specific business unit. It can include job titles, **direct reporting** relationships, areas of responsibility, and lines of communication among different job levels. We will discuss several organization charts as we describe the role and relationships of accounting departments.

Full-Service Hotels

Figure 3.1 contains two examples of organization charts for a full-service hotel. It includes four levels of responsibility divided into the two main types of business activities: **operating departments** and **staff departments**.

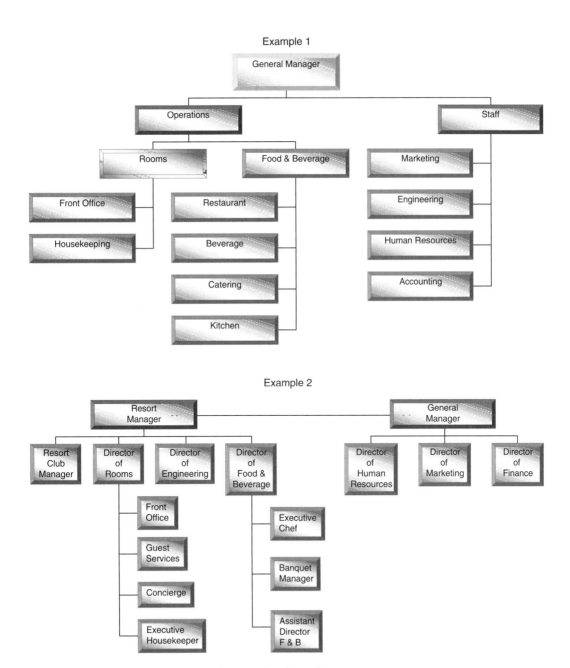

FIGURE 3.1 Full-service hotel organization charts.

General Manager

This is the top level of authority and responsibility. The **General Manager** is responsible for all the different activities and operations of the hotel. The General Manager relies on specific senior managers to operate the separate and distinct operating departments in the hotel. These are divided into two areas. The **operations departments** have direct interaction with paying or external customers and generate revenue and profits for the hotel. There are two main departments: the rooms department and the food and beverage department. The **staff departments** support the operating departments and their direct interaction is with internal customers—the operating department employees. There are four main departments: sales and marketing, human resources, engineering, and accounting.

Executive Committee or Leadership Team

The group of senior managers on the **Executive Committee** or Leadership Team has the direct responsibility for the overall operations of the departments under their leadership. These leaders directly report to the General Manager. They are experts in their operations, generally will have more than 10 years of experience, and will have worked in several hotels in several different positions. The General Manager relies on them to take care of the detailed aspects of operations, including product and service delivery, guest relations, service levels, revenues and profits, and employee development. Typical titles for these positions are listed in Table 3.1.

Department Heads

This group of managers has the direct responsibility for the operations of one specific department. **Department heads** report directly to an Executive Committee member and generally will have more than five years of experience in several hotels in several different positions. The Executive Committee member relies on Department Heads to take care of the daily operations of the department. Examples of key hotel department heads are the Front Office Manager, Executive Housekeeper, Director of Restaurants, Director of Catering, and Executive Chef.

TABLE 3.1
Executive Committee Titles

Operations	Staff
Rooms	**Sales and Marketing**
Resident Manager or Rooms Division Manager	Director of Sales and Marketing
	Human Resources
Food and Beverage	Director of Human Resources
Food and Beverage Director	**Engineering**
	Director of Engineering or Chief Engineer
	Accounting
	Director of Finance or Controller

Line Managers

This group of managers actually run the departments. **Line managers** are divided into the a.m., or morning shift, and the p.m., or afternoon/evening shift. They directly interact with the employees and the customers. They supervise and direct the employees in performing their specific responsibilities to take care of and service guests. They also deal directly with guests in the normal department operations or taking care of specific requests or handling specific guest problems and complaints. The line managers are also entry-level managers or managers in their first management position. Their job responsibilities include providing operational information to the accounting department, such as wage schedules, processing payroll, purchasing, physical inventories, Profit and Loss (P&L) Statement critiques, and revenue forecasting. Examples of line managers are Assistant Front Desk Managers, Assistant Housekeeping Managers, Assistant Restaurant Managers, Assistant Catering Managers, and Kitchen Managers.

The second example of a hotel organization chart demonstrates different responsibilities and relationships. Notice that the General Manager shares some of the primary responsibility with the Resort Manager. The Resort Manager has responsibility for the rooms and food and beverage, the main operating departments as well as for resort club operations (time share or vacation club) and engineering. Notice that there is also a difference in the departments reporting to the Director of Rooms and the Director of Food and Beverage. The Director of Human Resources, Director of Marketing, and Director of Finance along with the Resort Manager report directly to the General Manager.

This example offers a different way that a hotel can structure its operations. Each of these examples offers strengths and advantages depending on how the hotel chooses to operate. One is not necessarily better than the other, just different.

Accounting Departments

We will now discuss in detail the organization and structure of the Accounting Department. As we can see from the hotel organization chart, the Accounting Department is one of the staff departments with the Director of Finance or Controller responsible for all accounting operations and reporting to the General Manager. The accounting staff includes both managers and hourly employees. Figure 3.2 contains two accounting organization charts for a typical full-service hotel. Following are details about the positions and responsibilities of the accounting department.

Director of Finance/Controller

This Executive Committee member is responsible for all accounting department operations. Although there is a staff that actually perform these responsibilities, the **Director of Finance** is responsible for ensuring that all accounting information for the hotel is accurate, correct, and conforms to Generally Accepted Accounting Principles. Specifically, the Director of Finance does the following:

1. Prepares the monthly financial statements, primarily the P&L Statement, but also reconciles the Balance Sheet or Asset and Liabilities (A&L) Accounts and the Statement of Cash Flows.

2. Supervises all activities of the different accounting functions.

3. Prepares the annual operating budget and the annual capital expenditure budget.

4. Analyzes and critiques all monthly financial statements and weekly revenue and wage forecasts.

5. Is a financial advisor to all hotel managers and their operations.

6. Coordinates all communication with regional and corporate offices.

7. Prepares all financial statements and presentations for hotel owners.

Assistant Controller of Income Accounting and Operations

The **Assistant Controller** is often a department head and oversees several of the important aspects of accounting operations and their involvement with hotel department operations. These responsibilities include the following:

1. Assists the Director of Finance in hotel accounting activities including reconciling A&L Accounts, preparing P&L critiques, capital expenditure accounting, weekly revenue and wage forecasts, productivity analysis, and any other activities requested by the Director of Finance.

2. Closes each month and assists in the preparation of monthly P&L Statements, including adjusting A&L Accounts, processing transfers, verifying physical inventories, and coordinating corporate entries.

3. Performs hotel audits.

4. Assists rooms and food and beverage operations managers.

5. Supervises accounting employees in the following activities:

    a. *Income Journal*. Records all hotel revenues and prepares daily, weekly, and monthly revenue reports.

    b. *General Cashier*. Handles all the cash operations of the hotel, including verifying department deposits, preparing daily hotel deposit, maintaining hotel change bank, assisting with department bank audits, and assisting with all cash-handling activities.

    c. *Accounts Payable*. Processes the payment of all hotel purchases and invoices ensuring compliance with hotel purchasing procedures and coordination with operating departments. This includes proper coding of invoices to appropriate accounts, timely payments, maximizing discounts, and reconciling accounts payable.

    d. *Payroll*. Processing the payroll for hourly and management employees.

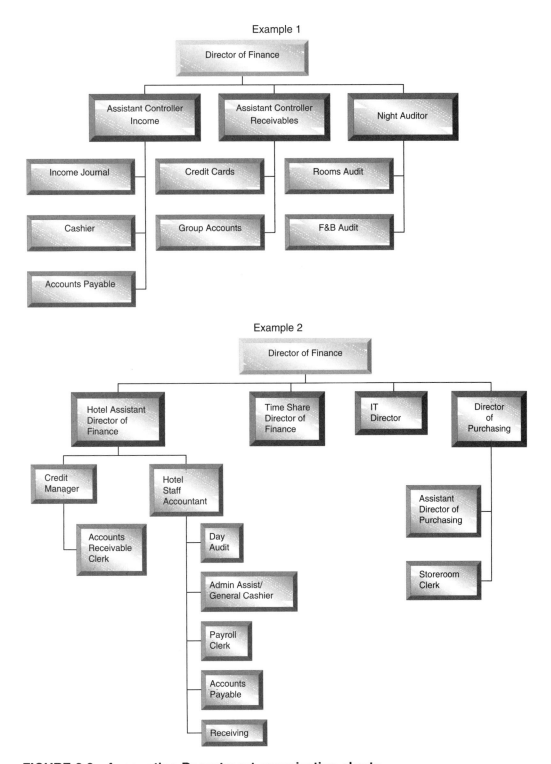

FIGURE 3.2   Accounting Department organization charts.

Assistant Controller Receivables

This manager is responsible for the billing and collection of all revenues and **accounts receivable** due the hotel. He or she oversees several areas of billing and collection and is especially involved in group accounts at larger convention hotels and resorts. These responsibilities include the following:

1. Assists the Director of Finance in hotel accounting activities including reconciling cash accounts (there could be many), reconciling credit card statements, and generating a positive cash flow for the hotel. These are important responsibilities because they have a major impact on maximizing cash flow for the hotel.

2. Assists in closing each month or accounting period and preparing financial statements.

3. Reviews the aging accounts to effectively manage current, 30- to 60-day, 60- to 90-day, and over 90-day accounts. Prepares information for bad debt write-offs and coordinates activities with collection agencies when necessary.

4. Coordinates group billings, including direct billing approvals, account preparation and review, and group account collection.

5. Supervises the employees in the following accounts receivable activities:

   a. Group account management including pre-meetings, account review during the group's stay in the hotel, and post-meetings to ensure proper authorization and processing of all group charges.

   b. Credit card collection, including the timely billing, processing, and collection of credit card payments. Reconciliation of all credit card charge-backs and guest disputes.

   c. Credit Manager in proper credit review and approvals and preparing information for credit and write-off meetings.

Night Auditor

This manager is responsible for the processing and auditing of all accounting and operational information for each day. She or he is also responsible for operating the all-night (or 11 p.m. to 7 a.m.) front desk shift. These responsibilities include the following:

1. Records and balances the day's transactions for each hotel department. This includes room revenues, food and beverage revenues, catering and meetings revenues, gift shop revenues, and any other revenue-producing departments.

2. Rolls the date after all accounting transactions are audited and in balance. This means closing all the information for the previous day and setting up all the information and systems for the next day.

3. Prepares daily management reports including daily revenue reports, discrepancy reports, and the next-day guest reservations.

4. Ensures that all guests checking in and out of the hotel are taken care of efficiently.

5. Supervises the employees in the following auditing activities:

   a. Rooms revenue posting and auditing.

   b. Food, beverage, and banquet revenue posting and auditing.

   c. Front desk clerks in front desk operations.

Smaller Hotels (Fewer Than 100 Rooms)

Smaller hotels do not generate the volume and range of revenues and expenses as do full-service hotels, and therefore they do not require an on-property accounting office. If they

WeKoPa Golf Clubhouse, Fountain Hills, Arizona
WeKoPa Golf Club

WeKoPa Golf Club is located east of Phoenix on the Ft. McDowell Yavapai Nation reservation. It has 18 spectacular holes of golf set in the Arizona Sonoran desert. Because it is located on a reservation, there will never be any buildings or roads to obstruct its natural beauty. A second 18 holes will be open in 2006 and a 250-room Radisson Resort next to the golf course will open in late 2005.

WeKoPa #14

The main departments in a Golf Club include golf operations, golf course maintenance, restaurant and lounge, and often banquets and catering for small meetings or social functions like weddings. The 10,000-square-foot clubhouse includes a full-service restaurant, bar, and conference room. What do you think will happen to the revenues for WeKoPa when the second 18 holes open up? What do you think will happen to the revenues for WeKoPa when the 250-room resort opens? Draw an organization chart for WeKoPa and show how you think these departments will report to the General Manager. (WeKoPa means Four Peaks in the Ft. McDowell Yavapai language. You can see the Four Peaks in the distance in the picture of the 14th hole.)

are part of a national hotel chain, the General Manager or owner will be responsible for providing daily operational information to the corporate accounting office. This person will then process the information into reports and return it to the hotel for its information and use.

If the hotel is privately owned, the owners will either assume the responsibility for all accounting information and reports or they will hire an outside accounting service to provide these services for them. Because these hotels are privately owned, they do not have as many reporting requirements and regulations as publicly owned hotels have. They do need to meet state and local tax-reporting requirements.

Individual Restaurants

Individual restaurants that are part of national chains have similar accounting relationships and reporting procedures as small chain hotels. Each individual restaurant is responsible for providing daily operating and accounting information to the corporate office, which processes the information and returns reports to the restaurant for its use. If the restaurant is privately owned, the same accounting responsibilities and relationships exist as for individually owned hotels.

Accounting Operations in Full-Service Hotels

The Accounting Department is a staff department that supports all other departments in the hotel with regard to accounting procedures and hotel operations. It works with these departments to provide services and information that will assist them in operating their departments on a daily basis.

Accounting Department Operations

The Accounting Department records and processes the previous day's hotel activities. Refer to the Accounting Department Organization Chart in Figure 3.2. Each day the individual sections within the Accounting Department receive the paperwork and records or processes the information to update accounts and prepare reports. Consider the following examples.

Income Journal

The **income journal** records the previous day's revenues in the appropriate account. Room revenues are recorded in individual accounts (or market segments) for transient, group, and contract. This includes the previous day's revenue and the month-to-date revenue. The same process is used for recording breakfast, lunch, and dinner revenues for a restaurant and revenues for breakfast, lunch, dinner, coffee breaks, receptions, meeting room rental, and audio/video for the Catering Department. Beverage revenues are recorded in liquor, beer, wine, and soft drink accounts.

The income journal also records and balances the method of payment for each account. For example, total room sales must equal or balance with cash receipts, credit card payments, and company or personal checks. This balancing function is important because it ensures that the revenue recorded equals money received.

Recorded Revenues	=	_Method of Payment_
Transient Room Revenues		_Cash Payments_
Group Room Revenues		_Credit Card Payments_
Contract Room Revenues		_Check Payments_
		Direct Billing/Accounts Receivable
Total Room Revenues	=	_Total Receipts and Deposit_

Here is an example for a typical day:

Transient room revenues	$12,500		Cash payments	$ 1,600
Group room revenues	4,800		Credit card payments	10,400
Contract room revenues	1,200		Check payments	2,500
			Direct billing	4,000
Total room revenue	$18,500 =		Total receipts/deposits	$18,500

General Cashier

The daily functions of the **General Cashier** are to collect, balance, and consolidate all of the operations department deposits into one deposit for the hotel, which goes to the bank each day. The General Cashier balances the cash and checks in each deposit to the same amounts posted for that day in the income journal account. In our example, the daily hotel deposit prepared by the General Cashier should be $4,100—the amount of cash and checks collected for the day.

The credit card payments and direct billing are not part of the hotel deposit until the actual checks are received. In our example, the credit card sales for the day of $10,400 will generally be received within 48 hours via electronic transfer directly into the hotel's cash bank account and will not be a part of any hotel deposit. The $4,000 direct billing should be received within 30 days, and the actual check would be added to the day's deposit on the day that it is received.

The General Cashier also maintains a change bank for the hotel. This consists of keeping an adequate supply of coin and small currencies—one-, five-, and ten-dollar bills—to be used by the hotel departments in making change for their customers. The General Cashier will send a change order to the bank at the same time the deposit goes to the bank. This change order will include larger currency of twenty-, fifty-, and hundred-dollar bills submitted by the hotel to the bank, which will be exchanged for smaller currency and returned to the hotel the next day.

Accounts Payable

Each day, the **Accounts Payable Clerk** will receive invoices to be paid. The procedures for paying invoices will include verifying information such as a manager's signature confirming the accuracy of the invoice and authorizing its payment, the amount to be paid, the date that it needs to be paid by, and the account that it will be coded or charged to. It is the accounts payable clerk's responsibility to verify this information before writing the check.

Accounts payable checks are generally written during the week and mailed once a week or on a daily basis to take advantage of discounts and to meet due dates. Much of this process is now done electronically on computers, and part of the accounts payable clerk's responsibility is to review and check the payments for accuracy and to ensure that they balance to the backup documentation.

Accounts Receivable

Each day, the **Accounts Receivable Clerk** receives all the direct billing accounts to be processed for collection. Direct billing is when a company has been preapproved to have its bill sent at the end of the function with payment being expected within 30 days from checkout. The two main categories of accounts receivable are credit cards and direct billing.

The credit card documentation for the day includes totals for each credit card. Individual guest room accounts are closed out or transferred to a credit card master account when the guest checks out. For example, the hotel might have 10 guests owing $1,800 pay their accounts by American Express. These 10 individual room accounts are zeroed out, transferred to the American Express master account, and sent to accounts receivable for processing. Another 15 guests might pay with Visa or MasterCard for $4,600 and $4,000, respectively. In our example, the total credit card billings of $10,400 for the day become $10,400 of credit card receipts within 48 hours when the electronic transfer of funds from each credit card company is deposited directly into the hotel's bank account.

The $4,000 of direct billing will be monitored by accounts receivable personnel to ensure that there are no problems and that the company will review, approve, and issue the check for payment in a timely manner. When the check is received, it will be added to that day's deposit.

The Accounts Receivable Department also handles guest disputes and problems. Credit card chargebacks occur when a guest disputes the charge on his or her credit card. Accounts receivable will research the problem and provide proper documentation, such as signatures and guest checks, that verifies that the charge is valid and correct; the department will then return the documentation to the credit card company so that it will rebill the customer.

Night Audit

The **Night Auditor** and his or her staff receives, audits, reconciles, and balances all the day's transactions; prepares daily reports that state total revenues; updates accounts; and ensures that all the day's transactions balance and are correct. A big challenge for the night auditor and his or her staff is to research and find problems or mistakes and properly correct them in a timely manner. They have to do this during the all-night shift when none of the employees or managers is available to answer questions or assist in finding mistakes. They must rely on their ability to research the paperwork and transactions to find and correct any problems.

With the development of new technologies some hotels are now able to perform the night audit functions the next morning. Modern property management systems and POS systems can perform the audit functions. These audit reports are reviewed the next morning. Therefore, day audits are now a common occurrence.

Hotel Department Operations and Relationships with Accounting

Each department in the hotel is responsible for providing the expected products and services to the customer following established hotel policies and procedures. The accounting department assists the other departments in following appropriate procedures. Following are examples of how an operating department might interact with accounting.

Front Office

Managers in the front office will work with the Income Journal Clerk by reviewing the daily room revenue information that they record. They can look at average room rates by market segment, rooms sold by market segments, and any adjustments to revenues in reviewing the previous day's operations. They can compare actual sales with forecasted, budgeted, and last year's sales. They constantly work with the General Cashier by requesting change for front desk cashiers, helping to research any cash-handling problems such as shortages in banks or deposits, and processing or reimbursing petty cash requests. They work with the Accounts Payable Clerk by forwarding invoices for payments, checking on account numbers, researching invoice problems, and generally ensuring that all invoices approved for payment are correct. They hand the day's work over to the Night Auditor at 11 p.m., who will check in any remaining guests and begin the process of auditing the day's work.

Restaurant and Catering

Managers in the restaurant and catering departments work with the accounting office in much the same manner as do the Front Office managers. Instead of market segments, these managers are interested in meal period information (breakfast, lunch, and dinner) to analyze their sales. The rest of their interactions are the same as those for the Front Office managers.

Staff Departments

The Sales and Marketing, Human Resources, and Engineering departments primarily interact with the Accounts Payable Clerk in processing invoices for payment. Because these departments have no revenues, they do not have any direct interaction with the Income Journal Clerk or General Cashier.

Monthly Preparation of Financial Reports

We need to refer back to the four steps in the Financial Management Cycle Presented in Chapter 2:

1. The Operations Department produces the numbers.

2. The Accounting Department prepares the numbers.

3. The Accounting Department and Hotel Management analyze the numbers.

4. Hotel Management applies the numbers to Operations to change and improve.

We have just discussed the first step—Operations produces the numbers. Now we will discuss the second step—Accounting prepares the numbers.

Hotels or restaurants prepare either monthly financial reports or accounting period reports. The process is the same for both. The difference is the time period covered. The monthly reports are prepared at the end of each month and include operating results for 28, 30, or 31 days depending on the month. Although this makes for consistent comparison to the same month for a previous year, there are some problems with comparing results to the previous month when that month might contain more or fewer days in it. For example, comparing February, March, and April results will involve 28 days, 31 days, and 30 days, respectively, of operating results. Comparing these three months will require some adjusting, such as calculating daily averages to make the comparisons more meaningful.

Accounting periods all have 28 days and four weeks. There are 13 accounting periods in a year, all with the same number of days in each period. This makes comparisons to previous periods or previous years consistent. Each week in an accounting period always begins on the same day, ends on the same day, and involves the same number of days. For example, a workweek could begin on Saturday and end on Friday. However, monthly financial statements are more common, and the 13 accounting periods only include 364 days so there has to be an adjustment every seven years to get back to an end-of-the-year close to December 31.

Regardless of whether a company is on a monthly or an accounting period basis, the process of closing the books and preparing the financial statements is generally the same. For consistency purposes, we will talk about monthly closings. The process of closing the month includes the following activities:

1. *Preclosing information.* Several days before the end of the month, invoices, physical inventories, and transfers documenting entries will be due to the Accounting Office. This is to give everyone time to review and check the numbers reported for accuracy. If a problem arises, there is time to recheck the information.

2. *Month end.* This is the first day of the next month. The Accounting Office goes through a process of closing out all of the hotel accounts and posts entries for the previous month. For example, the income journal, the cumulative sales recorded for the month, is totaled, balanced, verified, and then closed out. The income journal for the next month is then opened, and all of the income or revenue accounts are set up for the new month. The Accounts Payable Clerk verifies with hotel managers that all invoices that should be paid for and charged to that month have been

received and inventoried and there will be a clean and consistent cutoff for the month. Once all the necessary operating information is received from the hotel departments, the Accounting Office verifies the information and enters it into the proper accounts on the proper reports. The main report is the monthly P&L. All accounting entries that reflect hotel revenues and expenses for the month must be entered in the proper account on the monthly P&L. This includes entries to adjust accounts in the A&L so that the balances on the account books equal the balances of physical inventories or computer reports. The monthly P&L already has the budget and last year's information, and the month-end closing collects and reports the actual information for the current month.

3. *Postclosing review.* The first draft of the monthly P&L is available within one or two days. The Director of Finance and Assistant Controllers then review the information to correct mistakes or make allocations and adjust entries to finalize the information on the P&L. Although this is primarily an accounting function, the Accounting Managers will be talking with Hotel Managers to ensure that any corrections made are proper and accurate. When these entries are completed and entered into the computer system, the final monthly P&L is generated. This P&L will include results for the current month and year-to-date (YTD).

Accounting Operations in Restaurants and Smaller Hotels

The accounting operations of restaurants and smaller, select service hotels are handled in a similar manner. Chain restaurants such as Red Lobster and Chili's as well as select service hotels such as the Fairfield Inn and Hampton Inn are examples of this type of operation. The size and range of operations do not warrant an onsite accounting office. Therefore, these operations utilize regional or corporate accounting offices to provide required accounting functions.

The accounting process in these operations is based on daily communication with the **corporate accounting office**. The operating results at the end of the day are transmitted to the corporate accounting office where they are processed and returned to the hotel or restaurant. It is the General Manager's responsibility to ensure that required operating information is submitted in a timely and accurate manner. While the General Manager can delegate this responsibility to his or her managers, it is ultimately the General Manager's responsibility to make sure that all procedures are followed correctly.

Financial Statement Preparation

At the end of each day, the restaurant or hotel will close out the day's operating information accumulated in its POS system. This will include meal period revenues, customer counts, wage costs, and any other expenses for the day. The p.m., or closing manager, is responsible for ensuring that all the day's operating information is sent at the end of each day. The corporate accounting office collects, summarizes, and reports the information and returns it to the restaurant or hotel the next morning. The next day, the a.m., or opening manager, will review the information for accuracy and completeness and make any necessary corrections. This daily information also includes month-to-date information and is used by the restaurant managers in operating their restaurants.

A similar process is followed at the end of the month for the monthly closing. This process is more involved and includes taking physical inventories, verifying revenue and wage information, and ensuring the accuracy of the month-end cutoff date. The corporate accounting office prepares the monthly P&L and any other trend or summary reports and returns it to the restaurant in three to five days.

Customer counts and revenues are forecasted each week for the next two weeks. These forecasts update the budget for the upcoming weeks and are based on the current business conditions that the restaurant is experiencing. These forecasts are used to schedule wages and determine purchase quantities.

Purchasing and Inventories

Food, beverage, and operating supplies are purchased weekly through a centralized purchasing system. This computer program contains inventory level status, daily and weekly consumption amounts, prices, order quantities, and other pertinent purchasing information. The restaurant manager responsible for this function ensures that all the pricing and paperwork are complete and accurate; verifies delivery quantities, prices, and invoices; conducts month-end physical inventories; and processes invoices for payment.

Although it is an advantage to have a sophisticated purchasing system to use, it is the manager's responsibility to ensure that all information submitted is accurate. This requires a knowledge of restaurant standards and operations, of the accounting process, and of the importance of current and ongoing communication with the corporate accounting office to ensure that the system is working as intended.

Wage and Cost Controls

Along with food costs, wage and benefit costs are the largest and most important expenses to be controlled in operating a restaurant. Wage costs are reviewed daily to ensure productivity standards are met and waste minimized. This process starts with the preparation of the next week's wage schedule based on the average volumes and employee labor hours for the previous several weeks. Relationships between guest counts and labor hours are established and used to schedule and control wage costs.

The wage departments in a restaurant can be divided into service, bar and hostess, and kitchen or heart of the house. Wage standards are established for each of these departments, and then the wage schedules are prepared for the upcoming week based on forecasted customer counts. An additional part of managing wage costs is controlling overtime. Each overtime labor hour includes a 50% premium—in other words, an overtime labor hour costs 50% more than a regular labor hour.

Another reason controlling wage costs is so important is that for every wage dollar there is an associated benefit cost. Most companies provide benefits to their hourly and management employees. This cost is split between the company and the employees. Typically, a company can pay from 20% to 40% in benefit cost for every wage dollar. This means that for every wage dollar paid, the restaurant will pay an additional 20 to 40 cents for benefits. If a restaurant is effectively controlling wage costs, they will be effectively controlling benefit costs. If they are not effectively controlling wage costs, they will also not be controlling benefit costs.

Summary

The Accounting Department or Office in a hotel supports and assists the operating departments in a hotel. It interacts daily with these other departments exchanging information, assisting with problems, and preparing daily, weekly, and monthly management reports to be used by the operating departments in their daily business.

An organization chart describes the responsibilities and relationships provided by a department or business unit. The Accounting Department Organization Chart shows the different management levels and the functions or activities that the department is responsible for providing to the hotel. The typical management structure in the accounting office for a full-service hotel includes the Director of Finance, Assistant Controller, Night Auditor, and the hourly employees. The accounting functions are divided into the income responsibilities, accounts receivable responsibilities, and night audit responsibilities.

The Accounting Department provides important assistance to the other departments in the hotel. The operating departments provide operating information to accounting, and accounting prepares financial information for the other department managers to use. The relationships between accounting and operating departments can be linked back to the Financial Management Cycle. The first step is "operations produce the numbers"; in the hotel industry, that refers to the rooms, food and beverage, and other staff departments. The second step is "accounting prepares the numbers." That is what we have talked about in this chapter. Without operations, accounting would have no information to prepare and report.

Small hotels and individual restaurants rely on corporate or regional accounting offices to provide all accounting services. Each hotel or restaurant sends operating information at the end of the day to the centralized Accounting Office, which records the information and prepares reports that are sent back the next day to the hotel or restaurant. Accurate and timely communications are essential to the successful operation of these systems.

Hospitality Manager Takeaways

1. The Accounting Office offers support and assistance for all hotel managers. Employees in the Accounting Office take the operational information from the departments and prepare accounting reports for all managers to use as a management tool and to measure financial performance.

2. Hospitality managers have to know what operating information they need to provide to the Accounting Office so that the two departments can work together in analyzing and applying the financial information to improve hotel operations.

3. Hospitality managers need to understand and provide relevant operating information to the Accounting Office, and they must understand and be able to use the financial information prepared by accounting in operating their departments.

Key Terms

Accounts Payable—The accounting function responsible for paying all invoices of the hotel.

Accounts Receivable—The process of billing and collecting accounts settled after the guest or company has checked out of the hotel.

Assistant Controller—A manager in the accounting office who reports to the Director of Finance and oversees specific functions in the accounting office, either income operations or accounts receivable.

Corporate Accounting Office—A central location that provides accounting support and services for individual hotels or restaurants operated by the company.

Department Head—A manager who is directly responsible for a specific hotel department. Department heads report to an Executive Committee Member and have line managers and supervisors reporting to them.

Direct Report—The managers and positions who report directly to a senior manager.

Director of Finance—The Executive Committee Member directly responsible for all accounting operations in a hotel.

Executive Committee—The members of senior management who report directly to the General Manager and are responsible for specific hotel departments. Department heads report to an Executive Committee Member.

General Cashier—The accounting function responsible for maintaining change for the hotel and for collecting department deposits and consolidating them into one deposit that goes to the bank daily.

General Manager—The senior manager in the hotel who is responsible for all hotel operations. All positions and activities are the responsibility of this person.

Income Accounting—The section of the accounting office that is involved with recording income, paying expenses, and assisting other hotel managers.

Line Manager—The entry-level management position that has face-to-face interaction with the customers and is responsible for operating the different shifts of a hotel department.

Night Audit—The accounting office function that receives, audits, reconciles, and balances all of the day's transactions; prepares daily reports; and ensures that the previous day's transactions are correct and in balance.

Operating Department—A hotel department that records revenues and produces a profit by providing products and services to the guests.

Organization Chart—Describes the reporting relationships, responsibilities, and operating activities for a department or business unit.

Staff Department—A hotel department that assists and supports the hotel operating departments.

 ## Review Questions

1. Name the two operating departments and the four staff departments in a full-service hotel.

2. Identify three areas of the accounting office and describe what their duties and responsibilities include.

3. What management position is responsible for delivering products and services every day to the guests?

4. What management position is responsible for all of the operations of a hotel?

5. Describe the operations and responsibilities of a corporate accounting office.

6. Identify three types of operating/financial information that a corporate accounting office returns daily to a restaurant for its review and use.

7. What is the most important financial report for hotel department managers that is prepared monthly by the accounting department?

8. Explain the differences, advantages, and disadvantages of monthly P&Ls when compared to 28-day accounting period P&Ls.

The Profit and Loss (P&L) Statement

Learning Objectives

1. To understand the information contained in a Consolidated Profit and Loss (P&L) Statement

   a. Revenue and profit centers

   b. Expense centers

   c. Fixed or overhead expenses

2. To understand the different profit measures contained in a Consolidated P&L and what they mean

3. To become familiar with the different formats for Consolidated P&Ls

4. To understand the information contained in Department P&Ls

5. To understand the four main expense categories of Department P&Ls

6. To understand how the financial information on a Consolidated P&L is used as a management tool and to measure financial performance

Chapter Outline

Hotel Consolidated P&L Statements

   Revenue and Profit Centers

   Fixed Expenses or Investment Factors

   Hotel Profit Levels

Formats for a Consolidated P&L

   Title

   Horizontal Headings

   Vertical Headings

   Examples of Consolidated P&L Formats

Department P&L Statements

  Revenue Centers

  Expense Centers

  Fixed Expenses

Summary

Hospitality Manager Takeaways

Key Terms

Review Questions

This is the most important chapter in the book for a hospitality manager. The Profit and Loss (P&L) Statement is the financial statement that hospitality managers need to understand completely. It is the financial statement that they will use to measure the financial performance of their departments and to monitor and improve the daily operations of their departments. The P&L provides a way for managers to measure the financial performance of their departments by comparing actual monthly operations to the budget established for the month, to last year's monthly performance, to the previous month's performance, and to the most recent forecast.

The P&L is the financial report that involves hotel managers in all four steps of the Financial Management Cycle. First, the managers operate the departments that provide the products and services to customers that produce the numbers—revenues, expenses, and profits. Second, the managers ensure that the numbers that are submitted to accounting are accurate and consistent so that the financial reports prepared by accounting are accurate and useful. Third, hotel managers must be able to analyze and discuss the numbers to determine how well hotel operations are meeting established goals and budgets. This includes providing critiques and details of operations that can assist them and accounting managers in determining the best or next course of action to take regarding operating their departments. Fourth, hotel managers are the ones responsible for applying the numbers back to operations by implementing changes for improvement or corrections to solve problems.

The P&L also provides information that is connected to both the Balance Sheet (Assets and Liabilities [or A&L] Statement) and the Statement of Cash Flow. A hospitality manager who understands these relationships will be able to use these financial statements more effectively in operating their departments.

Hotel Consolidated P&L Statements

The Consolidated P&L for a hotel is a summary P&L that lists the department totals for revenues, profits, and expenses. Only the department totals for revenues, profits, and expenses are included in the Consolidated P&L. It is a true summary report showing the important financial results for each department in the hotel.

Revenue and Profit Centers

Both of these names refer to operating departments that produce revenues (sales) and profits. The terms *revenue* and *sales* are interchangeable. The terms **revenue centers** and **profit centers** are also interchangeable. Specifically, these departments provide products and services to the customers who pay for these services. Employees record the sales on cash registers or point-of-sale (POS) computer systems. That is why these operating departments are referred to as revenue centers. They receive and record revenues from customers. Examples of revenue centers in full-service hotels are the rooms department, restaurants, lounges, catering and banquets, the gift shop, and telephone departments. Resorts include these same revenue centers, as well as golf, spas, tennis, and recreation revenue centers. Exhibit 4.1 presents an example of revenue centers in a Consolidated P&L.

EXHIBIT 4.1

SAMPLE CONSOLIDATED P&L FOR A HOTEL

Flagstaff Hotel
Consolidated P&L Statement
June 30, 2004

	Current Period*				Year to Date*		
	Actual	Budget	Last Year		Actual	Budget	Last Year
Room Revenues	$100	$102	$ 95		$ 675	$640	$625
Telephone Revenues	6	6	5		34	35	34
Gift Shop Revenues	8	7	7		41	41	39
Miscellaneous Revenues	3	3	3		18	18	18
Restaurant Revenues	15	15	14		73	71	70
Beverage Revenues	6	6	6		29	30	29
Banquet Revenues	<u>23</u>	<u>20</u>	<u>18</u>		<u>150</u>	<u>140</u>	<u>135</u>
Subtotal F&B Revenues	$ 44	$ 41	$ 38		$ 252	$241	$234
Total Hotel Revenues	$161	$159	$148		$1,020	$975	$950

* Revenues are reported in thousands of dollars or (000).

Exhibit 4.1 shows the revenue for the current period and year-to-date (YTD) for the revenue centers of the hotel. This part of the Consolidated P&L only reports revenues. A quick review of the financial results for the current period shows that the hotel's actual sales of $161,000 were $2,000 over budget and $13,000 over last year. It is good financial performance when actual results exceed the budget and last year. The hotel's actual performance YTD is also exceeding the budget and last year's performance—actual revenue of $1,020,000 to a budget of $975,000 and last year's performance of $950,000.

The next section of the Consolidated P&L shows profits for the revenue center after all department operating expenses are paid. The direct costs of operating each revenue center are charged to each department, and the detail is shown by line account in the Department P&L. The total expenses are subtracted from the total revenues to produce total department profit for each revenue center. The consolidated P&L contains two entries for each revenue center: total revenues and total profits. That is why the two terms are interchangeable—revenue center or profit center. Both terms refer to operating departments that produce revenues and profits. Exhibit 4.2 presents an example of how department profits are shown on a Hotel Consolidated P&L.

EXHIBIT 4.2

SAMPLE PROFIT CENTERS OF A CONSOLIDATED P&L

Flagstaff Hotel
Consolidated P&L Statement
June 30, 2004

	Current Period*			Year to Date*		
	Actual	Budget	Last Year	Actual	Budget	Last Year
Room Revenues	$100	$102	$ 95	$ 675	$640	$625
Telephone Revenues	6	6	5	34	35	34
Gift Shop Revenues	8	7	7	41	41	39
Miscellaneous Revenues	3	3	3	18	18	18
Restaurant Revenues	15	15	14	73	71	70
Beverage Revenues	6	6	6	29	30	29
Banquet Revenues	23	20	18	150	140	135
Subtotal F&B Revenues	$ 44	$ 41	$ 38	$ 252	$241	$234
Total Hotel Revenues	$161	$159	$148	$1,020	$975	$950

	Current Period*			Year to Date*		
	Actual	Budget	Last Year	Actual	Budget	Last Year
Rooms Profit	$66	$67	$63	$439	$416	$406
Telephone Profit	1	1	1	6	6	6
Gift Shop Profit	2	2	2	11	10	10
Miscellaneous Profit	3	3	3	18	18	18
Restaurant Profit	2	2	2	12	12	11
Beverage Profit	2	2	2	12	12	12
Banquet Profit	8	7	6	53	49	47
Subtotal F&B Profits	$12	$11	$10	$ 77	$ 73	$ 70
Total Hotel Department Profit	$84	$84	$79	$551	$523	$510

* Numbers reported are in thousands of dollars (000).

This section of the Consolidated P&L shows the department profit for each revenue center. The profit numbers include all revenues less expenses for each department for the current period and YTD. A review of Total Hotel Department Profits of $84,000 for the period show that they are equal to the budget of $84,000 and $5,000 over last year's $79,000. The $551,000 of YTD profits are $28,000 over budget and $41,000 over last year. Again, these are good YTD financial results because the hotel's actual profits are over the budget and over last year's performance.

Expense Centers

Expense centers are the staff departments in a hotel. They can also be called deductions from income. They do not generate any revenues or profits. Their budget only includes expenses, which is why they are called expense centers. They only have total department expenses on the Consolidated P&L. These total expenses include wage expenses, benefit expenses, and other operating expenses for each staff department. Exhibit 4.3 is an example of the expense centers on a Consolidated P&L.

Three of these expense centers are based on allocations. They are Accidents, Training, and National Sales and Marketing. Allocation means that a set dollar amount or percentage of sales is charged to these departments each month. The money goes into a corporate account and is used to cover company or national programs. In the Accident Department, the company has one insurance policy that covers all the hotels. The alloca-

Crescent Moon Restaurant Patio
Four Seasons Resort, Scottsdale, at Troon North

This Four Seasons resort offers 210 casita rooms in two-story buildings located on 40 acres of the High Sonoran Arizona desert. This picture features the patio seating of the Crescent Moon Restaurant. Guests can dine inside or outside at this restaurant, enjoy outside lunch or dinner at the Saguara Blossom outdoor pool restaurant, dine at the Acacia specialty restaurant, or enjoy 24-hour casita dining. Note in the background the two-story casita buildings. This resort recently expanded the indoor meeting space to over 20,000 square feet. It also features 14 treatment rooms in the 12,000-square-foot spa.

From this information, list the name and number of revenue centers for the Four Seasons Scottsdale and draw an organization chart of how these departments report to an Executive Committee member and the General Manager. Since Four Seasons Hotels and Resorts are in the luxury market segment, do you think the rooms sales mix will be higher or lower than a typical resort? What do you think the different profit center percentages are in the high, shoulder, and low seasons? Do you think the Food & Beverage revenues rely on a higher average check or higher customer counts to maximize revenues?

tion charges each hotel the appropriate amount to cover employee and guest accident premiums and expenses for the specific hotel. The training allocation pays for a corporate training department that provides training to all the hotels. The National Sales and

EXHIBIT 4.3

SAMPLE EXPENSE CENTERS OF A CONSOLIDATED P&L

Flagstaff Hotel
Consolidated P&L Statement
June 30, 2004

	Current Period*			Year to Date*		
	Actual	Budget	Last Year	Actual	Budget	Last Year
General and Administrative	$12	$12	$11	$ 71	$ 72	$ 71
Heat, Light, and Power	7	7	6	43	42	40
Repairs and Maintenance	15	15	15	92	90	88
Accident Expense	4	4	4	25	25	24
Training Expense	2	2	2	12	12	12
Sales and Marketing	15	14	13	90	85	83
National Sales and Marketing	<u>6</u>	<u>6</u>	<u>6</u>	<u>70</u>	<u>68</u>	<u>66</u>
Total Expense Centers	$61	$60	$57	$403	$394	$384

* Numbers are in thousands of dollars (000).

Marketing allocation collects money from each hotel that is used at the corporate level to pay for national advertising and promotional campaigns and regional or national sales officers.

The rest of the expense centers include the wage, benefit, and operating expenses for the department. There is an Executive Committee Member in charge of each department who is responsible for managing all department expenses and ensuring that they are productive and within the established budget.

Fixed Expenses or Investment Factors

The last expense category on the Consolidated P&L is the **Fixed Expenses**, also known as **Investment Factors** or Overhead Expenses. These expenses are constant or fixed and are generally not affected by hotel volume levels or activity. They are the result of contracts, bank loans, fees, some taxes, and insurance policies. Often these costs are determined for the year and spread over each month in equal amounts. Examples of fixed accounts are lease expenses, bank loans, insurance costs, licenses and fees, and depreciation. Hotel management has little ability to control these expenses. They are already set and have to be paid for out of hotel revenues regardless of whether the hotel is having a good month or year or a bad month or year.

These fixed amounts can be large and difficult to pay unless the hotel is operating at high levels. During slow months or low seasons, these amounts remain the same or fixed and must still be paid. These are the difficult times for a hotel. However, when a hotel is busy and revenues and profits are increasing, these expenses do not go up but remain constant or fixed. So when the hotel is doing well, fixed expenses are more easily paid and should result in higher profits. When the hotel is not doing well, there is less money available to pay the fixed expenses, and this eats into profits.

Hotel Profit Levels

There are several levels of profits in a hotel, each measuring a specific aspect of hotel performance. Each Executive Committee Member is responsible for specific departments and performance. The profit terms can change from company to company, but the concepts and formulas are the same. We will discuss Department Profits, Total Department Profits, House Profit, Net House Profit, and Profit before and after Taxes.

Department Profits

The formula for **department profits** is revenues minus expenses equals profit. The Consolidated P&L records the revenues and profits for each operating department. The Resident Manager or Director of Rooms Operations is responsible for Rooms Department Profit and the Director of Food and Beverage is responsible for Restaurant, Beverage, and Banquet department profit. The Executive Committee Member, along with her or his management and hourly employees, can control or direct all the revenues and expenses for the departments.

Total Department Profits

The formula for **total department profits** is adding up and totaling the department profits for each operating department in the hotel. The Total Department Profits amount identifies the total profit dollars produced by the profit centers and, in our example, measures the management performance of the Resident Manager and Director of Food and Beverage in maximizing the profits for their departments. Total Department Profit is the dollar amount available to pay all other hotel expenses.

House Profit

Also called Gross Operating Profit, the formula for **House Profit** is Total Department Profit minus Total Expense Center Costs. The Expense Center costs represent the other costs incurred by the staff departments to support the operating departments in providing products and services to the guests. A specific Executive Committee Member is also responsible for each expense center and is expected to control costs and achieve productivity and budget standards for his or her department. Refer to Figure 3.1 in Chapter 3, the "Full-Service Hotel Organization Chart," and the departments listed in the expense centers section of this chapter to see the departments that make up expense centers and to identify the Executive Committee Member responsible for controlling that department expense.

House Profit is an important profit measure because it identifies hotel management's ability to maximize revenues, control expenses, and maximize profits. It is the hotel profit measure used to calculate management bonuses because the managers have the ability to affect and control procedures and activities to maximize profits and to minimize and control expenses. House Profit also identifies the profit or dollar amount hotel operations turns over to the General Manager to pay hotel fixed costs.

Net House Profit

Also called Adjusted Gross Operating Profit, the formula for **Net House Profit** is House Profit minus Fixed Expenses. This is the dollar amount or profit that remains after the hotel has recognized all revenues and paid all operating and fixed expenses. It is the profit amount the hotel has produced that is available to pay all applicable taxes and to be divided among the hotel owner and hotel managers based on management contracts. Ownership accounting is important because it identifies which fixed expenses, reserve accounts, and taxes will be paid by either the owner, the management company, or any other investors or business entity that has an interest in the hotel. Exhibit 4.4 is a Consolidated P&L through Net House Profit.

Profits before and after Taxes

Taxes are the last expense the hotel must pay. The term **Profit before Taxes** refers to the final dollar profit that has recognized and accounted for all hotel revenues and expenses. This includes the payment of several operational or sales taxes. The final expense is income taxes (or corporate taxes). Profit before Taxes is the profit amount that is subject to corporate taxes. The corporate tax is calculated and paid, and the remaining amount is **Profit after Taxes**. This is the final profit amount that is divided among any owners and management companies involved in operating the hotel.

Formats for a Consolidated P&L

Exhibits 4.1 through 4.4 show the Consolidated P&L format used by Marriott Hotels. The P&L is arranged to present the financial information in a logical and clear format. We will look at the organization and format for Consolidated P&Ls in this section. Three separate sections make up the format of a P&L.

Title

This is a basic but important part of any financial statement. The **title** gives the reader specific information about the financial statement so that the reader will know what the numbers represent. The title includes the following information:

1. Name of the hotel or restaurant
2. Type of financial statement

EXHIBIT 4.4

CONSOLIDATED P&L

Flagstaff Marriott
Consolidated P&L Statement
June 30, 2004

	Current Period*			Year to Date*		
	Actual	Budget	Last Year	Actual	Budget	Last Year
Room Revenues	$100	$102	$ 95	$ 675	$640	$625
Telephone Revenues	6	6	5	34	35	34
Gift Shop Revenues	8	7	7	41	41	39
Miscellaneous Revenues	3	3	3	18	18	18
Restaurant Revenues	15	15	14	73	71	70
Beverage Revenues	6	6	6	29	30	29
Banquet Revenues	23	20	18	150	140	135
Subtotal F&B Revenues	$ 44	$ 41	$ 38	$ 252	$241	$234
Total Hotel Revenues	$161	$159	$148	$1,020	$975	$950
Rooms Profit	$ 66	$ 67	$ 63	$ 439	$416	$406
Telephone Profit	1	1	1	6	6	6
Gift Shop Profit	2	2	2	11	10	10
Miscellaneous Profit	3	3	3	18	18	18
Restaurant Profit	2	2	2	12	12	11
Beverage Profit	2	2	2	12	12	12
Banquet Profit	8	7	6	53	49	47
Subtotal F&B Profits	$ 12	$ 11	$ 10	$ 77	$ 73	$ 70
Total Hotel Department Profit	$ 84	$ 84	$ 79	$ 551	$523	$510
General and Administrative	$ 12	$ 12	$ 11	$ 71	$ 72	$ 71
Heat, Light, and Power	7	7	6	43	42	40
Repairs and Maintenance	10	10	10	62	60	58
Accident Expense	4	4	4	25	25	24
Training Expense	2	2	2	12	12	12
Sales and Marketing	15	14	13	90	85	83
National Sales and Marketing	3	3	3	19	19	18
Total Expense Centers	$ 53	$ 52	$ 49	$ 322	$315	$306
House Profit	$ 31	$ 32	$ 30	$ 229	$208	$204
Fixed Expenses	20	20	20	120	120	120
Net House Profit	$ 11	$ 12	$ 10	$ 109	$ 88	$ 84

* Numbers are in thousands of dollars (000).

3. Time period covered for the financial statement

The financial information in Exhibits 4.1 through 4.4 is for the Flagstaff Hotel and is the Consolidated P&L Statement for June 30, 2004.

Horizontal Headings

The headings across the top of a P&L statement tell how the financial information is arranged and organized according to time periods and type of financial information reported. The **horizontal headings** include the following information:

1. The financial information for the current accounting period or current month

2. The YTD financial information, which cumulates the financial information for all accounting periods or months as of the current date

3. The actual numbers, budget numbers, and last year's numbers for the current accounting period or current month

4. The YTD actual numbers, YTD budget numbers, and YTD last year's numbers

5. Columns for the dollars and percentages for each of the previous categories

These horizontal headings arrange and organize the financial information so that it can be read logically and clearly.

Vertical Headings

The headings down the side of a P&L statement provide the names of the accounts or departments that the numbers will be organized into and reported for. The **vertical headings** include the following:

1. Revenue centers for operating department revenues. This includes the revenues for individual departments such as rooms and food and beverage and the total of the revenues for all the departments in the hotel.

2. Profit centers for operating department profits. This includes the profits for individual departments such as rooms and food and beverage and the total of the profits for all the departments in the hotel.

3. Expense centers for the staff or supporting departments. This includes the total operating expenses for each department that is an expense center and the grand total of all the expense centers in the hotel.

4. Fixed expenses, which identify those expenses that do not change from month to month and are constant. This department can also be called investment factors or overhead costs.

5. Profit levels including Total Department Profits, House Profits, Net House Profits, and Profits before and after Taxes.

Examples of Consolidated P&L Formats

Following are examples of other formats that can be used for Consolidated P&L Statements. We will start with the format that we have used in this chapter.

HOTEL P&L EXAMPLE 1

THE FLAGSTAFF MARRIOTT HOTEL

	Current Period or Month Actual Budget Last Year in Dollars and as a Percentage	YTD Period or Month Actual Budget Last Year in Dollars and as a Percentage
Revenue		
Rooms		
Telephone		
Gift Shop		
Restaurant		
Lounge		
Banquet		
Total Food and Beverage		
Other Income		
Total Revenues		
Department Profits		
Rooms		
Telephone		
Gift Shop		
Restaurant		
Lounge		
Banquet		
Total Food and Beverage		
Other Income		
Total Department Profits		
Expense Centers		
General and Administrative		
Credit Card Discounts/Commissions		
Heat, Light, and Power		
Training		
Accidents		
Sales		
Local Advertising		
National Advertising		
National Sales		
Total Expense Centers		
House Profit		
Investment Factors or Fixed Expenses		
Profit Contribution or Net Operating Profit		
Taxes		
Profit after Tax		

In the second and third formats, notice how the horizontal headings are moved around but essentially show the same financial information for the same time periods. The vertical headings are moved to the center of the P&L and have some of the same terminology and some that is new. They all measure specific areas and types of financial results.

HOTEL P&L EXAMPLE 2
THE FLAGSTAFF OMNI HOTEL

Current Period
Actual Budget Last Year
in Dollars and as a Percentage

Year to Date
Actual Budget Last Year
in Dollars and as a Percentage

Total Hotel Rooms
Total Rooms Occupied
Revenue Occupancy Percentage
Average Room Rate
REVPAR
Gross Operating Revenues
Room Revenue
Food Revenue
Beverage Revenue
Total Food and Beverage Revenue
Telephone Revenue
Other Revenue
Total Gross Operating Revenues
Department Profits
Rooms Department
Food Department
Beverage Department
Total Food and Beverage Department Profit
Telephone Department
Other Departments
Total Department Profits
Administrative and General
Management Fee
Advertising and Sales
Repairs and Maintenance
Heat, Light, and Power
Total Deductions from Income
Gross Operating Profit
Fixed Expenses
Earnings before Interest, Taxes, Depreciation, and Amortization

			Month							Year to Date			
Act	Act	Budget	Budget	Last Yr	Last Yr			Act	Act	Budget	Budget	Last Yr	Last Yr
$	%	$	%	$	%			$	%	$	%	$	%
					Occupancy Percentage								
					Total Average Rate								
					REVPAR								
					Total Rooms Revenue								
					Total Food Revenue								
					Total Beverage Revenue								
					Total F&B Revenue								
					Total Telephone Revenue								
					Total Other Departments Revenue								
					GROSS OPERATING REVENUE								
					Rooms Net Profit								
					F&B Net Profit								
					Telephone Net Profit								
					Total Other Departments Profit								
					TOTAL DEPARTMENT PROFITS								
					Administrative and General Department Total								
					Accidents Department Total								
					Repairs and Maintenance Department Total								
					Heat, Light, and Power Department Total								
					TOTAL DEDUCTIONS								
					Gross Operating Profit								
					Taxes and Insurance								
					PROFIT BEFORE FEES								
					Management Fees								
					Other Management Fees								
					Four Seasons Incentive Fees								
					NET OPERATING PROFIT								
					Rent Expense								
					Depreciation								
					Amortization								
					Other Expense								
					Gain/Loss Expense								
					Income Tax								
					NET PROFIT								

Notice how the horizontal headings in the following format for a restaurant P&L are arranged to show different time periods for financial results. This format focuses on the current monthly trend of financial results by comparing the current month to the two previous months. These results also show some guest count information in addition to dollar information in the YTD section. The vertical headings are again found in the middle of the P&L to separate the activity for the current month from the YTD activity. This is just a different way to present the financial information.

RESTAURANT P&L EXAMPLE 1

THE FLAGSTAFF RESTAURANT

	Monthly Activity			Year to Date Activity			
2 Months Ago	1 Month Ago	Current Month	Actual Last Year	Current Year (Dollars)	Per Guest	Last Year (Dollars)	Per Guest

Total Guests
Lunch
Dinner
Take-Out
Lunch Sales
Dinner Sales
Take-Out Sales
Total Food Sales
Total Beverage Sales
Total Add-on Sales
Total Sales
Food Cost
Nonfood Cost
Beverage Cost
Other Cost
Total Cost of Sales
Hourly Wage Cost
Management Cost
Benefit Cost
Total Wage Compensation
Variable Expenses
Manageable Expenses
Utilities Expenses
Other Expenses
Total Manageable Expenses
Facilities Expense
Marketing Expense
Total Restaurant Earnings/Net Income

These four examples show how the financial results of a business can be presented in different formats in a P&L so that readers can learn about the financial performance of a company or business. A company determines how it wants to organize the financial information in the P&L so that the information can be used both as a management tool and to measure financial performance. *A hospitality manager should be comfortable reading and using a Consolidated P&L in any format.*

Department P&L Statements

Consolidated P&L statements provide summary information of the financial operations of a hotel, including department totals for revenues, profits, and expenses. The **Department P&L Statements** provide detailed operating information for individual departments. They are the P&Ls that hotel managers use to measure the financial performance of revenues, profits, and expenses and as a management tool to help them operate their departments more efficiently and productively. In addition to the revenues recorded on a department P&L, there are four major **expense categories**: cost of sales, wages, benefits, and controllable or direct operating expenses. We will discuss in more detail revenue center department P&Ls and expense center department P&Ls.

Revenue Centers

The department P&Ls for revenue centers are composed of revenues, cost of sales, wages, benefits, direct operating expenses, and department profit. Exhibit 4.5 shows the format for a department P&L. Notice that the title and horizontal headings are the same; only the vertical headings or accounts are different. Within each major expense category are many individual line accounts that collect all the operating information for that particular expense. For example, the individual accounts under the wage category include management wages, hourly wages, and other wages. Individual line accounts in the direct operating expenses category can include the china, glass, silver, and linen accounts, as well as other accounts. During the month, each expense incurred is classified or coded to the appropriate expense account in each department. At the end of the month, the accounting office collects, records, and reports all the operating information by account. This is the financial information included in each account total on the department P&L.

Expense Centers

The department P&Ls for expense centers are composed of wages, benefits, direct operating expenses, and total department expenses. Because they do not sell any product or service, there are no revenues or cost of sales. All other expense categories are the same as in the revenue centers. Their main responsibility is to manage their expenses efficiently and stay within established budgets or forecasts.

Fixed Expenses

There is a separate department for recording the fixed expenses of a hotel. There is only one expense category, and that is fixed expenses. There are no revenues, cost of sales, wages, or benefits categories. Only single-line accounts that provide the total expenses

EXHIBIT 4.5

DEPARTMENT P&L FORMAT

Flagstaff Hotel
Restaurant Department P&L
June 30, 2004

	Current Period			Year to Date		
	Actual	Budget	Last Year	Actual	Budget	Last Year
Revenues						
Breakfast						
Lunch						
Dinner						
Total Revenues						
Food Cost						
Hourly Wages						
Management Wages						
Other Wages						
Total Wage Cost						
Medical Costs						
Insurance Premiums						
Vacation Pay						
Unemployment Insurance						
Total Benefit Cost						
China						
Glass						
Silver						
Linen						
Paper Supplies						
Menu Expense						
Sales and Promotion						
General Expense						
Total Direct Operating Expenses						
Total Restaurant Department Profit						

such as loan payments, lease payments, insurance costs, depreciation expenses, and licenses and fees are contained in the fixed expense department.

The individual department P&Ls are directly connected to the organization charts that were presented in Chapter 3. There will be a specific manager in charge of each individual department P&L. For example, in a large convention hotel or resort, the Food and Beverage Director will have final responsibility for many restaurant and bar outlets as well as the banquets and meetings departments. But she or he will have a department head who is directly responsible for all the restaurants. Examples of these department heads and their direct P&L responsibilities are shown here:

Director of Catering	Banquet and Meetings department P&L
Restaurant Manager	Restaurant department P&L
Room Service Manager	Room Service department P&L
Beverage Manager	Lounge or Beverage department P&L
Executive Chef	Kitchen P&L

The Food and Beverage Director will meet with each one of these department heads to review their operations and assist in any way. But it is up to the department head and her or his team of shift managers to operate their respective departments efficiently, meeting established goals, budgets, and forecasts.

One final type of department to mention is **allocation departments**. These types of departments have their monthly costs allocated back to the departments that use their services. Two examples of allocation departments are the Laundry Department that is allocated back to the laundry accounts in the rooms, restaurant, and banquet departments and the Employee Cafeteria, which is allocated back to the employee meal accounts in the benefit category for each department that has employees.

Summary

P&L Statements measure the financial performance of a business. Hotels use two main types of P&Ls: the Consolidated P&L and the Department P&L. The Consolidated P&L is mainly used to report and measure financial performance, whereas the Department P&L is used as a management tool to provide managers with more detailed financial information, which they can use to operate their departments.

The Consolidated P&L is a hotel summary P&L that is arranged by revenue centers, profit centers, and expense centers. It also has several levels of profit measures. Total Department Profit measures the profitability of all the operating departments. House Profit measures the profits remaining after expense center costs are deducted from Total Department Profits. It reflects management's ability to successfully maximize revenues and minimize expenses. Net House Profit is the profit remaining after fixed expenses are paid from House Profit and is a good measure of the financial profitability of a hotel.

The Department P&L provides specific financial information on the operations of each department. The six main categories on a Department P&L are revenues, cost of sales, wage expense, benefit expense, direct operating expense, and department profit. There are specific line accounts within each of these main categories that further break down and identify expenses so that they can be measured and effectively controlled. Hospitality managers spend a lot of time using their department P&Ls to help them operate their departments.

The P&Ls are organized in a format that enables the reader to easily read and identify financial information contained in the P&L. The format can be different, but the financial information contained in a P&L will generally be the same. There are three main areas in the format of a P&L. First, the title identifies the report, time period, and company name. Second, horizontal headings include current month or period financial information organized into actual, budget, and last year's and year to date financial information also organized into actual, budget, and last year. Third, vertical headings identify the department revenue, expense, and profit accounts and are organized with revenues at the top and profits at the bottom.

 ## Hospitality Manager Takeaways

1. The Consolidated P&L is a summary P&L for a hotel that reports total revenues, profits, or expenses for the departments in a hotel.

2. The Department P&L provides detailed operating information in specific line accounts for each individual department in a hotel. A specific hotel manager is directly responsible for the financial performance of each hotel department.

3. The total revenues and profits on each Department P&L are the same as the total revenues, profits, or expenses reported on the Consolidated P&L. In accounting terms, these numbers tie into or balance to each other on both P&Ls.

4. The Department P&L contains one revenue, four main expense categories, and total department profit or expense. Each of these main categories contains individual line accounts that collect all the specific revenues or expenses for the month that are classified or coded to each specific account.

5. Both Consolidated and Department P&Ls can have different formats that organize and report the financial results. Each company chooses the format that will work best for that particular company.

Key Terms

Allocations—The portion of an expense charged to a specific hotel for services received in connection with expenses incurred at the corporate level on behalf of all the hotels or restaurants in the company.

Deductions from Income—The same as expense centers. The direct expenses of staff departments that support the operating departments of a hotel by providing products and services to customers.

Department P&L Statements—A P&L statement for one specific department that includes all revenue and expenses in detail that are involved in operating that department.

Department Profits—The dollar amounts remaining in revenue centers/profit centers after the department recognizes all revenues and pays all expenses associated with operating that department for a specific time period.

Expense Categories—The four major categories for collecting and reporting department expenses: cost of sales, wages, benefits, and direct operating expenses.

Expense Center—A staff department that supports the hotel operating departments: sales and marketing, engineering, human resources, and accounting. It has no revenues or cost of sales, just wages, benefits, and direct operating expenses.

Fixed Expenses—Direct expenses of a hotel that are constant and do not change with different volume levels of hotel business.

Horizontal Headings—The headings across the top of a P&L that identify the type, time, and amount of financial information.

House Profit—The profit amount that includes all revenues and expenses controlled by hotel management and measures management's ability to operate the hotel profitably. It is calculated by subtracting total expense center costs from total department profits.

Investment Factors—Another term for hotel fixed expenses that are constant regardless of the volume levels of the hotel and include expenses like bank loans, lease payments, certificates and licenses, depreciation, and insurance expenses.

Net House Profit—Identifies the amount of profit remaining after all hotel revenues are recorded and all direct hotel expenses are paid. It is equal to house profit minus fixed expenses.

Profit after Taxes—The amount of profit remaining after corporate taxes are paid that is divided among owners, management companies, and any other entities having an interest in the hotel.

Profit before Taxes—The same as Net House Profit. The profit amount remaining after all hotel operating expenses have been paid.

Profit Center—An operating department that produces revenues that result in a profit by providing products and services to customers. It includes revenues, expenses, and profits and is a term that is interchangeable with *revenue center*.

Revenue Center—An operating product that produces revenues by providing products and services directly to customers. It includes revenues, expenses, and profits.

Titles—The top portion of a financial statement that tells the name of the company, the type of report, and the time period covered.

Total Department Profits—The summation of the individual department profits of a hotel. Provides the amount of profit resulting from the operating departments of a hotel.

Vertical Headings—The names of the departments, categories, and accounts on the side or center of a P&L that identify the type and amount of financial information recorded on the P&L.

Review Questions

1. Define and name the four main classifications of accounting information contained in a Consolidated P&L.

2. Define and name the five main revenue and expense categories contained in a Department P&L.

3. Name and describe four different profit levels and what they measure.

4. Name the three sections of the format for a P&L.

5. Draw the format for a Consolidated P&L using the three sections in question 4.

6. Draw the format for a Department P&L using the three sections in question 4.

7. Refer to the hotel organization chart in Chapter 3. Identify at least one hotel department that each Executive Committee Member is responsible for.

8. Why do you think this is the most important chapter in this book?

The Balance Sheet (A&L) and Statement of Cash Flow

Learning Objectives

1. To become familiar with other financial statements that are used to measure financial performance.

2. To understand the use of the Balance Sheet (also called the A&L) by hospitality managers and accounting managers.

3. To understand how the Balance Sheet is used with the P&L in managing operations.

4. To understand the difference between capitalization and working capital.

5. To understand the Statement of Cash Flow and its uses.

6. To understand the importance of liquidity and profitability.

Chapter Outline

The Balance Sheet or Asset and Liability (A&L) Statement

    Definition

    Working Capital

    Capitalization

Working Relationship between the Balance Sheet and the P&L Statement

    Managers' Use of Balance Sheet Accounts in Daily Operations

    Differences and Similarities between the Balance Sheet and the P&L

The Statement of Cash Flow

    Definition

    Cash Flow and Liquidity

    Classification of Cash Flow

    Source and Use of Funds Statement

Summary

Hospitality Manager Takeaways

Key Terms

Review Questions

There are three financial statements that have the greatest value in measuring the operations and financial performance of a business: the Profit and Loss (P&L) Statement, the Balance Sheet (or Asset and Liability [A&L] Statement), and the Statement of Cash Flow. We discussed the P&L in Chapter 4. In this chapter we will discuss the Balance Sheet and the Statement of Cash Flow.

Whereas the P&L is mainly used by hotel managers as a management tool and a measure of financial performance, the Balance Sheet and Statement of Cash Flow are also used by owners, bankers, and other outside institutions or agencies that have a financial interest in the business. They want to understand the financial strength and stability of a business that will permit that business to operate successfully and profitably over time. The P&L measures financial performance. *The balance sheet and statement of cash flow measure the ability of a business to sustain and produce profitable operations.* What resources does the business have, how effectively do they use them, and how sufficient are they in maintaining ongoing profitable operations?

This chapter discusses in detail the Balance Sheet and Statement of Cash Flow and how they are used primarily to measure financial performance but also as a management tool. Hospitality mangers should have a fundamental understanding of these two financial statements to go along with a strong and detailed knowledge of the P&L. This knowledge enables managers to discuss the financial aspects of their operations with senior management and to demonstrate the financial knowledge and skills presented in the career success model discussed in Chapter 1.

The Balance Sheet or Asset and Liability (A&L) Statement

The purpose of the **Balance Sheet** is to measure the financial status, value, and net worth of a business. It is also referred to as the A&L. It is prepared at the end of each month or accounting period as well as at the end of the year. The Director of Finance or the corporate accounting office is responsible for preparing the Balance Sheet each month and ensuring that the accounts are accurate and in balance.

Definition

The Balance Sheet measures the status or net worth of a business as of a specific date. It is like a snapshot in time. The Balance Sheet shows the amounts or balances in each account as of a specific date. It is called the Asset and Liability Statement because it shows the balances in each of the assets and liability accounts. It is called the Balance Sheet because, again, that is what it shows—the *balance* in each of the accounts at a specific time. Exhibit 5.1 on page 94 is an example of the Balance Sheet for the Flagstaff Hotel.

The Balance Sheet measures the value or worth of a business. Key characteristics of the Balance Sheet are as follows:

1. It measures the value or worth of a company at a specific point in time. For example, a Balance Sheet might be prepared at the end of the year, December 31. It is a snapshot of account balances at that specific point in time that identifies what a company owns (assets), what it owes (liabilities), and how it is owned (owner equity).

2. The **Fundamental Account Equation** describes the Balance Sheet. This equation is

$$Assets = Liabilities + Owner\ Equity$$

3. It is made up of accounts organized by asset, liability, or owner equity.

4. These accounts are divided into current accounts (less than one-year obligations), also referred to as working capital, and long-term accounts (longer than one-year obligations), which are referred to as capitalization.

5. Each account has a beginning balance, monthly activity, and an ending balance.

6. Unlike the P&L Statement, managers are not expected to provide critiques of monthly Balance Sheet activity. This is done by the Accounting Department.

7. Accounting managers balance monthly the accounts of a Balance Sheet.

8. Current accounts are used as working capital in operating the business. The definition of working capital is current assets minus current liabilities.

9. Long-term liability accounts and owner equity accounts are used as capitalization, which provides the money to start, renovate, or expand a business.

It is important for managers to understand the Balance Sheet because they use the current assets and current liability accounts (working capital) in the daily operations of their business. They are expected to efficiently use the assets of a business to operate it profitably. Following are definitions that describe important balance sheet accounts:

- **Current Assets**—Less than one-year life.

- **Cash**—Money that is in the cash bank account and available to use in daily business operations. It can be in a savings or checking account. It is the most liquid form of an asset. It is available immediately.

- **Accounts Receivable**—Dollar amounts that the company is owed for providing products and services to customers but that is uncollected. These accounts go through a direct billing process and are expected to be paid generally within 30 days. Credit cards and direct billing to companies are the two major parts of accounts receivable. It is the next most liquid asset after cash.

- **Inventories**—Supplies or materials that the company has purchased but not used in order to provide products and services to its customers. Examples of important inventories for hospitality operations are food, beverage, china, glass, silver, linen, cleaning supplies, and guest supplies. The company has purchased and paid for the inventory but has not put it to use. Inventory is not considered very liquid because it must first be converted into a final product, then sold, and then the proceeds collected and deposited into the cash account.

- **Prepaid Expenses**—Obligations of a hotel paid in advance and charged to department P&L accounts on a predetermined schedule such as monthly for six months or monthly for one year.

- **Long-Term Assets**—Longer than one-year life.

- **Property**—Land that is purchased to provide the building to produce products and services. This is the land on which a hotel or restaurant is located.

- **Plant**—The physical structure or building that houses the business operation. This is the actual hotel or restaurant building.

- **Equipment**—The machines and other assets that are used to produce the product or service. This is the kitchen equipment, guest room furniture and fixtures, restaurant tables and chairs, vehicles, washers and dryers, heat-light-power equipment, computer systems, and all other machines used in a hotel or restaurant.

- **Depreciation**—The portion of the total cost of property, plant, and equipment that is charged each year to the actual operations of a business. It is calculated by dividing the total cost by the number of years of useful production life to get the annual cost or depreciation charged to a specific year.

- **Current Liabilities**—Less than one-year obligations.

- **Accounts Payable**—Products or services received but not paid for that are due within one year. The invoices have been received, approved, and are in the process of payment.

- **Wages Payable**—Wages owed but not paid to employees who have performed the expected labor responsibilities. The employees have worked, but the paychecks have not been distributed or cashed.

- **Taxes Payable**—Taxes that have been collected but not paid to the appropriate tax agency. Taxes are typically paid quarterly or annually.

- **Advance Deposits**—Funds received from customers before the arrival date to guarantee sleeping rooms, meeting space, and other products or services. This can be a major current liability for resorts and convention hotels.

- **Accrued Liabilities**—Amounts owed for purchases received but not paid for at the end of month or end of period cut-off date.

- **Long-Term Liabilities**—Longer than one-year obligations.

- **Bank Loans**—Amounts owed to banks or other financial institutions that will be repaid over an extended number of years, generally from 5 to 30 years. Bank loans are used for capitalization including startup, renovation, or expansion.

- **Line of Credit**—A form of bank loan where a specific dollar amount is set aside for the business to use. The business may draw on or use these funds as needed. When used, they are repaid on similar terms as a bank loan.

- **Lease Obligations**—The land, building, or equipment that is leased, not purchased, and is recognized as a long-term liability according to the contract.

- **Owner Equity**—Investment in a company in the form of paid-in capital, common or preferred stock, and retained earnings.

- **Paid-in Capital**—The amount invested to start a company by the owners of a company or business. It is the dollar amount that they provide from their own financial resources.

- **Common Stock**—The amount invested by other individuals or institutions by purchasing common or preferred stock in the company or business. The value of this investment is determined by the price of the company stock as it is traded on the open market.

- **Retained Earning**—The portion of annual operating profits that the company keeps. It improves the strength of the Balance Sheet and the company as it grows each year.

The format of the Balance Sheet comes from the Fundamental Accounting Equation. The Fundamental Accounting Equation states that the dollar amount or value of assets must equal the dollar amounts or value of the liabilities and owner equity used to purchase the assets. In other words, what you *own* should equal what you *owe* to financial institutions in the form of loans or to owners in the form of investment.

$$Assets = Liabilities + Owner\ Equity$$

- An **asset** is a resource. In business, it is all the property of a business that can be applied to covering liabilities (Webster's dictionary).

- A **liability** is a debt. In business, it is something owed to another, a legal obligation (Webster's).

- **Owner equity** is possession and value and is defined in two parts. To *own* is to have or possess, and *equity* is the value of property beyond a liability (Webster's).

The Fundamental Accounting Equation shows these relationships and defines them with dollar balances and values. The Asset total amount must equal the Liability and Owner Equity amount. This ensures that all funds and transactions are accounted for according to accounting rules and principles. The rules and procedures that govern accounting in business are called generally accepted accounting principles, or GAAP. A business needs to collect, prepare, and report their accounting results according to these principles in order to be recognized as valid and accurate. Anyone who reads financial statements prepared in accordance with GAAP can have confidence in the accuracy and validity of the numbers contained in those statements. Exhibit 5.1 is an example of a Balance Sheet.

EXHIBIT 5.1
BALANCE SHEET

Flagstaff Hotel
June 30, 2004

ASSETS			LIABILITIES	
Current			**Current**	
Cash	$ 75		Accounts Payable	$ 60
Accounts Receivable	40		Wages Payable	40
Inventories	90		Taxes Payable	25
Total Current Assets	$205		Total Current Liabilities	$125
Long Term			**Long Term**	
Property	$125		Bank Loans	$150
Plant	200		Line of Credit	50
Equipment	150		Lease Obligations	25
Less Depreciation	50		Other Long-Term Obligations	0
Total Long-Term Assets	$525		Total Long-Term Liabilities	$225
Total Assets	**$730**		**Total Liabilities**	**$350**
			OWNER EQUITY	
			Paid-in Capital	$200
			Capital Stock	100
			Retained Earnings	380
			Total Owner Equity	**$380**
Total Assets	**$730**		**Total Liabilities and Owner Equity**	**$730**

We will now apply the financial information in Exhibit 5.1 to the characteristics of the Balance Sheet as an example.

1. Assets = Liabilities + Owner Equity

   or

   $730 Total Assets = $350 Total Liabilities + $380 Owner Equity or $730

   The Fundamental Accounting Equation is in balance because the $730 in total assets is equal to the $730 in total liabilities and owner equity.

2. Ending balances as of June 30, 2004, are as follows:

Current Assets	$205	Current Liabilities	$125
Long-Term Assets	$525	Long-Term Liabilities	$225
Total Assets	$730	Total Liabilities	$350
		Paid-in Capital	$200
		Capital Stock	$100
		Retained Earnings	$ 80
		Total Owner Equity	$380

These are the ending balances in the major accounts as of June 30, 2004. Anyone reading the Balance Sheet will rely on these numbers as being accurate as to the value or net worth of the Flagstaff Hotel as of this date.

3. Current Accounts | Long-Term Accounts

Current Accounts		Long-Term Accounts	
Current Assets	$205	Long-Term Assets	$525
Current Liabilities	$125	Long-Term Liabilities	$225
		Owner Equity	$380

The values or account balances in the current and the long-term balance sheet accounts are as shown as of a specific date—June 30, 2004.

4. Working Capital = Current Assets − Current Liabilities

   $80 Working Capital = $205 Current Assets − $125 Current Liabilities

   The Flagstaff Hotel working capital is $80. This tells us that the Flagstaff Hotel has $80 left as working capital reflected by the $205 already committed and invested in current assets and the $125 currently owed in current liabilities. The $80 is the remaining amount available for use in operating the business.

5. Capitalization = Liabilities + Owner Equity

   or

   $730 Capitalization = $350 Liabilities + $380 Owner Equity

This tells us that the Flagstaff Hotel has total assets of $730 and that the company was financed by $350 in debt or long-term liabilities and $380 in equity.

Working Capital

Working capital is the dollar amount provided for the daily operations of a business. It is invested in the current assets of a business, primarily in cash, accounts receivable, and inventory. The initial dollar amount invested as working capital is deposited in the cash account. Then it is invested in inventories as part of the process of providing products and services to customers (Figure 5.1). When a sale is made and the customer has not yet paid for the product or service, that dollar amount is identified as accounts receivable. When the credit card company sends electronic transfers as payment, or when individuals or companies send checks as payment, they are deposited directly into the cash account.

Working capital also involves the use of the current liabilities of a business, primarily in accounts payable, wages payable, and taxes payable. When the company receives materials and supplies that are used in providing products and services but has not yet paid for them, they are recognized as accounts payable. As the invoices documenting amounts received and prices charged are approved by department heads for payment, the accounts payable clerk processes a check and sends it out as payment. When the checks are mailed, the corresponding accounts payable is closed out and no longer recognized as a current liability. The same is true for wages owed employees and taxes owed government agencies. Wages owed employees are accrued until the paychecks are distributed and cashed. Taxes are collected during a specified time period—quarterly or annually—and then paid. Until they are paid, they are recognized as accounts payable.

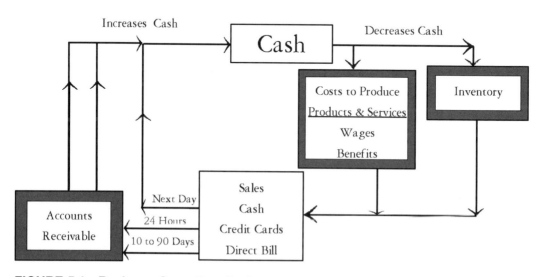

FIGURE 5.1   Business Operating Cycle.

The definition of working capital is current assets minus current liabilities. Another term closely associated with working capital is *liquidity*. Liquidity is the ability of a business to meet its short-term financial obligations. The larger the cash balances of a business, generally, the more liquid the company is or the more capable it is of paying its financial obligations. A company cannot afford to invest too much in inventory or let accounts receivable get too large. If that happens, it means that the company is taking longer to return cash to the cash account after it has been used to purchase materials and supplies or that the company is taking too long to collect accounts receivable and convert these balances into cash. That means that a company will have dollars tied up in large inventory and accounts receivable accounts rather than in the cash account where they can be used to operate the business.

Capitalization

Capitalization identifies the way a business obtains and uses money to start or expand the business. Capital is money or property that is used to create more money or property. Capitalization involves the use of long-term debt or owner equity (capital) as a way of obtaining the necessary funds or money to start a business. Technically, capital refers to the funds contributed to a company by the owners or stockholders. Capital also describes the net worth of a company (Webster's). We include long-term debt as well as owner equity in our definition of capitalization because long-term debt is another source of obtaining the necessary money or financing to start a business.

Referring to our example in Exhibit 5.1 and point 5, the capitalization of the Flagstaff Hotel is $730 and was obtained with $350 in long-term liabilities and $380 in owner equity.

Capitalization can be in the form of three activities. First is the initial startup costs of establishing a company, which involve purchasing mainly long-term assets. Second is capital replacement of older long-term assets as they wear out or become inefficient or obsolete with new long-term assets. Third is capital expansion, which is the use of capital to expand and grow the business. Capitalization provides the financial resources to invest in a business for the long term. These financial resources *should not* be used as working capital in the short term for the daily operations of a business. If a company has to use long-term capital to pay daily operating expenses, it is not generating sufficient revenues from its daily operations to cover operating expenses. This is a major liquidity problem that could result in a company not being able to pay its bills and eventually going out of business.

Courtyard Miami Airport South and Miami Airport Marriott Hotel

This 778-room 6-building hotel underwent a major conversion in 1995 that significantly changed the way it operated. It went from operating as a large 778-room full-service Marriott hotel to operating three different Marriott brands. It now operates three buildings as a 281 room Fairfield Inn by Marriott, one building as a 125-room Courtyard by Marriott, and two buildings as a 366-room full-service Marriott. The picture shows the Courtyard in the foreground and the original of the two 9-story full-service Marriott towers in the background. The Fairfield Inn is located on the right but not included in the picture.

As a result of this conversion from one to three different brands, revenues increased over 30%. What do you think the impact was of this revenue increase on cash flow for the property? Do you think the increase was in room rate or rooms sold? The owners invested a significant amount to convert this property from one brand to three brands. How did this conversion affect the Balance Sheet for this property? Is this conversion an example of capitalization or working capital? Do you think the owners received a good ROI (return on investment)? How would you calculate the ROI?

Working Relationships between the Balance Sheet and the P&L Statement

Managers' Use of Balance Sheet Accounts in Daily Operations

Hospitality managers work primarily with the P&L statement. It measures the financial performance of the department, hotel, or restaurant and is used as a management tool to improve operations. Managers should be focused on effectively managing their operations to produce the budgeted or forecasted results. The P&L results for a month help them review and evaluate actual performance and to plan on future performance.

Hospitality managers use the company's working capital (Balance Sheet amounts) in their daily operations. They primarily use the current assets of the company. They spend cash to purchase inventories (current asset, CA) or pay employee wages (current liability, CL) to produce products and services. They are expected to manage these accounts or expenditures according to budgets or company procedures. Working capital is both the amount a hotel or restaurant manager has to utilize for daily operations and the amount or balance in the cash account that is not spent and available for operations. Effectively managing the working capital in daily operations maximizes the working capital that is uncommitted and available for ongoing operations. Refer to the business operating cycle shown in Figure 5.1 to visualize these relationships.

Follow the arrows to see the flow of working capital in daily operations. The working capital provides current assets to produce products and services for customers. Notice that everything starts with the cash account. Current assets and operating expenses use cash. Inventory is a balance sheet current asset, and wages and benefits are operating expenses on the P&L Statement that are used to produce products and services. Production uses assets and incurred expenses.

When the sale occurs, cash payments are deposited directly into the cash account. Credit card sales go briefly into accounts receivable and then into the cash account when the electronic transfer of funds is received. Direct billing sales go to accounts receivable where they stay until the account is paid. Thirty-day accounts are acceptable, but accounts unpaid that are 30 to 60 days, 60 to 90 days, or more than 90 days tie up cash and put a strain on cash flow.

The more efficient a company uses its assets and the quicker it collects its sales, the better the cash flow and financial soundness of the company.

Several of the accounts in Figure 5.1 are revenue and expense accounts that are part of the P&L Statement. For example, the amount of wages payable (CL) on the A&L is determined by the amount managers spend in management, hourly, and overtime labor costs. These costs are immediately recognized on the P&L as expenses incurred in providing products and services to customers. The cost is recognized on the Balance Sheet as wages payable (CL) until the paychecks are written, issued, and cashed by employees. At that time, wages payable are decreased and the cash account is decreased. So the time associated with an accounting transaction is different for the P&L and Balance Sheet, but they will all be included in the same time period, usually a month or accounting period. The wage expense on the P&L is *for the month or accounting period*, and the cash and accounts payable are *at the end of the month or the end of the accounting period.*

The same relationship exists for inventories and operating expense. When a manager purchases guest supplies and linen for the Rooms Department, it will increase the rooms guest supplies and rooms linen inventory accounts when the supplies are received. The total expense is then recognized as accounts payable until the manager receives, approves, and sends the invoice to accounting for payment. When accounts payable sends out the check, accounts payable decreases and the cash account is decreased. At this point, the transactions only affect the Balance Sheet accounts—inventory (CA) and accounts payable (CL).

> Step 1 Transaction when inventory is purchased—Increase inventory and increase accounts payable.
>
> Step 2 Transaction when invoice is paid—Decrease accounts payable and decrease cash.

When the supplies are taken out of inventory and put into operations, the corresponding P&L expense accounts are charged. For example, if $2,000 of linen and $1,000 in guest supplies are taken out of inventory and put into operations, the inventory accounts are decreased by those amounts, and $2,000 is charged to the linen operating expense account and $1,000 is charged to the guest supply operating expense account on the Rooms Department P&L Statement.

Linen transaction	Decrease linen inventory account (CA)	−$2,000
	Increase linen expense account (P&L)	+$2,000
Guest supply transaction	Decrease guest supply inventory (CA)	−$1,000
	Increase guest supply expense account (P&L)	+$1,000

Differences and Similarities between the Balance Sheet and the P&L

Let's take some time to review the characteristics and transactions that affect the P&L Statement and the Balance Sheet.

Differences

1. The P&L shows financial transactions *over a period of time* like a month or year. The Balance Sheet shows financial information *at a specific time or date* like the end of the month or end of the year.

2. The P&L records revenues, expenses, and profit *amounts* incurred or spent during a specific time period. The Balance Sheet records account *amounts or balances* at the end of a specific time period.

3. The P&L *accumulates and totals* revenues received and expenses incurred over the month or accounting period. A new month starts with zero balances on the P&L. The balance sheet *records account activity* during the month or accounting period and the balance remaining at the end of the month.

4. The P&L is used by hospitality managers in operating their departments, and it measures the financial performance of the department. The Balance Sheet is also used by hospitality managers in operating their department, and it is also used by owners, investors, and outside financial institutions in evaluating the value and net worth of a business.

Similarities

1. Both statements are subject to generally accepted accounting principles (GAAP).

2. The hotel accounting department or corporate accounting department prepares both financial statements.

3. Both statements have accounts that are used as working capital.

The Statement of Cash Flow

The **Statement of Cash Flow** is the third financial statement used in measuring the financial performance of a company. It focuses on two areas of company operations. First is the cash account on the Balance Sheet. It identifies the movement of cash in and out of the cash account and the amount of beginning and ending cash balances are maintained. Liquidity is the key term and measurement. Second is the source and use of funds generated by the company in using accounts on the Balance Sheet in daily operations. Working capital is the key term and measurement.

Definition

The Statement of Cash Flow measures the amount of cash a company has and how cash flows through the company during the course of daily operations. The primary source of cash should be the revenues generated by the operations of a company or business. It should be sufficient to cover all expenses incurred to produce products, services, and profit. Key characteristics of the Statement of Cash Flow are as follows:

1. It involves the cash account of the Balance Sheet.

2. It has beginning and ending balances.

3. It shows how money is used in the daily operations of a business.

4. It measures liquidity.

5. It is a fundamental component of working capital.

6. It reflects the increases and decreases in Balance Sheet accounts.

Cash Flow and Liquidity

Several key elements of measuring and managing cash are important for hospitality students to know and understand. A business must pay as much attention to managing cash and maintaining sufficient cash balances as it pays to making an operating profit.

Cash Flow

The main reason that the cash account on the Balance Sheet is so important is that a company must maintain a large enough balance in its cash account to pay all operating expenses in a timely and efficient manner. Purchases of supplies and materials from vendors, payment of wages to employees, and paying long-term obligations such as bank loans on time are critical to the success of a company. The hotel's Director of Finance is responsible for managing the cash account so that no disbursements are made in payment of obligations unless there is money in the cash account to cover these expenses and obligations.

Cash increases come through revenues recorded on the P&L Statement as a result of operating activities. Specifically, the cash account increases with the daily hotel deposit of cash, traveler's checks, and individual or company checks received in payment of products and services provided by the hotel and directly billed to the customer. Each day, the hotel also receives electronic cash transfers directly into its cash account from the credit card companies in payment of guest accounts paid by credit card. Last, specific accounts billed directly to individual guests or companies progress through the accounts receivable cycle until the bill is approved by the customer/company and a check is processed and mailed to the hotel in payment of amounts owed the hotel.

Cash is a current asset on the Balance Sheet, so it always will have a beginning balance at the beginning of the month, activity during the month, and an ending balance at the end of the month. This activity in the cash account represents the cash flow of a company.

Liquidity

Liquidity refers to the amount of cash or cash equivalents that a company has to cover its daily operating expenses and that it maintains in its cash or cash equivalent accounts on the Balance Sheet. This includes the length of time it will generally take to convert a Balance Sheet account to cash. A short conversion time period reflects a liquid asset. A long conversion time period reflects a nonliquid asset. Let's look at some examples of asset accounts on the Balance Sheet that illustrate liquidity:

- *Cash.* **Cash** is the most liquid asset of all. It is available for immediate use.

- *Cash equivalents.* The next most liquid asset. These are current assets that can be converted to cash in a matter of hours—for example, 24 to 48 hours. Common stock, company and Treasury bonds, certificates of deposit, and overnight investments are examples of cash equivalents. They can be sold, and the receipts are usually deposited into the cash account within a matter of days.

- *Liquid assets.* Accounts that are on their way to becoming cash. Accounts receivable are an example of a liquid asset. The sale has been made, the invoice has been sent to the buyer, and payment is in the process of being made. Receipt of payment and deposit in the cash account can occur in a matter of days or weeks. The point to remember is that the next transaction of a liquid asset is that of being deposited into the cash account.

- *Nonliquid asset.* Accounts that are not close to being turned into cash. Inventory is an example of a nonliquid current asset. The fact that money is tied up in inventory means that it has not been sold yet. In fact, there are three categories of inventory reflecting three stages of liquidity:

    Finished goods. Inventory of assembled and completed products at the manufacturing plant that are waiting to be shipped, on the shelves of a distributor ready to be shipped to retail outlets, or on the shelves of retail outlets ready to be sold to customers.

    Work-in-process. Inventory that is in the process of being assembled into a final product. It is no longer raw material and will soon be finished goods.

    Raw materials. Inventory that has not been used yet to produce a product. It is sitting on shelves in the warehouse or in piles in the stockyard. It is a long way from being converted into cash.

    Generally, no estimates are made of when inventory will be converted to cash because of the status and many variables involved in managing inventories. Finished goods are much closer to being converted into sales and cash than work in process or raw materials. Finished goods are more liquid than raw materials or work in process.

- *Long-term assets.* Assets that are not intended to be converted into cash but to be used in the daily operations of the company over an extended period of time. They are involved in the capitalization of a company and represent assets that have a longer life, generally 1 to 50 years. They will only be sold or replaced when they are worn out, outdated, or fully depreciated.

It is important for a company to maintain acceptable levels of liquidity. Each industry has a set standard that identifies the amount of cash or cash equivalents that a company should maintain to have acceptable levels of liquidity. Two of those measures are working capital and the current ratio. Working capital is defined as current assets minus current liabilities. It implies that a company should have a higher amount of current assets than current liabilities. This means that the company owns more current assets than it owes in current liabilities. It is important to look at the direction or trend of working capital from month to month. Is it getting larger and stronger, or is it getting smaller and becoming a concern or a problem?

The current ratio is current assets divided by current liabilities and expresses this relationship in terms of a percentage. Again, a company would like a current ratio of more than 1, because that means that the company has more current assets than current liabilities. It is also important to look at the direction in which the current ratio is moving. Is it getting stronger or weaker? Is it high and safe or low and not safe? Industry standards will be applied to a company's current ratio to determine if it is acceptable and moving in the right direction or not.

We will use the financial information in Exhibit 5.1 to illustrate working capital and calculate the current ratio.

$$Working\ Capital = Current\ Assets - Current\ Liabilities$$
$$= \$205 - \$125$$
$$= \$80$$
$$Current\ Ratio = Current\ Assets \div Current\ Liabilities$$
$$= \$205 \div \$125$$
$$= 1.64$$

Classification of Cash Flow

Cash flow activities are classified into three main categories that describe the nature of the cash inflow or outflow: (1) operating activities, (2) investing activities, and (3) financing activities. Hospitality managers are primarily involved in the operating activity but should have a good understanding of financing and investing activities.

Operating activities include *cash inflow*, primarily from the sale of products and services to guests. This is the main reason for the existence of a company or business and is therefore the most important cash flow activity. Hospitality managers are directly involved in maximizing hotel and restaurant revenues. *Cash outflow* involving operating activities includes the payment of wages and benefits to employees, the payment for supplies and materials to vendors, and the payment of taxes and other expenses to appropriate agencies. Hospitality managers, again, are directly involved in managing and controlling expenses to maximize profitability, which should also result in the creation of a strong positive cash flow.

Investing activities include cash outflow that involves purchasing long-term assets or investing in marketable securities. When these investments are reversed, cash inflow is created. For example, if older equipment is sold or property is sold, this results in cash being received and deposited in the cash account; therefore this is a cash inflow. The same occurs when marketable securities are sold and cash is received, and deposited in the cash account. The Director of Finance, along with corporate senior management, is primarily involved with investing activities.

Financing activities involve the creation or use of cash for capitalization purposes. Cash inflow results from selling common stock or obtaining a bank loan. The cash account goes up. Cash outflow results from purchasing common stock or the repayment of a bank loan. The cash account is decreased, and the funds are used to buy the common stock or to repay the bank loan. Financing activities primarily involve the owner and management company working with the Director of Finance and General Manager in conducting financing activities.

Source and Use of Funds Statement

The **Source and Use of Funds Statement** is part of the Statement of Cash Flow and shows how cash is created or used among the different accounts on the Balance Sheet. It involves the changes in the balances of all the accounts on the Balance Sheet. It will be helpful to refer back to the Fundamental Accounting Equation in discussing the changes in individual balance sheet accounts that result in a source of funds or a use of funds.

$$Assets = Liabilities + Owner\ Equity$$

Let's begin with the following table, which separates sources and uses of funds and thereby demonstrates increases or decreases in the accounts.

Sources	Uses
1. Decreases in asset accounts	1. Increases in asset accounts
2. Increases in liability accounts	2. Decreases in liability accounts
3. Increases in owner equity accounts	3. Decreases in owner equity accounts

Sources of Cash

A decrease in an asset account means that the asset balance has gone down or declined and less money is contained in that account. For example, collecting $5,000 in accounts receivable (CA) means that accounts receivable is now $5,000 lower. The offsetting/ balancing entry is cash (CA), which increases $5,000. The decrease in accounts receivable is a source of funds or a source of cash. Another example is when food inventory (CA) of $3,000 is put into production. The accounting entry is a $3,000 decrease in inventory that was sold and a $3,000 increase in food cost on the P&L. Again, the decrease in inventory creates a source of funds. In both examples, money was freed up from a current asset account, which generated a source of funds.

An increase in liabilities also is a source of cash and means that the amount owed vendors or other companies has increased. Therefore it is a source of cash because the actual cash disbursement has been delayed.

An increase in owner equity is also a source of cash. This means that owners have made additional contributions to the company in the paid-in capital account or that individual investors have bought more of the common stock of the company or that retained earnings have increased as a result of operating profits. All of these transactions are a source of cash because the amount invested in the company in owner equity accounts has increased. For each of these transactions, the corresponding accounting entry is an increase in the cash account—a source of funds.

Uses of Cash

An increase in an asset account means that the balance in that account has gone up, which requires a cash outlay. For example, the company purchases and pays for $10,000 in materials, which increases the inventory account. That is a use of funds because $10,000 is used to purchase materials and increase inventory.

A decrease in liabilities is a use of cash and means the amount owed vendors or other companies has decreased because the company has made a payment to them. Using the same $10,000 inventory purchase example but not paying cash results in the following transactions:

Inventory + $10,000   Accounts Payable + $10,000

This part of the transaction is a source of funds because we the company *has not paid the $10,000 invoice*. The second part of the transaction, when the company pays the invoice, is represented this way:

Accounts Payable – $10,000   Cash – $10,000

This is a use of cash. When the decrease in accounts payable occurs, that is the time when the transaction is a use of funds.

A decrease in owner equity is a use of cash. This means that the paid-in capital account has decreased because one or several of the owners have taken money out of the account in the form of a cash disbursement. A decrease in the common stock account means that investors have sold the stock, resulting in a cash disbursement. The final activity is a decrease in retained earnings, which means that the company had an operating loss and money was taken from the retained earnings account to cover the loss. This also is a cash disbursement. In each of these owner equity transactions, the account value decreased, requiring a corresponding decrease in cash as cash was disbursed or paid to cover the transaction.

Summary

The Balance Sheet is the financial statement that measures a company's value or net worth as of a specific date in time. It is also called the Asset and Liability (A&L) Statement. The Balance Sheet is organized according to the fundamental accounting equation:

Assets = Liabilities + Owner Equity

Assets are resources or what a company owns.

Liabilities are debts a company owes.

Owner equity is who owns a company.

The main characteristics of a Balance Sheet are the following:

1. It measures the value or net worth of a company at a specific date in time.
2. The Fundamental Accounting Equation describes the Balance Sheet:

Assets = Liabilities + Owner Equity

3. It is divided into current and long-term accounts.
4. It has beginning balances, monthly activity, and ending balances.
5. It has monthly activity including increases and decreases.
6. The value of the asset side of the Balance Sheet must equal the value of the Liability and Owner Equity side of the Balance Sheet.

Capitalization refers to the way a company or business obtains and uses money to start or expand the business. It involves obtaining long-term debt or raising funds from investors by way of paid-in capital or common stock. Working capital is the amount of funds used by a business in its daily operations and is defined as current assets minus current liabilities. Hospitality managers use the assets in the Balance Sheet accounts in the daily operations of their departments.

The Statement of Cash Flow identifies the movement of cash in and out of the cash account in the daily operations of a business. It measures the amount of cash available and identifies how it is used. The cash account is the most important current asset account because it is used to purchase the other assets required to produce the products and services, and it is used to pay all operating expenses including the salaries and wages of employees making the products and services.

Cash flow activities are divided into three categories: operating activities, financing activities, and investing activities. Hospitality managers are primarily involved in operating activities as they manage their departments.

Liquidity is an important measurement of cash flow. It is the amount of cash or cash equivalents that a company has to cover its daily operating expenses. The dollar amount available in the cash account is immediately available for use in company operations and requires no time for conversion into the cash account.

Hospitality Manager Takeaways

1. **It is important for hospitality managers to have a general understanding of the Balance Sheet and Statement of Cash Flow. The daily operation of their department will affect both statements.**

2. **Working capital is the accounts on the Balance Sheet that hospitality managers use on a daily basis—primarily cash, inventories, and accounts payable.**

3. **Hospitality managers must understand the importance of liquidity, which is the ability to maintain sufficient cash account balances to pay all debts and operating responsibilities.**

4. **It is important for hospitality managers to understand the basic characteristics of the Balance Sheet and Statement of Cash Flow and be able to have a positive impact on them through the daily operations of their departments.**

Key Terms

Accounts Payable—Products or services received by a company but not paid for that are due within one year.

Accounts Receivable—What the company is owed for providing products and services to customers. Revenues recorded but uncollected.

Assets—The resources owned by a company that are used by that company in the production of products and services.

    Current—Assets that are used or consumed during a one-year time period.

    Long Term—Assets with a useful life of longer than one year.

Balance Sheet—The financial statement that measures the value or net worth of a business as of a specific date. Also called the Asset and Liability (A&L) Statement.

Cash—Funds that are in the cash account and available for use in daily business operations.

Classifications of Cash Flow—Operating activities, financial activities, and investment activities.

Fundamental Accounting Equation—Assets = Liabilities + Owner Equity.

Inventory—Assets in the form of materials and supplies that the company has purchased but not yet used in the production of products and services.

Liabilities—Obligations owed by a company.

　Current—Obligations that are due within one year.

　Long Term—Obligations that are due longer than one year from the current date.

Owner Equity—The amount invested in a company by owners or investors including paid-in capital, common stock, and retained earnings.

Source and Use of Funds Statement—A part of the statement of cash flow that shows how funds are created (source) and disbursed (used) among the different accounts on the balance sheet.

Statement of Cash Flow—Measures the liquidity and identifies the flow of cash in a company.

Review Questions

1. Explain the financial information contained in a Balance Sheet, and explain how it is used.

2. Describe working capital and capitalization, and explain what each is used for. Include the Balance Sheet accounts that are used in each process.

3. What accounts on the Balance Sheet will hospitality managers generally use in the daily operations of their departments?

4. List five characteristics of the Balance Sheet.

5. Compare and contrast liquidity with profitability.

6. Name the three classifications of cash flow.

7. Name three changes in Balance Sheet accounts that are a source of funds and three that are a use of funds.

8. Why is an increase in accounts payable a source of funds? Give an example.

9. List four characteristics of the Statement of Cash Flow.

Hotel Management Reports

Learning Objectives

1. To learn about internal hotel management reports.
2. To understand and be able to use Daily Revenue Reports.
3. To understand and be able to use revenue forecasting reports.
4. To understand and be able to use labor productivity reports.
5. To understand the relationship between revenue changes and profit changes.

Chapter Outline

Internal Hotel Management Reports

    Definition

    Types and Uses

Daily Reports

    Daily Revenue Reports

    Labor Productivity Reports

Weekly Internal Management Reports

    Weekly Revenue Forecast

    Weekly Wage and Cost Scheduling

    Profitability Forecasting

Monthly Internal Management Reports

    Monthly P&L Statement

    Profitability, Retention, and Flow Through

    Monthly P&L Statement Critiques

Summary

Hospitality Manager Takeaways

Key Terms

Review Questions

The three financial reports that we have discussed in previous chapters—the Profit and Loss (P&L) Statement, the Balance Sheet, and the Statement of Cash Flow—are used by both management and outside parties in evaluating hotel operations. We will now talk about two types of internal financial and management reports that hotel managers use:

- One report summarizes and presents the operating results for the previous day or week.

- The second report forecasts or schedules operations and functions for the next day or next week.

Managers use these reports to understand and evaluate past operations and to plan their daily and weekly future operations. They will make any necessary changes to daily operations to achieve budgets and forecasts or to respond to market or outside conditions.

Internal management reports are prepared by the accounting office and distributed to hotel managers for their use. Refer again to the Financial Management Cycle:

1. Operations produces the numbers.

2. Accounting prepares the numbers.

3. Operations and accounting analyze the numbers.

4. Operations applies the numbers to change or improve operations.

The reports that we will discuss in this chapter are examples of the Financial Management Cycle. Operations produces the numbers, whether they are good or bad. It is accounting's job to collect and prepare the management reports from these operational numbers so that managers can use them to identify and analyze operations. Then management can apply the information from the numbers to the next day's or week's operations. The goals are to understand what happened, why it happened, and how it can be changed or improved.

Internal Hotel Management Reports

Definition

An internal management report contains detailed operating information covering a specific time for a specific product, customer, department, or for the entire hotel or restaurant. It can contain the operational results for activities of the previous day or week, or it can contain the information required to plan the next day or week. Daily and weekly reports are used internally as management tools, whereas monthly reports are used both as a management tool and to report the monthly financial results for the three formal financial statements: the P&L, the Balance Sheet, and the Statement of Cash Flow.

These internal management reports are extremely valuable to operations managers. They are a guide—a true management tool—for them to use in managing their daily operations. The more a manager understands these reports, the better she or he will be able to use them to improve or change operations.

Types and Uses

Reports contain daily, weekly, monthly, and quarterly information. They include reports that provide actual operating information and financial information for previous time periods and reports that plan in detail for future time periods. Daily and weekly reports that provide the results of actual operations are used to forecast and schedule operations for the next day, week, month, or quarter. Table 6.1 illustrates the types and uses of internal management reports.

We will discuss these reports in detail, including examples of the reports used by some of the major hotel and restaurant companies. Keep in mind that one type of report provides historical operating information and the other type forecasts and schedules operations for the next week.

Daily Reports

The two most important daily reports provide information on revenues and labor costs. The names and formats of these reports can be different from company to company, but the content is the same. They focus on providing the actual operating results for the previous day and comparing those results with forecasts, budget, the previous month, and last year's information.

TABLE 6.1
Internal Management Reports

	Daily	Weekly	Monthly	Quarterly	Annually
Performance Reports—The Past					
Daily revenue report	X				
Daily labor report	X				
Weekly financial report		X			
Monthly P&L			X		
Profitability measurement			X	X	X
Planning Reports—The Future					
The daily room count	X				
The daily banquet schedule	X				
Weekly revenue forecast		X			
Weekly labor forecast		X			
Monthly revenue forecast			X		
Quarterly revenue forecast				X	
End-of-year revenue forecast					X

Daily Revenue Reports

This report is prepared during the night audit or day audit shift and collects and presents all of the operating information for the previous day. It can be called the Sales and Occupancy Report, the Daily Revenue Report, or the Gross Revenue Report depending on the company. All contain virtually the same information. We will discuss a Daily Revenue Report that is organized into the following section: (1) hotel daily revenue by department, (2) hotel daily room statistics, (3) Restaurant and Banquets Summary, and (4) hotel market segment information.

The *daily revenue by department* is organized in a similar format as the P&L Statement. The *title* provides the name of the hotel, type of report, and date of the report. The *horizontal headings* provide revenue for the day and compare it to the budget and last year's revenues. It also provides month-to-date accumulated revenue for actual, budgeted, and last year's totals. Managers can then evaluate how their current financial results compare to the budget and to the previous year for both time periods. The *vertical headings* show the individual revenue centers (or departments) for the hotel. Exhibits 6.1 and 6.2 are examples of daily revenue report formats for two major hotel companies:

EXHIBIT 6.1

SALES AND OCCUPANCY REPORT

Hotel Name
Sales and Occupancy Report
Date

Revenue by Hotel Department

	Today				Period to Date		
	Actual	Budget	Last Year's Actual		Actual	Budget	Last Year's Actual
Transient Rooms Sales							
Group Rooms Sales							
Contract Rooms Sales							
Part Day/Guaranteed							
Adjustments							
Net Rooms Sales							
Telephone Sales							
Gift Shop Sales							
Rents and Commissions							
Other Sales							
Subtotal							

Restaurant Sales
Lounge Sales
Banquet Sales
    Total F&B Sales
Total Hotel Sales
    Over/Under Budget

Rooms Statistics

	Today			Period to Date		
	Actual	Budget	LastYear's Actual	Actual	Budget	Last Year's Actual

Room Nights

Total Rooms in Hotel
Complimentary Rooms
Out of Order Rooms
Rooms Available to Sale
Rooms Rented
Rooms Vacant
Occupancy Percentage Available Rooms
Occupancy Percentage Total Rooms

Average Rate

Transient Average Rate
Group Average Rate
Contract Average Rate
Full Day Average Rate
Net Average Rate
REVPAR

Miscellaneous

Total Guests
Arrivals
Departures
Drive-Ins
Guaranteed No Shows

Restaurant, Beverage, and Banquet Summary

	Food Today			Beverage Today			Period to Date	
Sales	Customers	Average Check		Sales & Food Sales			Customers	Average Check
	Act. Bud. L. Y.			Act. Bud. L. Y.			Act. Bud. L. Y.	

Restaurant

Room Service

Specialty Restaurant

Lounge

   Total Restaurant and Beverage

Banquet Sales

Banquet Meeting Rooms

Banquet Other

   Total Banquet

Hotel Market Segment Information

	Today			Period to Date		
	Rooms Sold	Revenue	Average Rate	Rooms Sold	Revenue	Average Rate

Weekday

Regular

Corporate

Special Corporate

Discounts

   Total Transient

Corporate Group

Association Group

Other Group

   Total Group

Contract

   Total Weekday

Weekend

Regular

Corporate

Special Corporate

Discounts

   Total Transient

Corporate Group

Associate Group

Other Group

   Total Group

Contract

   Total Weekend

Group Business
Individual Groups Listed

Complimentary Rooms
Names Listed

Other Information
Contract Business
Out-of-Order Rooms
Walked Guests

As you can see, this is a lot of information. It is very complete and detailed. Each manager in the hotel will focus on the operating information for his or her department. The Front Office and Housekeeping managers will focus on room sales and statistics. The Restaurant, Lounge, and Catering managers will focus on food and beverage sales and statistics. Again, there is a lot of information in these reports, but each manager will focus on his or her own areas and will be familiar with trends, forecasts and budgets, recent events, and the status of the local economy. Working with the Daily Revenue Report each day will enable a hospitality manager to get familiar and understand better the operational results contained in the daily report and internal or external factors that affect those results.

Exhibit 6.2 is a second example of a hotel daily revenue report. This company organized the information into the following sections: (1) summary, (2) rooms sales and statistics, and (3) food and beverage sales and statistics. It includes labor productivities and profitability estimates.

EXHIBIT 6.2

REVENUE REPORT

	Today		Month to Date (MTD)		MTD Variance to Preliminary		MTD Last Year's Actual		MTD Variance to Last Year	
	Actual Preliminary Dollar Percentage		Actual Preliminary Dollar Percentage		Dollar Percentage		Dollar Percentage		Dollar Percentage	

Room Revenue

  Food Revenue

  Beverage Revenue

  Food and Beverage Other Revenue

Total Food and Beverage Revenue

  Telephone Revenue

  Other Revenue

Total Revenue

  Rooms Profit

  Food and Beverage Profit

  Telephone Profit

  Other Profit

Gross Operating Income

  Administrative and General

  Sale and Market ng

  Heat, Light, and Power

  Repairs and Maintenance

Total Overhead Expense

Gross Operating Profit (Estimated)

Rooms Sales and Statistics

Transient Revenue
Group Revenue
Less Allowances
Total Rooms Revenue
Payroll
    Administration
    Front Office
    Housekeeping
    Guest Services
    Transportation
    Reservations
Total Wages
Employee Benefit Percentage
Total Payroll
Other Expenses
Department Profit
Statistics
Available Rooms
Rooms Sold/Average Rate
    Transient
    Group
Total Rooms Sold/Average Rate
Complimentary Rooms
Total Rooms Occupancy/Average Rate
Occupancy Percentage
Hotel Guest and Guests per Room
Arrivals
Departures

Memo Statistics
Rack Rate
Discounts
Contracts
Wholesalers
Total Transient
Association
Corporate
Specialty Group
Travel Industry
Total Group
Labor Hours
Administration
Front Office
Concierge
Housekeeping
Guest Services
Transportation
Reservations
Total Labor Hours

Food and Beverage Sales and Statistics

Food Revenue
Restaurant
Specialty Restaurant
Rooms Service
Banquets
Total Food Revenue
Beverage Revenue
Restaurant
Specialty Restaurant
Room Service

Lounge
Banquets
Total Beverage Revenue
Other Banquet Revenue
Room Rental
Service Charge
Other
Net Food and Beverage Revenue
Food Cost
Payroll
Restaurants
Beverage
Banquet
Kitchen
Administration
Catering
Total Food and Beverage Wages
Employee Benefits
Total Payroll
Outside Labor
Other Expenses
Department Profit
Labor Hours
Restaurants
Room Service
Banquets
Total Food Hours
Total Beverage Hours
Total Kitchen Hours
TOTAL LABOR HOURS

121

This hotel company chooses to provide operating information such as costs and estimated profits for the day in addition to the revenues. This enables managers to relate revenues for the day to the costs incurred to produce those revenues. If they see problems, they can make changes and corrections immediately.

It is important to go back to one of the fundamental financial analysis concepts—comparing actual results to other measures to establish meaning. These daily reports provide the financial numbers that result from operations. These are compared to other operating time periods to show if operations are improving, if revenues and profits are increasing, or if established budgets and forecasts are being met. After reading these daily reports, a department manager can adjust revenue forecasts, labor schedules, or make other operational changes if necessary. These daily reports can be very effective management tools if understood and used consistently.

Labor Productivity Reports

The second example of a Daily Revenue Report also includes daily labor productivity and wage cost information. The managers in this hotel company have both revenue and labor information available to them on the same report. This is convenient, and by reviewing this report, they can make necessary changes.

The hotel company in the first example provides the labor and cost information in a separate daily labor report. This report contains detailed information and states the labor expenses for the previous day. These results are compared to budget or forecast numbers to determine if established labor guidelines have been met. Each department manager focuses on her or his specific department results. There are two parts to analyzing labor and wage costs: labor hours and wage cost percentages. Both are important.

Labor Hours and Labor Productivity

This measure of productivity does not include any dollar cost information. It relates units of labor to units of output. More specifically, what amount of labor hours is required to support a certain volume of business. A labor hour is defined as the number of hours one employee works in performing his or her job responsibilities. Typically, full-time employees are scheduled for an eight-hour workday and a 40-hour workweek. Any additional hours during the week will result in overtime. So our basic unit of labor hours measurement is an eight-hour day and 40-hour week. Examples of formulas and ratios used in the hotel and restaurant business are as follows:

1. *Labor hours per room sold.* The formula is total labor hours divided by total rooms sold. This measure is used by the front office and housekeeping departments. They have established guidelines that are used to prepare budgets and forecasts. If actual results are different from these guidelines, managers are expected to identify what caused the difference or variations and how to make any necessary corrections.

Photo: The Otesaga Hotel

Aerial View of the Leatherstocking Golf Course and Otesaga Hotel
Cooperstown, New York

This aerial view of the Otesaga Resort in Cooperstown, New York, highlights the resort's Leatherstocking Golf Course and Lake Otsego. The resort opened in 1909 with 136 guest rooms, five food and beverage outlets, 13,000 square feet of meeting space, and an 18 hole golf course. The Otesaga offers meal packages that include breakfast and dinner in the room rate. Because this resort is located in Cooperstown where the Baseball Hall of Fame is located, it enjoys a very busy summer season. This high season is extended into October because of the many people who come to see the beautiful fall foliage in the mountains.

The Otesaga closes for approximately five months during the winter. What effect will this have on the hotel's profitability? What expenses will it continue to incur while it is closed? What do you think the owners of the Otesaga have had to do over the years to keep the resort competitive with the newer resorts that have been built in the last 20 years? How do the owners and managers of the Otesaga have to plan the cash flow for the year when they are closed for five months?

2. *Rooms cleaned or credits cleaned per shift.* The formula is total rooms cleaned divided by one eight-hour shift. This formula is used by housekeeping. The number of rooms cleaned by one housekeeper on an eight-hour shift can range from as few as 12 at a resort to as many as 18 at full-service or limited-service hotel.

3. *Labor hours per customer.* The formula is labor hours divided by total customers served in the restaurant. This relationship describes the number of labor hours required to service or take care of a corresponding customer volume level.

These formulas are used to calculate the number of labor hours required to work based on forecasted rooms sold or customers. They are true measures of labor productivities because they relate labor input in labor hours to products and services produced in terms of rooms sold or customers served. They do not involve any cost dollars or revenue dollars.

Wage Cost Percentage

This productivity measure compares the wage cost in dollars to revenue produced in dollars. It converts the labor productivity to dollars. The relationship now measures the dollar cost in wages incurred to the corresponding revenue levels resulting from rooms sold or meals served. Examples of wage cost percentages are as follows:

1. *Front office wage cost.* The formula is total front office wage cost in dollars (front desk, reservations, bellmen, concierge) divided by total room revenue in dollars. The resulting wage cost percentage measures this relationship. A hotel will have budget and forecast guidelines to achieve expected productivities and the actual wage cost percentage will be compared to these guidelines to determine if expected productivities are achieved.

2. *Wage cost per occupied room.* This formula has two steps. First, labor hours used times average hourly wage rate equals wage cost in dollars. Second, wage cost in dollars divided by rooms sold (same as rooms occupied) equals wage cost per occupied room. This shows how well managers are controlling labor dollar costs as they relate to rooms sold.

3. *Housekeeping wage cost.* The formula is total housekeeping wage cost in dollars (housekeepers, housemen, public space, supervisors) divided by total rooms revenue in dollars.

4. *Restaurant wage cost.* The formula is total restaurant wage cost in dollars (servers, bussers, hostess) divided by total restaurant revenue in dollars.

Labor productivities like labor hours per occupied room are the truest measure of productivities because they just measure labor input with labor output. It is the main measurement to managing wages. The next productivity identifies the dollar cost incurred to produce products and services and the dollar revenue resulting from the sale of products and services. This is the best measure of the financial relationship between expenses and revenues. Both are useful in managing operating departments.

It really does not matter whether labor productivity is included in one report or in two separate reports. What is important is that the daily productivity reports are used and applied to make department operations run smoother and produce maximum revenues and profits.

Weekly Internal Management Reports

These reports are also used to review and critique the previous day and the previous week and to forecast and prepare for the next week. These weekly reports are the primary reports used by managers because operations are planned for in weekly time periods. Revenues are forecasted for the entire week, wages are scheduled for the week, employee schedules are posted, and all operations are planned in weekly planning meetings. The week is the key planning and measurement time period. Although managers are concerned with the daily operations, the planning generally involves a weekly time period. The two most important weekly reports again involve revenues and wages.

There are two main uses for the weekly reports: forecasting to prepare for upcoming operations and evaluating and critiquing the past week's operations. First, managers look at the budget that was prepared for the upcoming week. This will be the starting point for their weekly plan. Second, managers review recent reports and business volume levels to see if the budget should be adjusted upward or downward. Third, managers prepare the revenue forecasts and wage schedules for the next week based on this information. This becomes the weekly forecast and will be the main planning document for their department. Hotel operations will be conducted daily based on this schedule. This part of the weekly report is about forecasting and planning.

The second use of weekly reports is evaluating and analyzing the previous week's performance to see how actual operational results compared with the budget or forecasted operations. Fourth, managers analyze actual performance and compare it to the budget and the forecast. Any differences or variations will be analyzed and critiqued to identify both good and bad results. If a problem exists and forecasted revenues or productivities are not achieved, it is important to identify if the entire week had problems or if there were big problems for only one day. What caused the problem? Was the problem a result of lower revenues or higher costs?

Fifth, managers evaluate how accurate their forecast for the week was compared to actual operations. Because a weekly forecast is prepared only several days before the week starts, it should be fairly accurate. Results from the previous week are available to help prepare as accurate a forecast as possible. It is important to evaluate the accuracy of the forecast as well as the actual performance because the weekly forecast is the document that is used to plan the details of the next week's operations. Managers should be close in their forecasts to build reliability and credibility. A poor forecast can result in poor performance in controlling costs as well as maximizing revenues and profits. Sixth, managers apply what they learned from the weekly results to operations and use this information to forecast the next week's operations.

Weekly Revenue Forecast

As discussed previously, the weekly revenue forecast is the first step in planning operations for the week. It is typical for hotel management to have a weekly selling strategy meeting on Monday or Tuesday to prepare a detailed, day-by-day forecast for the upcoming week that includes detailed daily revenue information such as daily rooms sold, daily arrivals and departures, the average rate, and daily revenues. The weekly forecast is then distributed to all managers for their use in planning the week. They will also look at the next month in more general terms to see if any significant changes are expected that will affect their weekly schedules.

Weekly Wage and Cost Scheduling

The next step is to take the weekly revenue forecast and schedule the wages required for each day's operations. This is usually due on a Wednesday. Ratios and formulas are used to convert daily rooms sold or customer counts into daily wage schedules for each department. The labor hours and wage expenses for the week are then totaled and ratios calculated to ensure that the weekly productivities are maintained. Adjustments are made to get productivities in line. For example, if the housekeeping labor hours per room sold is too high, the housekeeping manager should determine which day or which wage department is above the wage standards and reduce the labor hours to get to the expected productivity levels. If higher wage levels are required, the manager needs to document why and what work will be completed.

Profitability Forecasting

The last area to forecast is profitability. This is done by adding other operating expenses to the forecast. These are generally based on historical averages and are often relatively fixed expenses. Forecasted profits are calculated by subtracting all forecasted expenses from forecasted revenues. By completing profit forecasts for the week, they can be compared to budgeted weekly profits to ensure that both revenue and expense forecasts are in line and will meet expected or budgeted productivities and profitability.

Monthly Internal Management Reports

Everybody on the management team uses monthly reports, and that is why they are so important. We again focus on the monthly P&L Statement and how it is used by internal management as well as external investors, bankers, and other interested parties. It is analyzed in great detail to measure financial performance and describe the operations for the month.

Monthly P&L Statement

This is the financial statement that gets the closest scrutiny and is used the most in analyzing financial performance. This close analysis enables the monthly P&L to become a useful management tool. It describes not only the operational performance of a department but also what financial results that operational performance produces. The P&L is a common ground for discussion of financial performance because it is the financial statement that is used most by internal and external parties.

The monthly Consolidated P&L Statement provides a summary of each department's revenues and profits for the revenue centers and a summary of each department's total expenses for the expense centers. It is used to review the overall performance of a hotel by presenting the big picture. Comparisons with the budget—or with the previous month or the previous year—show if the financial performance of the hotel is improving, staying the same, or declining. It also identifies which departments are underperforming and which departments are overperforming.

The monthly Department P&L Statements provide the detailed operating results by department. This is where the analysis of department operations begins. Department managers can see the financial results of the decisions and activities that they have made during the month in operating their departments. Each line account in revenues and expenses can be examined to see if established operating plans and expected productivities were achieved. It is the primary responsibility of the department managers to know and understand the operations that produced the numbers. They are assisted in evaluating their monthly Department P&L Statement by their Executive Committee member, the Director of Finance, or another member of the accounting office. This is the third step of the Financial Management Cycle—evaluate and analyze the numbers.

Profitability, Retention, and Flow Through

This aspect of financial analysis is important because it goes beyond comparing the monthly financial results of a department with the budget and forecast, as well as comparing them to last month or last year. It involves identifying revenue, expense, and profitability changes from the budget or the forecast. There is an expected relationship between increases and decreases in revenues and how they increase or decrease expense and profitability.

Refer back to Chapter 2 and the section on trends. One important trend in financial analysis is to identify the relationship between revenue, expenses, and profits. Department managers are expected to be able to forecast increases and decreases in revenues compared to the budget and recent forecasts. They are also expected to be able to manage expenses to maintain productivities and produce the maximum profit given the forecast change in revenues.

There are several important terms that we need to understand before we go on:

- **Incremental** refers to an increase, something gained or added. This term is used in financial analysis to describe revenues, expenses, or profits beyond what was expected. If sales increase, what are the corresponding increases in expenses and profits? They should all increase in varying increments. Analyzing the incremental revenues, expenses, and profits will identify where the department did well and where it did not do well.

- **Fixed expenses** refer to expenses that remain constant regardless of the volume and level of business. Fixed expenses do not change from month to month.

- **Variable expenses** refer to expenses that increase or decrease directly with the volume and level of business. Variable expenses change each month based on business volume.

- **The Cost Management Index (CMI)** is the formula used to identify what level of expenses and profits is expected given incremental changes in revenues. The formula expects higher levels of profits with higher levels of revenues and can be used to forecast expenses and profits that should result from incremental revenues. Terms used by two hospitality companies to describe this process are **retention** and **flow thru**. These terms measure how much profits go up and down as a percentage of how much revenues go up and down.

- **Variation** refers to something that is slightly different from another of the same type. In financial analysis, variation is the difference between numbers—for example, the variation between actual and budgeted numbers or between actual numbers for this year and those for last year.

To illustrate the concepts of retention and flow thru, we will use several examples. We start with the Rooms Department budget and forecast for a month. We will identify incremental revenues and the effect they are expected to have on expenses and profits at the new revenue level:

	Forecast		Actual		Difference/Variation	
	Dollars	Percentage	Dollars	Percentage	Dollars	Percentage
Room Revenue	$600,000		$625,000		+$25,000	+4.2%
Management Wages (fixed expense)	11,000	1.8%	11,000	1.8%	0	0
Hourly Wages (variable expense)	36,000	6.0	37,000	5.9	+$ 1,000	+2.8
Contract Cleaning (fixed expense)	2,000	.3	2,000	.3	0	0
Guest Supplies (variable expense)	8,000	1.3	8,400	1.3	+400	+5.0
Reservation Cost (variable expense)	20,000	3.3	20,500	3.3	+500	+2.5
Total Fixed Expense	$ 13,000	2.2	$ 13,000	2.1	0	0
Total Variable Expense	64,000	10.6	65,900	10.5	+1,900	+3.0
Total Expenses	$ 77,000	12.8%	78,900	12.6	+1,900	+2.5
Total Profit	$523,000	87.2%	$546,100	87.4%	+$23,100	+4.4%

Retention or Flow Thru = $23,100 or 92.4% ($23,100/$25,000)

The forecast for the Rooms Department was $600,000 in room revenue and a $523,000 Rooms Department Profit. The forecasted profit percentage is 87.2%, which means that .872 cents out of every revenue dollar will be profit. Actual Room Revenue was $625,000, or $25,000 over forecast. Therefore, incremental revenue was $25,000. We can also calculate the percentage increase of the $25,000 incremental revenue, which is +4.2% ($25,000/$600,000). In other words, revenues were 4.2% higher than forecast.

Now let's look at the increase in expenses that resulted from the $25,000 incremental revenue. Fixed expenses did not change, so the incremental $25,000 in revenue incurred no additional fixed expense. Fixed expenses remained at $13,000. The fixed expense percentage will therefore decrease from 2.2% to 2.1%. This percentage decreases because the revenue increased without a corresponding increase in fixed expenses. We can therefore assume that for every incremental dollar increase in revenue, there will be no incremental increase in fixed expenses.

Variable expenses have a direct relationship with revenue—when revenue goes up, variable expenses should go up; when revenue goes down, variable expenses should go down. It is the department manager's ability to control and manage variable expenses such as labor costs that can have a positive or negative effect on profits. In our example, variable expenses increased $1,900, or 3.0%. This was the incremental amount of variable expenses incurred to support the $25,000 and 4.2% increase in room revenue. The variable cost percentage declines slightly from 10.6% to 10.5%.

The resulting profit increases $23,100 from $523,000 to $546,100, or +4.4%. The incremental revenue of $25,000 generated an incremental profit of $23,100. Stated in terms of percentages, 92.4% ($23,100/$25,000) of the incremental revenue of $25,000 resulted in an incremental profit of $23,100. This is a very high percentage and would indicate that the managers did a good job in controlling expenses.

The financial concept of retention or flow thru involves setting guidelines for the expected amount and percentage of incremental profit that will result from incremental revenue. Two examples of hospitality company standards are a 60% retention of incremental profits at Hotel Gross Operating Profit and the other is 50% flow thru at Hotel House Profit. The 60% retention standard would expect $15,000 of incremental profit and the 50% flow thru standard would expect $12,500 of incremental profits. In our example, the rooms department managers exceeded the guidelines by producing +$23,100 in incremental profits.

Keep in mind that the retention and flow thru standards are for Gross Operating Profit or House Profit. There are also specific department standards. For example, the rooms department retention standard is 80%, and the food and beverage department retention standard is 55% for one hotel company. The 92.4% actual retention in our example exceeded the room retention standard of 80%.

All department managers are responsible for controlling and managing expenses to achieve guidelines and standards. It is equally important for the Director of Engineering to control the repairs and maintenance expenses as it is for the Restaurant Manager and Housekeeping Manager to control the expenses of their departments. If each department does its part in managing expenses, the overall hotel productivity as measured by Gross Operating Profit or House Profits will achieve the goals and standards set.

Monthly P&L Statement Critiques

This refers to the process of analyzing the monthly department and consolidated P&Ls to evaluate the financial performance and to determine what action to take next. The critiques should be prepared by department heads and line managers and reviewed by the Director of Finance and Executive Committee member. The objective is to evaluate the numbers and explain what happened, why it happened, and what action will be taken as a result of the analysis. It is equally important to identify positive changes in revenues and profits *as well as* negative changes in revenues and profits.

The department P&L critique involves a narrative that identifies major variations and explains the causes of the variations in the accounts on the department P&L Statement. The focus should be on the largest dollar accounts and the largest variations from budget or forecast in terms of dollars and percentages. For example:

1. If revenues increased or decreased, which market segments or meal periods had the largest variation? Was it in rate or volume? Was it in one week or each of the weeks in the month?

2. If food or beverage costs increased, did the increase originate in the full-service restaurant, specialty restaurant, or banquet department? What caused the cost increase, and how will it be corrected?

3. If wage cost increased, did the increase originate in housekeeping or the front office for the rooms department? Did it originate in the restaurant, banquets, or kitchen for the restaurant department? Was it caused by increased labor hours or wage rates? What was the cause of the increase?

4. If other operating costs increased, which account reflected the increase? What caused the increase? How will it be corrected?

The Department P&L critique explains what happened and how the department will improve operations in the next months. It is important to remember that identifying the cause of increased revenues and profits is just as important as identifying the cause of problems that decrease profits. The department manager will want to know what actions produced the improvements and do what she or he can to keep those procedures or actions in place so that the improved operations will continue.

Summary

Internal management reports are essential to the successful operations of any hotel or restaurant. The entire hotel or restaurant management team uses these internal reports to evaluate past performance and to determine appropriate action to take in the upcoming months to ensure acceptable performance in the future. This is the third step in the Financial Management Cycle—operations and accounting analyze the numbers. Department heads and line managers implement and critique these reports with the assistance of the Director of Finance and their Executive Committee member.

Internal management reports cover two time periods. The first report contains actual operations from the previous day, week, or month. This looks back at completed operations and describes what has happened. The second forecasts revenues, expenses, and profits for the upcoming day, week, or month and is used to plan for expected business levels in the future. This report looks forward and forecasts what the managers expect and plan to happen.

There are daily, weekly, monthly, and quarterly reports. Although operations are managed daily, they are planned for in weekly forecasts and schedules. The monthly reports are the main financial reports and are used by both internal managers and external parties or stakeholders in the hotel's operations.

It is extremely important to understand the concepts of incremental revenues and the expected impact that changes in revenue will have on retention or flow thru to profits. These terms describe the guidelines set for managers to assist them in controlling expenses and maintaining expected productivities. Because some expenses are fixed, there should be no increase in them if revenues increase. That will have a positive effect on profitability. Likewise, there is no decrease in fixed expenses if revenues decline. This will have a negative effect on profitability. All department managers are expected to manage their variable expenses whether revenues increase or decrease.

Hospitality Manager Takeaways

1. **The ability of hospitality managers to understand and use internal management reports is essential to the successful operation of any department.**

2. **The Daily Revenue Report summarizes the previous day's results and can include revenues, statistics, and labor productivities. This is one of the most important management tools that a manager can use.**

3. **Weekly reports are used for planning and scheduling upcoming operations.**

4. **Retention and flow thru are essential financial concepts that identify management's ability to control expenses given incremental changes in revenues. This is a direct responsibility of department managers.**

5. **Managing variable wage costs is critical to maintaining productivities and maximizing retention or flow thru.**

Key Terms

Cost Management Index (CMI)—The formula that identifies what level of expenses and profits are expected given incremental changes in revenues.

Fixed Expense—Expenses that remain constant regardless of the volume and level of business.

Flow Thru—Measures how much profit goes up or down as a percentage of the change in revenue.

Incremental—An increase, something gained or added. In financial analysis it describes additional revenues, expenses, or profits beyond what was expected.

Retention—Same as Flow Thru.

Variable Expense—Expenses that increase or decrease directly with the volume and level of business.

Variation—Something slightly different from another of the same type. In financial analysis, variation is the difference between a planned number and an actual number—for example, the difference between actual results and budget.

Review Questions

1. Compare the format of a P&L Statement with a Daily Revenue Report. What is the same and what is different?

2. What information does the Daily Revenue Report contain, and how does a hospitality manager use it?

3. Explain how fixed and variable wage expenses are used to maintain labor productivity standards.

4. How are weekly revenue forecasts used to plan expenses for the upcoming week?

5. Define *retention* and *flow thru*. Why they are important?

6. How do department managers use retention and flow thru to manager their departments?

7. Define *incremental*. How is it used in financial analysis?

8. List three formulas for calculating labor productivities and percentages.

Revenue Management

Learning Objectives

1. To understand the importance of maximizing revenues.

2. To understand why REVPAR is so important for maximizing hotel revenues.

3. To understand revenue management systems—Yield Management.

4. To understand rate structures and selling strategies.

5. To be able to read, understand, and use revenue management reports.

Chapter Outline

REVPAR: Revenue per Available Room

    Definition

    Why REVPAR Is Important

    How REVPAR Is Used

Rate Structures and Market Segments

    Definitions

    Establishing Rate Structures

Revenue Management Systems

    Definition

    Yield Management

    How Yield Management Is Used

    Using Yield Management in Different Types of Hotels

Selling Strategies

    Definition

    The Process

    Yield Management Critiques

Summary

Hospitality Manager Takeaways

Key Terms

Review Questions

This chapter discusses the importance of revenue management in operating a hotel. The two primary ways of maximizing profits is first to maximize revenues and second to control and minimize expenses. Understanding the policies, procedures, and tools that are available to maximize revenues and being able to use them effectively are valuable skills for any hospitality manager, particularly in the rooms department. A hotel that is meeting or exceeding revenue budgets is a much more enjoyable place to work and provides managers a better opportunity to maximize profits because revenues are helping rather than hurting profitability. It is challenging for hospitality managers to maximize profits when a hotel is under-performing based on its revenue budgets and forecasts.

Revenue management relies on historical room revenue information contained in a computerized program called Yield Management or Demand Tracking. Yield management programs contain historical information organized by day of arrival (DOA) and compare the current year's booking pace to the historical average. The booking pace determines appropriate selling strategies that a hotel can put in place to maximize room revenues for a specific day of arrival.

This chapter covers the different aspects of revenue management. All managers need to have a good understanding of how their hotel generates revenues. It will help them understand how their particular department fits into the total operations of the hotel.

REVPAR: Revenue per Available Room

Definition

Revenue per Available Room (REVPAR) is total room revenue divided by total rooms available. It combines room occupancy and room rate information to measure a hotel's ability to maximize total room revenue. It is the best measurement of maximizing total room revenue because it identifies the hotel's ability to manage *both* occupancy (rooms sold) and average rate in maximizing room revenues. A hotel must effectively manage both to maximize total room revenue.

There are two formulas for calculating REVPAR. The REVPAR calculated each way might be slightly different as a result of rounding. Typically, the occupancy percentage is rounded to one decimal point—87.3%, for example. Average room rates are rounded to two decimals points—$76.23, for example. Let's look at the formulas:

$$REVPAR = Occupancy\ Percentage \times Average\ Room\ Rate$$

or

$$Total\ Room\ Revenue \div Total\ Available\ Rooms$$

Applying the first formula to our example results in a $66.55 REVPAR:

$$\$66.55\ REVPAR = 87.3\%\ Occupancy\ Percentage \times \$76.23\ Average\ Room\ Rate$$

Following are characteristics of REVPAR that this example demonstrates:

1. REVPAR is measured in dollars and cents.

2. REVPAR will always be lower than the average room rate. The only exception is if the hotel is running at 100% occupancy. Then REVPAR and average room rate will be the same. REVPAR can *never* be higher than the average room rate.

3. You need to know both the hotel occupancy percentage and the hotel average room rate to calculate REVPAR, or

4. You need to know the total room revenue and the total available rooms in the hotel to calculate REVPAR.

This leads to our second REVPAR formula:

$$REVPAR = Total\ Room\ Revenue \div Total\ Available\ Rooms$$

To calculate REVPAR using this formula, we need to know the total room revenue (a variable) for the day and the total number of rooms in the hotel (a constant). To continue our example, let's use a 400-room hotel. That is the only additional information that we need to calculate REVPAR with this formula. It will require three steps:

1. *Calculate rooms sold.* We need this number to calculate total room revenues. We can calculate rooms sold by applying our 87.3% occupancy percentage to our 400-room hotel:

$$400\ Total\ Rooms \times .873\ Occupancy\ Percentage = 349.2\ Rooms\ Sold$$

Because we cannot sell .2 of a room, we round to 349 rooms sold.

2. *Calculate total room revenue.* The formula is

$$Rooms\ Sold \times Average\ Room\ Rate$$

or

$$349\ Rooms\ Sold \times \$76.23\ Average\ Room\ Rate = \$26,604\ Total\ Room\ Revenue$$

3. *REVPAR = Total room revenue divided by total available rooms.* Make sure to use the 400 *total available rooms* in the hotel and not the 349 *rooms sold.* Our REVPAR is

$$\text{\$66.51 REVPAR} = \text{\$26,604 Total Room Revenue} \div \text{400 Total Available Rooms}$$

Let's compare our two REVPARs:

$$\text{\$66.55 REVPAR} = 87.3\% \text{ Occupancy Percentage} \times \text{\$76.23 Average Room Rate}$$
$$and$$
$$\text{\$66.51 REVPAR} = \text{\$26,604 Total Room Revenue} \div \text{400 Total Available Rooms}$$

There is a difference of 4 cents. Which one is right? The difference is the result of rounding, so technically the $66.51 is the best answer because it is calculated using total room revenues and total available rooms in the hotel. However a 4 cent difference on a $66.51 REVPAR is insignificant, so either formula can be used. It is important to use the same REVPAR formula to be consistent and ensure that all REVPAR calculations are reliable and useful.

Why REVPAR Is Important

REVPAR measures both the ability to sell the most rooms (occupancy percentage) and the ability to achieve the highest average room rate. Therefore REVPAR includes *two financial measures* and identifies how the hotel is combining the two strategies of maximizing rooms sold and maximizing the average room rate to maximize total room revenue. Together they form a strong and useful financial measurement. They require the hotel management team to be good at managing *both measurements.*

If a hotel's selling strategy focuses only on one of these measurements, it can miss significant opportunities to maximize total room revenue with the other measurement. For example, a hotel can focus on maximizing its occupancy percentage and to accomplish this goal, managers might set low room rates to sell more rooms. If a hotel is running a 92% occupancy, which is very high compared to the industry average, which might be in the low 60% range, it probably dropped its room rates significantly lower than its competitive set. If a hotel is running a $48 average rate and its competitive set is achieving a $65 average rate, the hotel is missing out on an additional $17 in average rate. We refer to this as leaving money on the table. The important questions the hotel's management has to ask is, can the hotel increase total room revenues by increasing its average rate and is it willing to run a lower occupancy percentage as some customers go elsewhere because of the higher average rate?

The same issue applies to average room rate. A hotel might set its room rates too high and lose customers as a result. Using the same example, if our hotel is achieving a $65 average rate compared to the competitive set's average rate of $55, but running a 60% occupancy compared to the competitive set's average occupancy percentage of 78%, then our hotel is probably not maximizing revenue. Again the hotel is leaving money on the table because of a high average rate that might turn away potential customers, resulting in a lower occupancy percentage.

In each of these examples, the hotel is doing well in one of the revenue measurements. To accomplish this, it is probably not doing well on the other measurement. That is what makes REVPAR so important. REVPAR requires a hotel to be evaluated on its ability to *manage and maximize both rate and occupancy measurements*.

How REVPAR Is Used

REVPAR is used in several ways. Because of its importance, it is used as a management tool that assists the hotel management team in maximizing room revenues. It is also used to measure financial performance by outside investors who are evaluating investments. It is contained in P&L Statements for a hotel and the annual reports for a corporation. It is the most important measurement of how well a hotel is able to maximize room revenues. If a hotel is maximizing room revenues as measured by improvements to past results and by comparisons to competitors, it makes it much more possible for the hotel management team to efficiently manage expenses to maximize profits. Specific uses of REVPAR are as follows:

1. It is used as a measure of the hotel management team's ability to maximize total room revenue.

2. It is used to compare the hotel performance to similar hotels in the same market area. This is called the hotel competitive set.

3. It is used to measure the hotel's progress in consistently increasing total room revenue compared to previous years and the budget.

4. It is used by owners, outside investors, and other financial institutions to project future room revenues and cash flows.

REVPAR is used in many reports. It is calculated daily and included on the Daily Revenue Report. It is used in weekly forecasting. It is used in preparing the annual operating budget. It is used in corporate annual reports. This demonstrates its importance in the daily operations of individual hotels.

Photo: Hyatt Hotel and Resorts

Hyatt Regency Maui Resort

This 815-room Hyatt resort is located on 40 beachfront acres on Ka'anapali Beach on the Hawaiian island of Maui. Its food and beverage operations include 5 restaurants, poolside snack bar, 7 lounges, and an authentic Polynesian Luau. The 25,000 square feet of indoor meeting space includes a 17,000-square-foot ballroom. An additional 40,000 square feet of outdoor meeting space is also available. This resort has expanded water recreation that includes a half-acre swimming pool, 150-foot water slide, 4 miles of beaches, and scuba diving activities.

The Hyatt Regency Maui Resort is able to attract large group business because of the large number of guest rooms, the wide range of meeting space, and all the recreational activities offered by a beachfront resort. Do you think the Director of Revenue Management spends more time on transient or group business? With 815 rooms, do you think the strategy to maximize room revenue is based on achieving higher room rates or higher occupancy? What effect will the large amount of indoor and outdoor meeting space have on the transient/group market segment mix? How profitable do you think the Banquet Department is and how will Banquet Revenues effect the decision to accept or reject a piece of group business? Would you accept a large, lower-rated piece of group business with significant banquets and activities or hold out for higher-rated transient room reservations?

Rate Structures and Market Segments

Definitions

We defined *market segments* in Chapter 1 as customer groups defined by preferences, buying patterns, and behavior patterns. These similar characteristics enable hotels to create promotions, packages, and rates that meet the different expectations of each market segment. The hotel identifies market segments that it will be able to compete in and then advertises to attract customers in those market segments to the hotel.

Rate structures are the range of room rates that a hotel establishes for different market segments. They can be year-round room rates or seasonal room rates. They are published, and the hotel uses them to attract customers. Customers view the rates of a hotel, compare them to rates at other hotels, and choose which hotel they will stay in based on rate, experience, location, and the expected overall value of the service they will receive.

Establishing Rate Structures

Hotels use several factors in establishing room rates for their hotel. These include the following:

1. Rates of their primary competition

2. Age of the hotel, including recent renovations and improvements

3. Perceived value of the products and services delivered by the hotel

4. Location

5. Cost of the hotel and the return on investment (ROI) required by investors

6. Any competitive advantages that the hotel might have over its competition

Room rates are generally set for one year. They are established based on information from actual rates for the previous year, marketing studies, inflation rates, competitor's actions, renovations or improvements, and the expectation to increase total room revenues. It is a detailed process to change the established rate structure, and that is why room rates are generally set for a year at a time. The exception is seasonal properties where a rate structure is established each year for each of the seasons.

The room rate structure involves setting specific rates for specific market segments ranging from the highest to the lowest rates. Historically, the central point of room rate structures is the regular rate or rack rate. This is the room rate that is available to all of the different reservation systems selling rooms at a hotel, including travel agencies, airlines, and car rental companies, and generally the first room rate quoted at central reservation centers (800 numbers). All other rates are calculated based on increases or decreases from the rack rates. Let's look at a sample room rate structure for a full-service hotel and a limited or select service hotel:

	Full-Service Hotel	**Select-Service Hotel**
Concierge	$135	Not available
(upgraded rooms and service)		
Regular or rack rate	$119	$75
Corporate rate	$109	$69
(preference to business travelers)		
Special corporate rate	$100–$75	$65–50
(company special rates based on volume)		
Discounts		
Super saver	$ 89	$55
Weekend	$ 75	$50
Government/military	$ 65	$40

These rates are examples of how a hotel might set its rate structure. The concierge rate is the highest rate because it includes special amenities and services similar to first class on an airline. The regular or rack rate is considered the standard room rate that the hotel would like to get for all of its rooms.

The remaining rates are all forms of discounted rates from the rack rate. The corporate rate is a slightly discounted room rate extended to individual business travelers recognizing both the company and the individual's amount of time spent on the road on business. Often, the corporate rate has the highest rooms sold mix percentage, especially for the full-service market segment. Special corporate rates are the next level of discounted rates and are negotiated directly with each company. The degree of the discount is based on the number of room nights generated annually. A company that produces 200 rooms annually might receive a slightly discounted rate of $100 at our full-service hotel, whereas a company producing 1,000 rooms per night annually might receive a larger discount and a $75 rate. The discount rates reflect lower rates that are available during the slower time periods. They involve the biggest discounts because the hotel is running lower occupancies during this time. Our full-service hotel might run an 85% occupancy midweek but fall to 50% on weekends. The discounted weekend rates are a strategy to occupy more rooms during slow times at a lower room rate.

In setting the room rates at a hotel, there is a logical relationship between the various rates. Generally the discounted rates will be either a fixed dollar amount lower between each market segment, such as a $10 or $15 discount, or a fixed percentage discount lower, such as a 10% or 15% discount. The rate structure is orderly and intended to accomplish two goals that seem to be the opposite of each other: maximize room revenue with higher rates on the upper end and maximize room revenue with more rooms sold stimulated by lower room rates on the lower end. Customers are looking for lower rates, and lower rates generally do not maximize room revenues. This is the challenge of hotel management when setting room rates—how to balance maximizing room revenue and customer satisfaction.

At least once a year, hotels set new rates for the upcoming year. On occasion, they might change rates during the year based on new market conditions that warrant new room rates. Also, if the hotel completes a room redo and the hotel is refreshed and updated, it is typical for management to increase room rates at that time to reflect the better condition of the hotel and its facilities.

Revenue Management Systems

Definition

Revenue management systems are computer programs that utilized past historical information to project future room occupancies and revenues. They not only contain several years of historical room rate and occupancy information, they also include computer programs that utilize this information to assist managers in projecting future demand and rooms sold. These programs are referred to as Yield Management or **Demand Tracking** systems.

Yield Management

We will use the term **yield management** to describe computer programs used in identifying past rooms sold activity and trends and projecting rooms sold for future dates. This includes the number of rooms sold for every day in the future and the associated room rate. Generally the historical information of the hotel for the previous four to five years is combined to provide historical averages and buying patterns.

What Yield Management Is

Yield Management is the computer program that organizes a hotel's historical information by **day of arrival (DOA)**. This includes room rates, rooms sold, and room revenue by market segment. It tracks the number of rooms sold for each arrival date in the future. Directors of Revenue Management or Reservation Managers can compare the progress of reservations for any future DOA and compare it to the **historical average** for that date. The status of current reservations booked is called the **booking pace**, and it is compared to the historical average for that day of arrival. Yield Management reports determine whether the booking pace of this year's reservations for a specific DOA is ahead of or behind the historical average pace. Let's use an example to illustrate these points for a 400-room hotel. Yield Management provides the following information:

Day of arrival: June 1

Today's date: May 1

Number of days until the DOA: 31

Booking pace or the number of current reservations for the DOA: 275

Historical average of number of reservations 31 days before the DOA: 300

This information tells us that 31 days before the DOA of June 1, the hotel has 275 reservations booked compared to the historical average of 300 reservations booked 31 days before the DOA. The hotel booking pace is behind the historical average by 25 reservations. The selling strategy team will review this information and then decide what strategy to put in place to try and catch up and sell more rooms for the DOA. The team still has 31 days to affect the number of rooms sold. A typical strategy at this point will be to open up all discounted rates for the DOA in an attempt to stimulate reservations by offering lower, discounted room rates.

Now let's look at the Yield Management information two weeks later:

1. DOA: June 1

2. Today's date: May 15

3. Number of days until the DOA: 16 days

4. Booking pace or number of current reservations booked for the DOA: 320

5. Historical average of number of reservations 16 days before the DOA: 325

This information tells us that 16 days before the DOA, the hotel is now only five reservations under the historical average. The actual booking pace for the previous two weeks has been higher than the historical average, resulting in the hotel being down only five rooms from the historical average. The hotel is catching up. The selling strategy at this time could remain the same by keeping all discounts open, indicating that the hotel is willing to continue selling discount reservations in an effort to book more reservations to maximize room revenues. Or the selling strategy could change and restrict the lower discount rates but keep the higher discount rates open. The Director of Revenue Management will be the main person interpreting the information from Yield Management and helping the other managers to decide what selling strategy to implement.

Here is one more example:

1. DOA: June 1

2. Today's date: May 25

3. Number of days until the DOA: 7 days

4. Booking pace or number of current reservations booked for the DOA: 350

5. Historical average of number of reservations 7 days before the DOA: 340

This information, gathered one week before the DOA of June 1, tells us that the booking pace for the hotel is now 10 reservations ahead of the historical average. The hotel has not only caught up to the historical average number of reservations seven days before the DOA of June 1, but has booked 10 more reservations. The selling strategy would now probably change and discount rates would be closed, forcing remaining reservations to be booked at a higher rate. The hotel would choose this selling strategy because it has 10 more reservations booked, indicating a higher demand than historical averages. Higher demand means a higher probability of selling more rooms. The hotel will now implement a selling strategy to maximize rates by closing discounts to maximize total room revenue.

Yield Management's historical averages for any DOA reflect the historical average of the total number of actual rooms sold at a specific number of days before the DOA. It could be 400 rooms sold (a perfect sellout), or 375 rooms sold (a 93.8% occupancy, which is very good), or 200 rooms sold (a 50% occupancy, which is not good). The total number of rooms sold for the DOA reflects the historical average for that DOA whether it is high or low, good or bad.

How Yield Management Works

As the example shows, Yield Management not only provides the number of actual reservations booked for a specific DOA, but it also provides information that tells whether reservations are being booked at a faster or slower rate (the booking pace) than the historical average for any date before the DOA. This is valuable information for hotel managers to have as they determine the best selling strategy to implement to maximize total room revenue.

Yield Management provides a hotel with a historical number of reservations booked to compare with actual reservations booked at any point in time before the DOA. A Director of Revenue Management looks at the Yield Management Report daily on his/her computer to search for trends. These managers enter a specific DOA and compare the current booking pace to the historical average. Then they make any appropriate changes to the selling strategy that will help maximize total room revenue for each DOA.

The fact that a hotel has 300 reservations on the books as of a specific number of days before a specific DOA has little meaning by itself. However, when it is compared to a historical average of 325 reservations or 275 reservations, the hotel knows whether it is booking reservations at a faster pace (325 rooms) or a slower pace (275 rooms) and can implement an appropriate selling strategy in each situation. Once again, financial analysis involves comparing current actual results with other numbers. In this example, the current actual information (the booking pace) is compared to historical information (the historical averages).

How Yield Management Is Used

Hotel management uses Yield Management as a tool to maximize total room revenue. It provides the hotel with a daily status of total room reservations made, the average room rate, expected room revenues, and the pace or progress at which reservations are being made for a specific future DOA. It reflects the current status of demand for hotel rooms. This information or booking pace is compared with historical averages that show the current demand, which are then compared with the historical demand.

This information enables hotel management to consider room rates, rooms sold, and the reservation booking pace in managing reservations to maximize total room revenue. Managers can implement selling strategies to increase rooms sold or to increase room rates. They can change the selling strategy daily based on the updated information and room status that Yield Management provides.

Using Yield Management in Different Types of Hotels

All types of hotels in all types of markets and locations can use Yield Management. This is because Yield Management includes the historical and current information for any hotel. How that hotel uses the information can be very different. Let's look at some examples.

Corporate Hotels (Airports and Suburban)

The example we just discussed is similar to a corporate hotel. The main market segments are transient (business and pleasure) and then group. The transient segments, especially business travelers (corporate and special corporate), tend to make their reservations within days rather than weeks or months ahead. That results in many room reservations being booked within the last two weeks of the DOA. It is typical for a corporate hotel to book 25% to 50% of its room reservations within the last three weeks before the DOA.

Group Hotels (Downtown or Suburban)

These hotels have a higher number of group rooms than transient rooms. Because groups require a block of sleeping rooms and a certain amount of meeting space, they require certain types of hotels. To ensure that groups can obtain the required number of sleeping rooms and meeting space, they book their reservations more in advance—typically 6 to 12 months ahead. These reservations are called group room blocks and can include from 5 to 300 rooms per night—a nice way to sell a lot of rooms. Group rooms generally have a lower average room rate because of the higher volume. They also generate significant revenues for the Banquet and Food and Beverage departments. The booking time period for group hotels is very different than corporate hotels. Because most of the rooms are booked more than three months before the day of arrival, as little as 5% to 10% of reservations are booked within the last three weeks of the DOA.

Resorts and Convention Hotels

These types of properties book group blocks as far as five to six years before the day of arrival. This is because many conventions are very large, requiring 500 to 1,000 sleeping rooms per night and a large amount of space for meetings and banquet functions (+50,000 square feet). To be able to secure this number of sleeping rooms and amount of meeting space, large corporations and associations book their meetings five to six years in advance. The same is true at resorts, where the high or prime season involves only a couple of months. During these months the demand is typically very high. Large corporate and association groups book five to six years in advance to ensure that they can conduct their meeting when and where they want.

Group functions requiring 100 to 300 sleeping rooms and less meeting space still book their functions two to four years in advance to ensure that they can conduct their meeting when and where they want. This is especially true at resorts. The further ahead of the meeting date a company books the rooms, the better the chances that it can meet when and where it wants to meet. It is possible for these groups to book within one year but only if demand is slow, and there is greater risk that the company might be unable to find a resort with the amount of sleeping rooms and meeting space required.

Selling Strategies

We have mentioned *selling strategy* several times in this chapter. Let's talk about selling strategies—what they are and what they do.

Definition

Selling strategy refers to the decisions and actions taken by hotel management to maximize room revenues. Selling strategy meetings are held once a week, and that is where yield management information, group room block pickup, and other room revenue information is discussed and the best selling strategy identified and implemented.

The Process

The selling strategy process involves the Director of Revenue Management (the specialist), the Director of Sales and Marketing, the Director of Finance, the Director of Rooms Operations, the Front Office Manager, and the General Manger. They will discuss all the relevant information and determine the best strategy to put in place to maximize room revenues.

Selling strategies typically do not involve changing rate structures but opening and closing specific rate categories, arrival dates, and lengths of stay to maximize total room revenue. All of these actions affect total room revenues by either increasing the number of rooms sold or increasing/decreasing the room rates of reservations booked. Yield management provides the most detailed and valuable information used in determining selling strategies.

For example, if the booking pace for a specific DOA is significantly under the historical average, the selling strategy will probably be to open all discounts and do everything possible to sell rooms. This strategy should result in more rooms sold but at lower, discounted rates. This is okay because the booking pace is below the historical average. That generally means that the hotel will not be close to selling out and will probably have many unsold rooms. A room sold at a lower average rate is preferable to an unsold room.

Let's look at another example where the booking pace is significantly higher than the historical average for a specific DOA. This means that the demand for hotel rooms is higher than the historical average, and therefore there is a higher probability of more rooms being sold for the DOA. The selling strategy will probably be to close or restrict all discounts and ensure that all future room reservations are booked at the higher corporate, rack, and concierge rates. This strategy should result in higher room rates. That should be okay given the higher demand. The expectation is that the hotel will still be able to sell the remaining unsold rooms at the higher rate because of the stronger demand.

When the selling strategy is decided at the selling strategy meeting, the Director of Revenue Management is responsible for changing the available rates to all agencies and organizations that have access to booking reservations from the hotel inventory. They do this by closing off the discounted rates. This means that travel agencies, central reservations offices, hotel and car rental companies, the hotel reservation staff, and the hotel front desk can only book room reservations in the higher rate categories.

Let's look at how the proper selling strategy can maximize room revenues for a sold-out night at our 400-room hotel. Let's assume that one week before the day of arrival, we have sold 350 rooms at an average rate of $75. Yield Management tells us that this booking pace is 25 rooms higher than the historical average, and therefore we will almost certainly have a perfect sellout—400 occupied rooms for the DOA. We will now compare two revenue possibilities for selling the remaining 50 rooms.

First, let's assume we do not change our selling strategy and leave the discounted rooms open and available for sale. We can assume that the average room rate for the final 50 rooms will be the same $75 that Yield Management has calculated for the 350 reservations already made. The expected incremental revenue will be $3,750, which is 50 rooms sold × $75 average rate.

Second, let's assume we change our selling strategy to close all discounted room rates. The remaining 50 rooms will be sold at the corporate rate of $99 and rack rate of $115. The average rate of these 50 rooms will be somewhere between these two rates. Let's use $105 as an average. The expected incremental revenue for these 50 rooms sold increases to $5,250 or 50 rooms sold × $105 average rate. By closing the discounts, the hotel increases its average room rate from $75 to $105, generating an incremental room revenue of $1,500 (the difference between $5,250 and $3,750).

The advantages of dynamic selling strategies is that they can take advantage of current daily updates to change selling strategies to maximize room revenues for a specific DOA. In fact, during high-demand times, a hotel might change its selling strategy several times during the day. Yield Management is the key because of the detail of current reservation information that it provides. The Director of Revenue Management can pull up individual DOAs and implement appropriate selling strategies at any time during a day. Obviously, Yield Management is most useful in high-demand time periods when it is extremely valuable in maximizing room revenues. But it is important to understand that Yield Management can also maximize room revenues in slow time periods by identifying them early so appropriate selling strategies can be put in place to produce the highest room revenue possible during slow times. It would be a major mistake for a hotel to have discount restrictions in place when Yield Management indicates that the hotel is only going to achieve a 50% occupancy for a specific DOA. All discount rates should be open and available during slow times. Once again, it is better to sell a room at a lower, discounted rate and generate some incremental revenue than to have it unsold—another example of leaving money on the table.

Yield Management Critiques

The last step in the yield management process is to evaluate the selling strategies and the results they produced for a specific DOA or week. The critique process is the same as that of critiquing monthly profit and loss (P&L) performance. Did the selling strategies produce the expected results? Questions included in the critique might be the following:

1. Did the implemented selling strategies produce the desired results?
2. Were selling strategies quickly and efficiently communicated to all reservation outlets and selling agencies?
3. Were there any reservation turndowns or lost revenue opportunities?
4. Were there any problems or surprises that need to be considered in the future?
5. Did the yield management process work as intended?
6. Do any changes need to be made to the selling strategy process?

Summary

Maximizing total room revenues is a major priority for every hotel management team. It involves managing room rates and rooms sold in the best balance to maximizing room revenue. It is also the first step and probably the most important step in maximizing total hotel profits. If a hotel is increasing total room revenue from year to year and meeting budgeted and forecasted room revenue, it makes managing and controlling hotel operating expenses much easier.

The process of maximizing total room revenues involves four important processes. First is effectively managing REVPAR (revenue per available room). REVPAR is total room revenue divided by total available rooms in the hotel. This means doing a good job of managing average rates and maximizing total rooms sold.

Second is developing a competitive yet profitable room rate structure for the hotel. Setting the different rates offered to customers at appropriate levels is important for maximizing rooms sold and total room revenue. Rates should be competitive in the market, reflect a good value to customers, reflect the investment in the hotel and the operating cost requirements, and reflect any competitive advantage that the hotel might have.

Third is utilizing a yield management system to provide historical and current reservation information that will assist in maximizing total room revenue. Yield Management is a computer program that compares the current year's booking pace of reservations for a specific day of arrival (DOA) to the historical average booking pace for the DOA.

Fourth is developing and implementing successful selling strategies that will assist all reservation partners and hotel employees in using the hotel room rate structure and current status of room reservations to maximize total room revenues. Selling strategies are developed at weekly meetings and changed daily to react to current rooms sold status.

Effective room revenue management is one of the most important elements of successful hotel operations. It enables the hotel to have flexibility in the use and management of expenses to maintain or improve the hotel's physical structure and provide more and better services and amenities. A hotel that consistently produces lower room revenues than budgeted will not have the revenue and cash flow necessary to keep the hotel in a strong competitive position.

Hospitality Manager Takeaways

1. REVPAR is the most valuable measurement for maximizing total room revenues. It requires hotel management to be efficient in both maximizing rooms sold and maximizing the average room rate.

2. Yield Management is the most valuable tool used by hotel management to maximize total room revenue. It compares the current reservation booking pace to historical booking averages for a DOA and is used to decide on the best selling strategy to maximize total room revenue.

3. The selling strategy team is responsible for reviewing all reservation information including Yield Management information and implementing the best strategy to maximize total room revenue.

4. Room rates for a hotel are generally set annually for several specific rate categories based on the hotel's largest market segments.

Key Terms

Booking Pace—The current rate at which reservations are being received for a specific DOA. The booking pace is compared to historical averages to determine if demand is stronger or weaker than historical averages for a specific DOA.

Day of Arrival (DOA)—The focus point of Yield Management. All historical reservation averages and trends for a specific arrival day in the future.

Demand Tracking—The part of Yield Management that utilizes computer programs to provide historical information of reservation booking patterns that provide historical averages and trends for the hotel.

Historical Average—Average reservation information based on four or five years of hotel information.

REVPAR—Revenue per Available Room. Total room revenue divided by total rooms available. It combines room occupancy and room rate information to measure a hotel's ability to maximize total room revenues.

Rate Structure—A list of the different room rates offered by a hotel.

Selling Strategy—The actions and decisions of the senior management of a hotel concerning opening and closing room rates, arrival dates, and length of stay to maximize total hotel room revenues.

Yield Management—The computer reservation tracking system that combines current reservation booking information with historical reservation booking information. It is used to implement selling strategies that will maximize total hotel room revenue.

Review Questions

1. What are the two formulas for REVPAR?

2. Why is understanding and using REVPAR information so important to maximizing total room revenue?

3. Explain the relationship between room rates and market segments.

4. What is DOA, and why is it such an important part of Yield Management?

5. How is the booking pace used with the historical average in Yield Management?

6. Who is on a hotel's selling strategy team? Which one is the most important?

7. What selling strategy should a hotel implement when the booking pace is under the historical average pace?

8. What selling strategy should a hotel implement when the booking pace is over the historical average pace?

Comparison Reports and Financial Analysis

Learning Objectives

1. To understand the importance of hotel revenue and profit analysis and how they are explained and analyzed.

2. To understand what variation analysis is and how it is used.

3. To learn the key formulas and uses of variation analysis.

4. To understand the format and uses of the STAR Market Report.

5. To understand and be able to use internal and external financial reports.

Chapter Outline

Profitability: The Best Measure of Financial Performance

>   Definition
>   The Difference Between Analyzing Profits and Analyzing Revenues
>   The Impact of Department Profits on Total Hotel Profits
>   Maximizing and Measuring Total Hotel Profitability

Review of Chapter 2: Foundations of Financial Analysis

>   Comparing Numbers/Results to Give Them Meaning
>   Measuring and Evaluating Change in Financial Analysis
>   Percentages as a Tool in Financial Analysis
>   The Importance of Trends in Financial Analysis

Variation Analysis

>   Definition
>   Formulas and Ratios Used in Variation Analysis
>   Key Hotel Ratios That Measure Hotel Financial Performance

STAR Market Report

    Definition

    What the STAR Market Report Contains

    How the STAR Market Report Is Used

Summary

Hospitality Manager Takeaways

Key Terms

Review Questions

In the previous chapters we have presented material on numbers and how they are used to measure financial performance. At this point, students should be forming a solid foundation of financial knowledge and a good understanding of what financial analysis is, what it tells you, and how it is used in explaining hotel operations. The next concepts that we will discuss are other financial reports and methods of financial analysis used to compare and analyze hotel operations.

This chapter refers back to earlier chapters that presented basic accounting concepts and methods of financial analysis. A solid foundation of these fundamentals should now be in place. The next step is to learn about some helpful internal and external reports that can be used in analyzing and comparing operating results. Notice that we always start with operating performance, followed by the analysis of the financial results that operations produce.

Internal comparisons are made to company budgets, forecasts, previous months or periods, and established goals or standards. External reports are market or economic reports that are useful in comparing hotel operating and financial results with a competitive set, the industry average, or other external financial information.

Profitability: The Best Measure of Financial Performance

Definition

Profits are defined as revenues minus expenses—a rather simple formula that is very important in measuring financial performance. In actual hotel operations, this formula is used in a variety of ways that result in specific profitability measures. Profits can be measured at several levels of any business. Let's review some of the key profit levels that are included in hotel Profit and Loss Statements (P&Ls):

Department Profit = All of a Department's Revenues − All of a Department's Direct Expenses

Total Department Profits = The Sum of All Hotel Department Profits, Which Is the Same as the Sum of All Revenue or Profit Centers

House Profit or Gross Operating Profit = Total Department Profits − the Total of All Expense Departments

or

Total Department Profits − Deductions from Income

Net House Profit or Gross Operating Profit = House Profit − Fixed Expenses

Profit before Taxes = Net House Profit or Adjusted Gross Operating Profit − Owner Fees or Management Fees

Profit after Taxes = Profit before Taxes − Taxes

Profits are the best measure of financial performance because they include the two major factors of financial performance: maximizing revenues and minimizing expenses. Maximizing total hotel revenues is important, but it is only one step. Controlling and minimizing expenses is also important and is the second step. Maximizing profits requires management to be efficient in both areas. Together, revenue and profit analysis explain virtually everything about the financial performance of a hotel or restaurant.

The Difference between Analyzing Profits and Analyzing Revenues

Analyzing revenues is totally focused on the relationship between rate and volume in the effort to maximize total hotel revenues. It involves establishing rate structures, defining market segments, utilizing yield management information, setting selling strategies, and comparing rate and occupancy results with internal and external reports. Specific hotel managers are responsible for maximizing hotel revenues.

Analyzing profitability not only includes revenue analysis but also expense analysis in all department and expense line item accounts. Each specific expense category is evaluated on the effect it has on the hotel's ability to efficiently provide products and services for its customers. These expenses include fixed and variable expenses, direct and indirect expenses, and operating and overhead expenses. Specific hotel managers have the direct responsibility for managing specific revenue segments and controlling specific expense line accounts to maximize the profits of their departments.

The most important expenses to be analyzed and controlled are food cost and wage cost. These are two big expense accounts and can become major problems and drains on profits if they are not properly managed and controlled. Wage costs are even more important because they directly affect the benefit costs. If wage costs go up and are over budget, benefit costs will also go up and be over budget.

Finally, there are many more expense line accounts to be managed than revenue line accounts. This requires the attention of all hotel managers in every department in the hotel. Each must be effective in managing and controlling expense accounts if hotel profits are to be maximized. If each manager effectively controls his or her department expenses, the total hotel expenses will be in line and total hotel profits will be maximized.

The Impact of Department Profits on Total Hotel Profits

As we mentioned earlier, all department profit dollars are not created equally. This means that each department that is a profit center has a different expense structure. Some have more expenses that result in lower department profits, and some have fewer expenses that therefore result in higher department profit. The larger convention hotels and resorts have more profit departments and profit centers than typical full-service hotels and therefore can generate a larger Total Department Profit.

Let's look at two examples of full-service hotels and identify the profits associated with each department. Remember that a revenue center and profit center are the same and we can use these terms interchangeably. They are two terms that describe operating departments that produce revenues and profits. Also remember that the department profit percentage shows how much of a department revenue dollar will make it to the "bottom line" as a profit dollar.

Profit Center	Full-Service Hotel	Convention Hotel Resort
Rooms department	65%–75%	70%–80%
Banquets/catering departments	25%–35%	30%–40%
Full-service restaurant	0%–10%	5%–15%
Specialty restaurant	None	10%–20%
Bar and lounges	30%–40%	30%–45%
Gift shop	25%–30%	25%–35%
Golf club	None	25%–35%
Spa	None	25%–35%

Let's examine the impact that these examples have on profitability:

1. The Rooms Department has the highest profit percentage because there is no cost of sales. The rooms are re-rented every night, not consumed (like food and beverage items) or purchased (like gifts and clothing); therefore, there is no cost of sales. In other revenue departments, cost of sales can range from 30% to 40% for food and be about 50% for clothing, so it is a major expense category. This explains why the Rooms Department profit is so much higher than the other profit departments.

2. The room rates of the Rooms Department generally are much higher than the average checks in restaurants or gift shops. This also increases the Rooms Department profit percentage.

3. Convention hotels and resorts generally have higher average room rates and higher food and beverage menu prices that help to increase their department profit percentages.

4. The more revenue departments in a hotel, the more sources of profits to increase Total Department Profits, House Profits/Gross Operating Profit, and Net House Profit/Adjusted Gross Operating Profit.

5. Restaurant departments have the lowest profit percentage because of the many expenses required to prepare and serve food. Both food cost and wage cost will run between 30% and 40% each, benefits will range between 10% and 15%, and other direct operating costs will range between 10% and 15%. This leaves little room for error if the restaurant is to be profitable.

6. Specialty restaurants are generally more profitable because they have higher average checks.

7. It is financially beneficial for restaurants to serve liquor because liquor has lower wage costs and lower cost of sales, resulting in higher liquor profitability. This helps the overall financial performance of the total food and beverage outlets including banquets.

8. The Banquet or Catering Department is more profitable because its food functions can be planned with specific prices and customer counts, resulting in more efficient operations and higher profitability. For example, a dinner banquet for 500 people with a set menu and $30 average check can be planned for and produced with greater efficiency than opening a restaurant for the evening and waiting to see how many customers come, what the average check will be, and what the total revenues will be.

The Director of Finance and the General Manager of a full-service hotel generally spend a great deal of their time on the rooms and food and beverage operations for two very different reasons. First, the Rooms Department is important because it generates the most revenues and profits. A well-run Rooms Department means there will be higher cash flow and greater financial resources to operate the rest of the hotel successfully. The Rooms Department is a good example of a department that focuses on maximizing revenues. Second, the Food and Beverage Department is important because of the complexity and detail of its operations. Food and beverage operations have to be well managed to control all of the different expenses to achieve a profit. If this department is not operated well, operations could produce a loss rather than a profit. Restaurant departments are good examples of departments that focus on controlling and minimizing expenses in addition to maximizing revenues.

The different department profit percentages discussed here provide a good example of mix percentages, presented in Chapter 2. One dollar of revenue in each of these departments will produce different dollar amounts of profit. The management team of a well-operated hotel knows and understands this and plans daily operations to consider the department profit that will result from the forecasted department revenues for the week. *To maximize hotel profitability, expenses must be minimized and revenues maximized.*

Maximizing and Measuring Total Hotel Profitability

There is a partnership in a hotel that enables the hotel to use all the operating and financial resources available to maximize profitability. This partnership is between the staff departments and the operating departments. The goal of the four staff departments (Sales and Marketing, Repairs and Maintenance, Human Resources, and Accounting) is to provide specialized support for the operating departments (Rooms, Food and Beverage, Golf, Spas, Retail). The operating departments are responsible for taking care of guests and generating revenues and profits for the hotel. Their focus should be on providing the best products and services to the guests of the hotel and ensuring that the guests want to come back.

The partnership and support that the Accounting Office and the Director of Finance provide are the operating managers is extremely important in successful hotel operations. Because accounting and finance can become complicated and demanding, it is important that the Director of Finance provide these services and knowledge to both department managers and senior management. It is equally important that the department managers provide accurate numbers to the Director of Finance so that together they have all of the knowledge and resources necessary to identify problems and trends, develop corrective action, and determine the best way to implement changes so that improvements are made and goals met. It is a true partnership with specialized knowledge and experience brought to the relationship by each manager and department. A strong financial and operating team is essential to the successful operations of the hotel.

It is also important to understand the services and support the other staff departments contribute to the successful operations of a hotel. The Sales and Marketing Department works hard to establish good rate structures, implement successful selling strategies, attract profitable group business, and develop good marketing and advertising programs. The Repairs and Maintenance Department works constantly to ensure that the equipment in the hotel is working efficiently and that the hotel looks sharp both inside and out. This is a big job! The Human Resource Department ensures that good employees are hired, provides training and development, handles employee problems, and takes care of payroll and benefit administration. If each of these departments does its job, the hotel will be operating at a high level and have a much better chance of meeting the goals and budgets established to measure hotel performance and profitability.

Review of Chapter 2:
Foundations of Financial Analysis

Chapter 2 introduced fundamental accounting concepts and methods of financial analysis that are used to analyze numbers and results. We will now use this material and these methods to analyze internal operations, including both revenues and profits. We are also able to use this information to compare individual company performance with industry standards and external reports.

In this chapter, we will now focus on *applying the foundations of financial analysis* presented in Chapter 2 to our company performance. Variation analysis utilizes all of these fundamentals. Let's review them again.

Comparing Numbers/Results to Give Them Meaning

Numbers need to be compared to a standard and to other numbers to give them meaning. Variation analysis expands this definition by providing ratios and formulas that assist managers in comparing a company's monthly, quarterly, or annual performance. Variation analysis helps in two ways. First, it allows for an internal comparison of company performance to last year's results, to established plans such as the annual budget and current forecast, or to the previous month's performance. Second, it allows for an external comparison of performance to averages of like hotels in a company, to industry standards and averages, or to external reports such as the STAR Market Report.

Measuring and Evaluating Change in Financial Analysis

Changes in company performance are identified by comparing actual performance to previous performance or to an established goal or measure. Variation analysis expands this definition by identifying changes in company performance in terms of dollars, units, or percentages. The comparisons mentioned in the previous paragraph identify and calculate the amount of both positive and negative changes. Companies plan on improving their operations and performance from year to year, and actual results are compared to these planned changes (budgets and forecasts).

Percentages as a Tool in Financial Analysis

Percentages measure relationships and changes in operating performance. They always involve two numbers and provide another measurement in financial analysis beside dollar or unit changes. Percentages identify the size of a change compared to a standard. This is very important information. For example, a $1,000 change in revenues compared to $50,000 in revenues is a 2% increase. That same $1,000 change in revenues compared to $200,000 in revenues is only a 0.5% increase. These percentages tell us that the $1,000 change in the first example is a larger and more significant change than the $1,000 change in the second example.

The four types of percentages used most often in financial analysis are cost percentage, profit percentage, mix percentage, and percentage change. Each of these percentages is an important part of variation analysis.

The Importance of Trends in Financial Analysis

Trends are important because they show the size, direction, or movement of business activity, industry averages and standards, and national and world economies. Variation analysis compares the operating and financial trends of a company with the trends of other hotels or restaurants in the company, industry trends, stock market trends, or national or world economy trends. Variation analysis also identifies both positive and negative changes in the operating and financial trends of a company. Particularly valuable is comparing a company's revenue, expense, and profit trends in seeking to improve operating results and financial performance.

Photo: Rancho Las Palmas Marriott Resort & Spa

Sunrise Terrace
Rancho Las Palmas Marriott Resort and Spa
Rancho Mirage, California

This 422-room resort that opened in January, 1979, was the first resort built and operated by Marriott Hotels and Resorts. It is a part of the Rancho Las Palmas Country Club development that included 27 holes of golf, 25 tennis courts, and over 850 club home owners and members. In 1999, a second ballroom was added, bringing the total meeting space to 41,000 square feet. A two-story 20,000-square-foot spa was also added as part of the resort's expansion and renovation. It was also the first resort to open east of Palm Springs and opened the expansion into the Coachella Valley. Today there are more than eight other major resorts including another Marriott, a Renaissance, Westin, Hyatt, and La Quinta resorts.

The original competitive set would have included resorts in Southern California and Arizona. Now the competitive set is located in the Coachella Valley and includes a wide range of amenities, meeting space, and room rates. If you were asked to identify the current competitive set, would you focus on similar room rates, similar number of guest rooms, similar meeting facilities, similar recreational activities, similar room rates, or location? All of the above would be a safe answer, but how would you identify your primary competition and create a valuable competitive set?

Variation Analysis

Definition

Variation analysis involves identifying the difference between actual operating performance and established standards. These standards can be last year's actual performance, the previous month's actual performance, the budget for this year, or the most current forecast. Variation analysis relies on accurate financial information to identify both good and bad variations in operating activities. Therefore, variations can be positive, reflecting better performance than the standards, or they can be negative, reflecting worse performance than the standards.

Variation analysis also includes identifying and examining the causes of changes in operations. It identifies the variations of each line account, which collects all the financial information for a specific expenses category. The variations in the operating results of a hotel or restaurant are described and measured in the line accounts contained in the financial statements produced each month or accounting period.

Variation analysis is used to describe the results in revenue, expense, and profit accounts. Some of these accounts have several variables and some have just one variable. Variables are the different components involved in an account and can be revenue or expense. Two variables mean that two components can be managed and analyzed. Variation analysis shows the impact that each component has on the total of each account. For example, examining average room rates and volume in room revenues or average wage rates and labor hours in hourly wage analysis both include two variables. Let's look at some of the main accounts and the variables that are measured in analyzing revenue and expense accounts.

Account or Line Item	Variable
Room revenue	Average rooms rates and rooms sold/occupancy percentage
	Market segments
	Weekday and weekend
Restaurant revenue	Average check and customer counts
	Meal periods
	Beverage capture rates
Wage cost	Average wage rate and labor hours
	Management, hourly, and overtime wage categories
	Labor hours per occupied room

Most of the remaining expense accounts involve only one variable. Examples are food cost, china, glass, silver, guest supplies, linen, and so on. The total expenses in one variable account involve purchase amounts, inventory variation amounts, and transfer amounts in and out of an account. Larger line accounts such as food cost are more complicated, have many entries, and can be more difficult to manage and control. For example, total food cost for a restaurant could involve more than 100 entries each month to accurately identify the total food cost for the month. Compare that to linen cost, which will probably have fewer than five entries for the month.

Formulas and Ratios Used in Variation Analysis

Five major classifications of ratios are used in financial analysis. Each classification involves one or more of the three financial statements: the P&L Statement, the Balance Sheet, and the Statement of Cash Flow. There are a few ratios that involve information from two of these financial statements. The five classifications are as follows:

1. *Activity ratios.* A group of ratios that reflect hospitality management's ability to use the property's assets and resources. These ratios primarily involve dollars and statistics from the P&L Statement. Consider the following examples:

   a. Total Occupancy Percentage = Rooms Occupied ÷ Total Rooms

   b. Available Occupancy Percentage = Rooms Occupied ÷ Total Available Rooms for Sale

   c. Average Occupancy per Room = Total Guests ÷ Total Rooms Occupied

   d. Food Inventory Turnover = Cost of Food Sold ÷ Average Food Inventory

2. *Operating ratios.* A group of ratios that assist in the analysis of hospitality establishments operations. These ratios are also primarily from the P&L Statement. Examples are as follows:

   a. Average Room Rate = Total Room Revenue ÷ Total Rooms Sold

    b. REVPAR = Total Room Revenue ÷ Total Rooms or Average Room Rate × Occupancy Percentage

    c. Average Food Check = Total Food Revenue ÷ Total Customers

    d. Food Cost Percentage = Total Food Cost ÷ Total Food Revenue

    e. Wage Cost Percentage = Department Wage Cost ÷ Department Revenue

3. *Profitability ratios.* A group of ratios that reflect the results of all areas that fall within management's responsibilities. These ratios involve information from three areas: the P&L Statement, the Balance Sheet, and information from publicly traded stock exchanges. Examples are as follows:

    a. Profit Margin = Profit ÷ Revenue (This can be for a department or the entire hotel.)

    b. EBIDTA = Earnings before Interest, Depreciation, Taxes, and Amortization

    c. Return on Assets = Net Profit ÷ Average Total Assets

    d. Return on Owner Equity = Net Profit ÷ Average Owner Equity

    e. Earnings per Share = Net Profit ÷ Average Common Shares Outstanding

    f. Price Earnings Ratio = Stock Price per Share ÷ Earnings per Share

4. *Liquidity ratios.* A group of ratios that reveal the ability of an establishment to meet its short-term obligations. These ratios are from the Balance Sheet and P&L Statement. Examples are as follows:

    a. Current Ratio = Current Assets ÷ Current Liabilities

    b. Acid Test Ratio = Cash and Near Cash Assets ÷ Current Liabilities

    c. Accounts Receivable Turnover = Total Revenue ÷ Average Accounts Receivable

5. *Solvency ratios.* A group of ratios that measure the extent to which the hospitality operation has been financed by debt and is able to meet its long-term obligations. These ratios are also from the balance sheet. Examples are as follows:

    a. Solvency Ratio = Total Assets ÷ Total Liabilities

    b. Debt-Equity Ratio = Total Liabilities ÷ Total Owner Equity

Key Hotel Ratios That Measure Financial Performance

Many ratios are used in analyzing and evaluating the financial performance of a hotel. The main ratios are divided into revenue, profit, and expense categories. We will discuss and prioritize the most important ratios in each category. Notice that most of these ratios were mentioned in the five ratio classifications previously discussed.

Revenue

Variation analysis is used to examine two different aspects of the actual revenues generated by the hotel. It seeks to identify where differences occurred and what caused them.

The first analyzes rate and volume. The second compares actual performance to another standard such as budget, forecast, last year, or last month. The three primary measurements used in revenue variation analysis are rooms sold or occupancy percentage, average rate, and REVPAR. Let's examine rate and volume.

1. *Rooms sold or occupancy percentage.* This is the volume measurement of the revenue equation: Revenue = Rate × Volume. Variation analysis measures the actual number of rooms sold each night compared to the budget, forecast, or last year's rooms sold. The difference between the actual number of rooms sold and the budgeted number of rooms sold, for example, is the rooms sold variation. In our 400-room hotel, if the budgeted number of rooms sold is 360 and the actual number of rooms sold is 375, the rooms sold variation is +15. The hotel sold 15 more rooms than budgeted, which is a positive variation—more rooms sold than the budget anticipated.

   Rooms sold can also be stated in percentage terms, which is the occupancy percentage. In our example, the hotel's budgeted rooms sold prediction of 360 equates to a 90% occupancy rate. The actual rooms sold, 375, equates to a 93.8% occupancy rate (notice that we round to one decimal from the 93.75%). Our analysis of rooms sold variation now has a second measurement—15 more rooms sold, or 3.8% higher occupancy. We have now identified what part of any room revenue variations were the result of volume—selling more rooms.

2. *Average rate.* This is the rate measurement of our revenue equation: Revenue = Rate × Volume. Variation analysis measures the actual average room rate compared to the budget, forecast, or last year's average room rate. The difference between the actual average room rate and the budgeted average room rate is the room rate variation. In our 400-room hotel, if the budgeted average room rate is $75 and the actual average room rate is $74, the average room rate variation is $1. The hotel's average room rate is $1 lower than budgeted, which is a negative variation—a lower average room rate than the budgeted average room rate. We have now identified what part of any room revenue variations were the result of average room rate.

3. *REVPAR.* Revenue per Available Room (or **REVPAR**) combines both rate and volume into one measurement. It is the first operating and financial statistic that managers examine when analyzing total room revenues because it includes both rate and volume—the average room rate and the rooms sold/occupancy percentage. The difference between the actual REVPAR and the budgeted REVPAR is the REVPAR variation.

Let's continue our analysis with the average room rate and occupancy percentage information from our previous examples:

	Actual	Budget	Variation
Rooms sold/occupancy percentage	93.8%	90.0%	+3.8% points
Average room rate	$74	$75	−$1.00
REVPAR	$69.41	$67.50	+$1.91

An analysis of our example shows that actual REVPAR of $69.41 was $1.91 above the budgeted REVPAR of $67.50. Stated as a percentage, the $1.91 variance is 2.8% over the budgeted REVPAR. That is a positive variation. The next step is to identify whether rate or volume or both contributed to this positive variation. In our example, there is a positive occupancy or volume variation but a negative average rate variation. The fact that the overall REVPAR variation is positive tells us that the positive occupancy variation of 3.8 percentage points has a larger impact on REVPAR than the negative average rate variation of −$1.

The second aspect is the comparison of actual performance to a standard. We already started this process in our example. The importance of comparing the actual occupancy percentage, average room rate, and REVPAR to a standard is that it describes the direction and degree of actual performance. Comparing actual performance to last year's performance shows where and how much operations have improved or declined from the previous year. It compares yearly actual financial results. Comparing actual performance to the budget shows how actual results compare to the operating plan or budget for the year. It compares actual performance to planned or budgeted performance. Comparing actual performance to the forecast involves the most current operating plan that includes the current trend and current economic environment. The forecast updates the budget and is the most recent plan, so it should be the most accurate plan. It compares actual performance to the latest plan.

The best financial situation is to have actual operating and financial performance exceed all three measures: last year, the budget, and the forecast. The next best situation is to exceed last year but not meet the budget. This comparison shows that operations have improved over last year, which is always important, but did not improve enough to meet the budget. This could be because an aggressive budget was set. Another good situation is to meet or exceed the forecast. This is because the forecast represents the most current plan or projection. To meet or exceed last year and the forecast is very good financial performance even if the budget is missed. It is important to show improvement in at least one comparison because that indicates operations are moving in a positive direction.

Profit

Variation analysis is used to examine hotel profits at several different levels. The formula for profit is revenue minus expenses. Revenues have already been analyzed at this point, so the focus of profit variation analysis will be on the expense accounts. There are three aspects of profit variation analysis. The first analyzes the impact of revenues and expenses on profit. The second defines what profit level is being analyzed—department profits, house profit or gross operating profit, and net house profit or adjusted gross operating profit. The third compares actual performance to another standard such as last year, the budget, or the forecast.

The first step is to examine revenues and expenses:

1. *Revenues.* This part of profit analysis was completed in the previous section as rate, volume, and REVPAR were examined and compared. Refer to number 1 under "Revenue" for the details.

2. *Expenses.* The next step of profit variation analysis involves examining the different expense categories. The detail of operating expenses are included in the Department P&L and include the major cost categories of cost of sales, wages, benefits, and direct operating expenses.

The second step is to define what profit level is being analyzed. Following are the different profit levels that are examined as a part of variation analysis:

1. *Department Profits.* This is the dollar profit for the revenue/profit centers, and the formula is department revenues minus department expenses.

2. *Total Department Profits.* This is the sum of the department profits for all the revenue/profit centers in the hotel.

3. *House Profit.* This is the dollar profit that measures management's ability to control all the operating expenses in the hotel. The formula is Total Department Profits minus total Deduction Department Expenses/Total Expense Centers.

4. *Net House Profit.* This is the final profit measure that includes all hotel revenues and expenses. The only remaining expense is the distribution of profits between hotel owners and hotel management companies and taxes due. The formula is House Profit minus fixed or overhead expenses.

The third step is to compare the actual performance to a standard. This analysis is the same as described in the revenue section. The actual profit performance at each level is compared to last year, the budget, and the forecast. Any differences or variations are then identified. The revenue variations were identified in the revenue analysis, so the focus is on examining the differences in the expense categories of the different profit levels and the impact that has on each of the profit measurements.

Expense

In the "Profit" section above, we discussed how expenses are analyzed. Managing expenses is a critical part of any hospitality manager's job. Let's look at what she or he will be expected to manage in each of the major expense categories:

1. *Cost of sales.* Managers will be expected to meet the budgeted food cost in dollars and percentages each month and year to date. This will require that they effectively manage food and beverage purchases and inventory levels, assist in taking accurate physical inventories and reconciling these totals with the book inventory, oversee storeroom rotation to ensure quality and freshness, organize transfers to other food departments, and coordinate all numbers and financial information with the Accounting Department.

2. *Wage cost.* Managers will be expected to be able to forecast and control the hourly wage expense given weekly increases and decreases in expected revenue volumes. This includes maintaining productivity levels as well as acceptable customer service levels. Overtime is also an important wage expense to manage.

3. *Benefit cost.* Managers control this major expense category by controlling hourly wages.

4. *Direct operating expenses.* This cost category can have many line accounts that managers must control. This includes purchasing, verifying and processing invoices, taking physical inventory, processing transfers, and critiquing monthly operating expenses compared to budget. Examples of these accounts are china, glass, silver, linen, cleaning supplies, guest supplies, and paper supplies.

A detailed understanding of controlling all expenses and the ability to adjust them up or down given business levels is an important skill for any hospitality manager. There will always be pressure to maintain productivities and stay within the expense budget. A manager's ability to skillfully control expenses will have a major impact on department profits.

STAR Market Report

Definition

The **STAR Market Report** is published monthly by the Smith Travel Research Company. It provides rate, occupancy, and REVPAR information for a specific hotel and its competitive set. The report covers one year and provides a hotel with information to compare its monthly current operations with its **competitive set** and with its previous year's operations. It provides valuable trend information as well as the opportunity to compare a specific hotel's performance with its competitive set.

The competitive set will only include hotels considered **primary competition**. Other hotels that are considered **secondary competition** are not included in the competitive set. Then hotels are not considered direct competition because they offer different services and often have different room rate structures.

What the STAR Market Report Contains

The STAR Market Report contains confidential information regarding rooms sold, room rates, and REVPAR. This confidential information cannot be shared directly among competitors because of monopoly and price-fixing laws. Smith Travel Research Company collects this information for a minimum of five hotels and converts it into averages. This is called the *competitive set*, and the averages for the competitive set are compared with the actual results for a specific hotel. This will also include information on the **market share** of the hotel and the competitive set.

Any hotel can purchase this service from Smith Travel. A hotel identifies what hotels it wants included in its competitive set and agrees to provide its own monthly actual rooms sold, occupancy percentage, average room rate, and REVPAR information to Smith Travel to be included in the research company's information database. Smith Travel then *combines and averages* the information for the total competitive set. The report that it sends back to the hotel will contain the specific information for the purchasing hotel and the average information for the competitive set. The hotel can then compare its operating results to the competitive set and its own past performance.

We will look at the format for a twelve-month market share report. The format contains the same three categories that P&L Statements contain: title, horizontal headings, and vertical headings.

Hotel Name

Report Name

Report Date

	Each Month January–December Actual Results	Last 12 Months Average	Last 3 Months Average	YTD
Specific Hotel				
Occupancy Percentage				
Average Room Rate				
REVPAR				
Room Supply Share				
Room Demand Share				
Room Sale Share				
Percent Change from Prior Year				
Occupancy Percentage				
Average Room Rate				
REVPAR				
Room Supply Share				
Room Demand Share				
Room Sale Share				

Market
    Occupancy Percentage
    Average Room Rate
    REVPAR
Percentage Change from Previous Year
    Occupancy Percentage
    Average Room Rate
    REVPAR

This sample format shows the amount of information and the detail of the information that is available for hotel managers to use. Notice that this is only a room revenue report and does not include any food and beverage or banquet sales information. The members of the selling strategy team will review this report and look for trends and comparisons that will assist them in developing better strategies and making better decisions to maximize total room revenue.

There are several other market and financial reports available from Smith Travel Research including the Market Position Report.

The hotel will focus on two primary areas. First, it will compare its results for the current month to those from the previous month and to its quarterly and yearly averages. The hotel will focus on the size and direction of change from its previous results. Second, the hotel will compare its results for the current month to the results of the competitive set. The hotel will identify where its results are better or worse than the competitive set and then will determine if the difference is due to a single-month event or an ongoing trend. If the hotel results are below the competitive set, managers will need to ask what improvements are being made, has any progress been identified, or is the hotel still underperforming the competitive set? If the hotel results are above the competitive set, is the hotel maintaining, increasing, or decreasing its advantage? The hotel will be interested in both comparing its actual results to the competitive set and identifying if improvements are being made that reflect good management of the hotel's room revenues.

How the STAR Market Report Is Used

A great deal of operating information is contained in the monthly STAR Market Reports. There are several different types and formats, which provide specific month-to-month and total-year operating information. These include many trends and provide good comparison information. The hotel management team analyzes this information and compares its operating results to the competitive set's operating results. A hotel that is well run would expect its results to be better than the results for the competitive set.

Summary

The ability to effectively manage and critique revenues and expenses is an essential skill for all hospitality managers. Making or exceeding budgeted profits is equally important for maintaining customer satisfaction in the successful operations of a business. Both are important for maximizing profits. Profits are the most examined financial measurement used both internally by the senior management of a company and externally by investors, bankers, and other financial agencies.

Variation analysis is the process of examining financial results to identify differences or variations from expected results and performance. Identifying where variation occurs and determining the size and cause of variations are important elements of financial analysis. Specific ratios and formulas are used to determine the effectiveness of actual operations to the historical performance of established budgets or forecasts. Ratios can be divided into five types: (1) activity ratios, (2) operating ratios, (3) profitability ratios, (4) liquidity ratios, and (5) solvency ratios.

Variation analysis applies the methods of financial analysis presented in Chapter 2 to the actual performance of a company. These key methods of financial analysis are (1) comparing numbers to give them meaning, (2) measuring and evaluating the change in numbers and financial results, (3) using percentages as a tool for describing financial performance, and (4) utilizing trends to evaluate current financial performance.

Management is also expected to use external information to evaluate financial performance. This includes comparisons to like hotels or restaurants within the company, comparisons to industry averages, and comparisons to competitive sets within the company's market. The STAR Market Report includes several types of revenue management reports that enable a company to compare its performance with the average performance of competitors within its primary market. This is called the competitive set, and it provides a specific hotel with average operating information for a group of competitors in its market.

Hospitality Manager Takeaways

1. A hospitality manager must develop a solid understanding of department and hotel profits. This includes the ability to manage operations to maximize profits and the ability to identify and critique variations from the budget and forecast.

2. An important financial skill is the ability to use ratios and formulas in variation analysis. The manager who can effectively identify, explain, and correct operating results will have a major competitive advantage and will possess an important skill for maximizing profits.

3. Understanding external reports is essential for hospitality managers to effectively manage their operations. The STAR Market Report provides valuable information about the operations of a specified hotel competitive set.

Key Terms

Competitive Set—A group of five or more properties selected by individual hotel management. A competitive set enables hotel managers to compare property performance with external direct competition.

Market Share—Total room supply, room demand, or room revenue as a percentage of some larger group.

Primary Competition—A group of similar hotels that compete for the same customer. Hotels that you lose business to are primary competition.

Ratios—Formulas that define relationships between numbers and are used in financial analysis.

REVPAR—Revenue per available room. Total room revenue divided by total rooms available. It combines room occupancy and room rate information to measure a hotel's ability to maximize total room revenues.

Secondary Competition—A group of hotels that offer competition but provide different rates, services, and amenities and therefore are not considered direct or primary competition.

STAR Market Report—Monthly reports published by Smith Travel Research that provide a hotel with rate, occupancy, and REVPAR information for a specific hotel and its competitive set, including trends and comparisons.

Review Questions

1. Name two important variables for maximizing revenues.
2. Name two important variables for controlling expenses.
3. What is the impact of different department profit percentages on total hotel profits?
4. Define variation analysis, and tell why it is an important tool in financial analysis.
5. Name one important ratio from each of the five ratio classifications, and tell why you think it is important in financial analysis.

6. Discuss the relationship of the four elements that make up the foundation of financial analysis and why they are an important part of variation analysis.

7. What key information is provided in the STAR Market Report?

8. How is it used in the operation of and financial analysis of a hotel?

Forecasting: A Very Important Management Tool

Learning Objectives

1. To understand the fundamentals of business forecasting.

2. To understand the different uses of forecasts.

3. To understand the different types and time periods of forecasts.

4. To be able to prepare revenue forecasts.

5. To be able to prepare wage forecasts and wage schedules.

Chapter Outline

Forecasting Fundamentals

    Definition

    Last Year, Budgets, and Forecasts

Types and Uses of Forecasts

    Forecast Relationships with Last Year and the Budget

    Weekly, Monthly, Quarterly, and Long-Term Forecasts

    Revenue, Wage, and Operating Expense Forecasts

Revenue Forecasting

    The Importance of Room Revenue Forecasts

    Volume: The Key to Forecasting

Wage Forecasting and Scheduling

    Wage Forecasting Fundamentals

    Labor Standards, Forecasting, and Ratios

Summary

Hospitality Manager Takeaways

Key Terms

Review Questions

Problems

Forecasts are used to assist managers in the short-term operations of their businesses. More than any other financial document, forecasts are the key management tool used to plan the details of the daily operations for the next week. Like the operating budget, forecasts look to the future and assist management in the detailed planning of operations for the next week or month. They involve the shortest time period (daily and weekly) and are the last financial document prepared in advance of actual daily operations. For example, weekly revenue forecasts are used to develop weekly wage schedules as a business prepares for the next week of operations.

The major inputs to a forecast are, first, the historical daily averages provided by Yield Management or other demand tracking programs; second, the established budget; and third, recent events that affect the current operating environment of the business. Yield Management looks to the past and provides detailed information on daily room revenue actual results. The operating budget is the formal annual financial plan for a business and is prepared once a year. It is generally approved by December for the next year and does not change. *Forecasts are used to update the budget.* Recent events and trends in the marketplace need to be considered. The forecast is the management and financial tool that adjusts the budget to reflect these changes. It is then used to plan the details of each day's operations. Forecasts can both increase or decrease budget numbers based on historical information, recent market information, and current trends.

Forecasting takes the original budget, current market conditions, and trends, and combines them with ratios and formulas to calculate revenues or labor hours that help plan daily operations in detail for the next week. Forecasts for the next month or accounting period will be more general in nature. Ratios identify the relationships between the two components of revenues (rate and volume), the two components of wages (rate and labor hours), and the important components of other operating expenses. *Ratios and formulas are used to calculate appropriate expense levels in relation to different revenue levels.*

This chapter discusses revenue and wage forecasting—how they are prepared and how they are used. The chapter builds on the information presented in the revenue management chapter.

Forecasting Fundamentals

Definition

Forecasts are the financial documents that update the operating budget. Whereas the operating budget is a permanent financial plan for a year, the forecast is flexible and provides a way to makes changes to the budget to reflect current trends and economic/market conditions. Budgets are generally prepared in the fourth quarter of the current year for the next year. The budget for the first quarter is current, being only a couple of months old. However, the budgets for the third and fourth quarters are more than eight months old and many changes may have occurred in the marketplace that would affect the budget and the operations of a business. Forecasts are therefore valuable management tools used to update the budget so that it reflects current business levels and conditions.

Forecasting is not an exact science, and forecasts are not expected to balance or tie into other financial numbers. Forecasting involves using current information and combining this information with established ratios and formulas to estimate or project future business levels and operations. These ratios are based on existing relationships between revenues and expenses. These ratios can be applied aggressively or conservatively depending on the current management strategy.

Last Year, Budgets, and Forecasts

There is a logical progression for the preparation of financial documents used as management tools in operating a business. Two aspects are involved. The first is historical in nature, and the second is forward looking and looks to the future.

All financial documents used in the planning of business operations start with last year's actual financial performance. This is the historical aspect of financial planning. These numbers are facts and are the results of actual business operations for previous months or years. They become the foundation for preparing the operating and capital expenditure budgets for the next year. If last year's financial results are good, a business will try to continue the strategies and plans that produced those successful financial results. If last year's financial results are not good, then a business will identify changes and improvements that will produce the intended financial results. In both situations, the annual budget will lay out the details for the next year's operations including the expected financial results. It is the first and most formal financial document that plans for the future.

Once the annual operating budget is prepared, the next step is to update the budget by preparing forecasts that reflect any changes in the current market or economic conditions and the current trends in volume and revenues. Forecasts plan for the future, are short term in nature, and are intended to be flexible. They are the last planning document and are prepared by using the latest and most current actual market trends and information. The weekly revenue forecast and the weekly wage schedule are used to plan the specifics of daily operations for the next week. When the week is completed, actual financial results are compared to the forecast, the budget, and last year's actual results. Major variations are analyzed and financial critiques are prepared to explain the causes and discuss solutions.

In review, the progression of financial documents used in planning business operations begins with last year's actual results that are used to prepare the annual operating budget. The budget is then updated during the year by preparing forecasts, which update the budget and provide management with the most current information to plan the next week's daily operations.

Types and Uses of Forecasts

Forecasting Relationships with Last Year and the Budget

As we have discussed throughout the book, the main uses of numbers and financial reports are to measure financial performance and provide a management tool to use in operating a business. The Profit and Loss (P&L) Statement is the main financial report used to measure financial performance. The Balance Sheet and Statement of Cash Flows also provide useful financial information for measuring financial performance. Forecasting mainly involves financial activity that is included in the P&L. Therefore, the P&L will be the focus of forecasting in this chapter. One exception is the importance to owners and managers of forecasting the required cash flow to maintain daily operations. Cash flow forecasting is generally performed by the accounting office.

The forecasting relationship with last year's actual results and the budget for the current year can be illustrated with the following time line:

1. Last year's actual results will be shown by each week.

2. Management will determine what are realistic improvements or achievable growth objectives for next year.

3. Management and accounting will prepare the formal operating budget, a detailed financial plan by day, week, month, and year outlining the financial goals for the next year.

4. The final operating budget will be approved for the next year containing specific monthly or accounting period financial plans including dollar amounts, percentages, and statistics. This budget is approved and distributed to all departments and will be used for the entire year.

5. Before the beginning of a month or accounting period, the Accounting Office will provide a weekly breakout of the budget for each department.

6. Each department will then review the budget for the next week. If there are no meaningful changes, the department will use the weekly budget as its weekly forecast and will plan the next week—day by day—according to the budget numbers.

7. If there are meaningful changes—either increases and decreases—the department managers will update the budget by making changes that reflect more accurately the current business environment. The changes that update the budget become the weekly forecast.

This time line demonstrates the process that takes actual financial performance (last year) and projects it into the future with a formal annual financial operating plan (the budget). The last step is to review the budget, make any changes or updates (the forecast), and use this information to plan the details for the next week's operations. A forecast column is rarely included in the monthly P&L. Forecasts are, however, included on internal management reports that are generally reviewed daily and weekly. This includes reviewing actual revenues and labor costs and comparing them to the forecast, the budget, and last year. Any changes or differences are explained in variation reports called critiques.

The fact that weekly forecasts are not generally included in the monthly or accounting period P&L does not mean they are not important. It means that they are used primarily as an internal management tool to plan, operate, and analyze the daily and weekly operations. In fact, operations managers spend more time with the weekly financial information than with the P&L. This is because they use the forecasts daily in their operations, critique the variations daily and weekly, and make any necessary changes that will improve performance. Effectively using the weekly forecasts and other internal management reports generally leads to better financial performance on the monthly or period P&L Statements.

Weekly, Monthly, Quarterly, and Long-Term Forecasts

The **weekly forecast** provides the plans and details of operations for each shift and day of the week. Daily revenue reports and daily labor productivity reports are distributed the following day. These are compared to the weekly forecast and provide operations management with the detailed results of the previous day and week to date operating results. This includes efforts to maximize revenues and efforts to minimize expenses day by day. The shift or line managers have the direct responsibility to run their departments according to the most recent forecasts. They, with their employees, make the numbers happen. Therefore they spend a lot of time reviewing, analyzing, changing, and forecasting their operations.

An essential part of the weekly forecast is the critique that analyzes last week's results. Companies have weekly forms that are useful for capturing the actual, forecast, budget, and last year's information. Recent technology developments provide a vast amount of detailed information almost instantaneously for managers to use. The strongest operations managers in any business will possess both operating skills and financial knowledge so they can make the best use of the daily and weekly information. Weekly reports are primarily internal management reports. They provide information that measures financial performance, but their main use is as a management tool.

Monthly forecasts or accounting period reports are used equally as a management tool and to measure financial performance. These are formal reports that are distributed inside and outside the company to interested stakeholders. They provide the actual financial results of operations and compare them to the budget and to last year. Rarely is the forecast included on a formal P&L Statement. Critiques are also prepared for the formal P&L, and operations managers and accounting managers use the weekly critiques to explain the operations for the month. Operations managers are expected to prepare these critiques and review them with their direct manager or, in the hospitality industry, with their Executive Committee Member. Then the critiques are presented to and discussed with the General Manager. The final step usually involves providing this information to the regional or corporate office and to the appropriate owners.

Quarterly forecasts are primarily used to plan and project the financial performance for the next one or two quarters. Senior management as well as owners are interested to see and review what level of business can be expected in the near future. Whereas operations managers, along with the accounting department, can prepare these longer-term forecasts, they will not spend as much time on quarterly forecasts as they will on daily and weekly forecasts.

The final forecasts are the long-term forecasts, which are not as detailed as weekly and quarterly forecasts but are intended to give the general direction of expected business operations in the future. These long-term forecasts are more general in nature and will probably be prepared by the accounting office. They will include sales and profit projections and average rate, occupancy, and REVPAR projections. Companies can include different time periods in their long-term forecasts. Marriott looks at the next six accounting periods. Four Seasons includes an end-of-year forecast that combines the current year to-date actual performance with a forecast to the end of the year so that management will always have an idea of how the end-of-year actual/forecast performance compares to last year's actual results and the current year's budget. This is important to the owner in planning for cash inflow or outflow.

Revenue, Wage, and Operating Expense Forecasts

Weekly forecasts focus on the most important financial elements of operating performance. In the hospitality industry, this means focusing primarily on revenues and labor costs.

Maximizing revenues, as we have discussed in previous chapters, involves analyzing past performance and forecasting expected levels of performance in the future. Revenue forecasts are critical to the success of any business because, in addition to forecasting expected revenues, they are used to plan and schedule appropriate expense levels. Operations managers need to plan changes in operating expenses to handle the forecasted business levels. If a business does not forecast revenues for the next week or month, it is managing out of the rearview mirror and can get caught in some difficult situations by not seeing and adjusting to changes in the market and its business levels.

The key component of revenue forecasting is volume. Specifically, this is rooms sold for room revenues, customers for restaurant revenues, and labor hours for wage schedules. How many customers are projected to stay at the hotel or eat in the restaurant? Operations managers need to schedule appropriate labor costs and order appropriate materials and supplies to properly service the expected rooms sold or customer counts. This involves volume levels and not average rates. For example, if a hotel is forecasting $50,000 more in revenue for the week and it is all the result of higher average rates, the hotel will not have any more guests in the hotel than the budget specifies. No changes need to be made to wages or operating expenses. However, if the additional $50,000 is all the result of selling more rooms, then operations managers will need to schedule more employees and purchase more supplies and materials to provide expected products and services to their additional guests.

Controlling labor costs is the next most important responsibility of operations managers in all departments. In the hospitality industry, total hotel wage costs are generally 30% to 35% of sales and also produce another 10% to 15% in benefit costs. Because most of the labor costs are in hourly wages, which are a **variable expense**, managers are expected to schedule more or less wages based on the forecasted volume levels. Managers must control their hourly wages to maintain productivities and profit margins. This means sending employees home early on slow days as well as calling employees in on busier days in response to short-term changes in business volumes. It also means changing work schedules for the next few days if business has slowed down or picked up since the most recent weekly forecast was made.

Wage costs are all about hourly wages. Changing labor hours to reflect business levels is essential for managing and minimizing wage and benefit expenses. This also includes controlling overtime, which is a very expensive use of labor. Management costs are generally fixed and therefore are not subject to changes in business levels like hourly wages are.

The last expense to control according to business levels is operating costs. This primarily includes managing the food costs in the restaurant and banquet departments. These are the largest expenses in the food and beverage departments and are also subject to the changing business levels. It is important to manage food inventories because a high percentage of food is subject to time and perishability. Other operating expenses—such as cleaning supplies, guest supplies, china, glass, silver, and linen—cannot be controlled as quickly as wage and food costs. However, they are not perishable and can be used over many months and even over many years. To control these expenses, managers must pay close attention to purchasing and receiving, invoicing, physical inventories, and interdepartmental transfers. They will primarily use the monthly or accounting period budget to control these expenses.

Clubhouse Gallery Golf Club
Tucson, Arizona

The Gallery Golf Club opened the North Course in 1998 and was the first private club to open in Tucson in over 30 years. Nestled against the foothills of the Tortolita Mountains, it offers spectacular views to go along with spectacular golf. It got its name from over 100 gallery quality works of art in the Gallery's dining room and lounge. In 2003, the Gallery opened the South Course. Because it is a private golf club, the clubhouse includes member locker rooms in addition to the golf pro shop and food and beverage operations. Memberships also offer a significant source of revenues. Members generally own a home at the Gallery but memberships are also sold to prospective Gallery home buyers.

How was the Gallery's forecasting of revenues affected by the addition of the second golf course? Would you prepare one daily revenue forecast or one for each golf course? What is the impact the second golf course might have on memberships? Would you maximize golf course revenues by focusing on higher greens fees (rate) or higher rounds of play (volume)?

Photo: Bill Lesch

10th Hole Gallery South
Gallery Golf Club

Revenue Forecasting

The Importance of Room Revenue Forecasts

Room revenue forecasting is the starting point for maximizing all hotel revenues and minimizing all hotel expenses. These are the two most important financial goals for any operations manager. Identifying the causes of increases or decreases in actual business levels, understanding financial ratios and formulas used in revenue forecasting, and preparing accurate and useful forecasts are essential to the success of any department or business.

Room revenue forecasts are also used to prepare restaurant and banquet revenue forecasts. To forecast revenues for the hotels restaurant, the restaurant manager will consider the following details included in the room revenue forecast:

1. Total rooms sold or occupied for each day

2. Number of guests per room

3. Number of group rooms occupied

The manager will then look at the banquet weekly forecast to determine what percentage or number of guests will be attending meal functions provided by banquets. This will affect the number of guests available to dine in the restaurant.

To forecast banquet revenues, the banquet manager uses guaranteed customer counts as well as the number of group rooms in the hotel. The revenue forecast includes the actual number of rooms picked up by a group, and it tells the banquet manger if the meal function will meet the number of customers guaranteed in the contract.

Several other revenue departments will forecast their revenues based on room sales. These include the Gift Shop, Telephone, and Recreation departments, among others, which will use a formula based on room revenue forecasts. For example, these departments can use sales per occupied room to forecast their department sales. The Gift Shop will have a historical average sales per occupied room. Managers will use this amount and multiply it by the number of occupied rooms for the day or week to develop their forecasts.

Volume: The Key to Forecasting

We will emphasize one more time that all forecasting is based on **volume** or business levels. Each revenue department applies a formula based on rooms sold or hotel guests to calculate and forecast its department revenues. Examples of formulas used include the following:

1. Rooms Occupied × Average Sales per Room = Department Sales

2. Rooms Occupied × Average Guests per Room = Total Hotel Guests

3. Total Hotel Guests × Average Check per Guest = Department Sales

4. Total Hotel Guests – Banquet Guests × Average Check per Guest = Department Sales

Any of these formulas can be used to calculate and forecast the revenue for a specific department. Notice that these formulas require an expected volume level stated as total rooms occupied or total guests. This volume number is then applied to an average room rate, average guest check, average expenditure per room, or other formula to calculate a department sales forecast. The next section provides more details and examples of how rooms occupied and number of guests are used to prepare wage schedules and other cost control plans and schedules.

Because of the nature of **fixed costs** they are generally not changed from the budgeted amounts when included in forecasts. Variable costs are changed based on **ratios** that identify the relationship between different expenses and the volume of revenues or sales.

The formula for room revenue is

$$Rate \times Volume$$

Room revenue forecasting applies this formula with current actual information to determine the next week's forecast. Steps in the process of preparing weekly room revenue forecasts begin with forecasting volume levels and then applying an average rate to calculate or forecast total room revenues.

1. Historical averages are used to provide a starting point for forecasting. This can be average rooms sold for each day of the week for room revenues and average customers per day and meal period for restaurants.

2. Current trends and market conditions are then applied to these averages. If a hotel has been busier than usual for the last several weeks, the revenue forecast prepared will probably be higher than the historical averages. If a hotel has been slower during the previous weeks, the historical numbers will be adjusted downward when weekly forecasts are prepared. In each of these examples, the operations managers will add or delete 5, 10, 20, or any other number of rooms from the historical averages to reflect current demand and market conditions.

3. Often forecasts are prepared for each market segment and then added together to get the total room revenue forecast. For example, transient rooms sold are forecasted based on information from a yield management program, whereas group rooms sold are forecasted based on group room blocks and the actual pickup of rooms held in the room block.

4. The last step is determining an average rate to apply to each room sold or average check to apply to each customer. Historical room rates and average checks are the starting point, and then adjustments are made based on any room rate increases or

menu price increases. This process can also be done by market segment or meal period. The more detailed the forecasting of rooms sold and average rates, the more accurate the forecast should be. Forecasting total rooms sold for the week and using one average rate for the week will give a very general forecast. Forecasting volumes and average rates by market segment and meal period will result in more detail and accuracy.

Wage Forecasting and Scheduling

Wage Forecasting Fundamentals

Managing and controlling wage costs are the biggest responsibility of hospitality managers in maintaining productivities and profit margins. The reasons for this are as follows:

1. Wages are the largest expense of each revenue department in hospitality operations. The only exception is retail, where cost of goods sold is generally higher. Total wage costs in a full-service hotel will be in the 30% to 35% range.

2. Hourly wages are variable, and therefore hourly wage schedules can be prepared and adjusted based on the volume levels of current revenue forecasts.

3. Each wage dollar produces an associated benefit cost, generally in the 25% to 40% range. Controlling wage expenses also results in controlling benefit expenses.

Managers in revenue departments spend a great deal of time reviewing revenue forecasts and then preparing wage schedules that appropriately reflect volume levels. This is the primary way that labor productivities and profit margins are maintained.

Labor Standards, Forecasting, and Ratios

Many ratios and forecasts can be used in preparing wage schedules that maintain expected productivities. The primary methods used in a hotel relate to the rooms department and food and beverage departments.

The Rooms Department

Total Labor Hours per Occupied Room =
Total Department Labor Hours ÷ Total Occupied Rooms
Wage Cost per Occupied Room =
Total Department Wage Cost in Dollars ÷ Total Occupied Rooms
Wage Cost Percentage =
Total Department Wage Cost in Dollars ÷ Total Department Revenues

Housekeeper labor hours based on rooms cleaned per eight-hour shift, or numbers of housekeeper room credits per shift.

Front desk clerk labor hours based on check-ins per eight-hour shift.

Front desk cashier labor hours based on check-outs per eight-hour shift.

Restaurant Departments

$$Total\ Labor\ Hours\ per\ Cover/Customer\ Count =$$
$$Total\ Department\ Labor\ Hours \div Total\ Covers/Customer\ Counts$$
$$Wage\ Cost\ per\ Cover/Customer\ Count =$$
$$Total\ Department\ Wage\ Cost\ in\ Dollars \div Total\ Department\ Revenue$$
$$Wage\ Cost\ Percentage =$$
$$Total\ Department\ Wage\ Cost\ in\ Dollars \div Total\ Department\ Revenue$$

Server labor hours based on number of tables per shift or number of covers/customers per shift.

These ratios are applied to the forecasted volumes that produce weekly revenue forecasts for both the rooms department and all food and beverage departments.

Summary

Forecasting is an important management tool for any business. It is the process of reviewing past performance and combining it with present trends and market conditions to project business volume for the next week or month. It is important for a business to be aware of the economic conditions in its market and the actions and performance of its primary competitors.

Forecasting includes projecting future revenues and scheduling future expenses to maintain productivities and profit margins. This all starts with volumes as expressed in rooms sold or customer counts. The amount of activity in a hotel or restaurant will require an established level of wages and other operating expenses to deliver the expected products and services. As business volumes increase, additional wages and operating expenditures will be necessary to properly deliver these expected levels of service. Likewise, when business levels decrease, these wage and operating expenses will also need to be reduced to maintain productivities and avoid unproductive waste in wage and operating costs. It is important for operations managers in any business to possess adequate forecasting skills that will enable them to adjust operating expenses with expected levels of business.

Hospitality Manager Takeaways

1. Weekly forecasting of revenues and wages for the next week is a critical factor in maximizing revenues, controlling expenses, and maintaining productivities.

2. Volume—rooms sold and customer counts—is the starting point of all forecasts.

3. There is a direct relationship between revenue volume and variable expenses.

4. Forecasting is primarily a management tool that has a major impact on maximizing financial performance.

Key Terms

Fixed Expenses—Expenses that are relatively constant and that do not change with different business levels and volumes. Secretaries in sales and accounting clerks are examples of fixed-wage positions.

Forecast—A type of report that updates the budget.

Monthly Forecast—A forecast of revenues for the next month including average rates and volumes for specific market segments, departments, or meal periods.

Quarterly Forecast—A forecast that projects revenues over a longer time period and is completed by adding together the forecasts for each month of the quarter.

Rate—The part of the revenue equation that provides the dollar price that guests or customers are willing to pay to secure a room or meal. Typically, average room rates and average guest checks are used to calculate total room or restaurant revenues. It also provides the hourly rate of pay for wage forecasting and scheduling.

Ratios—Formulas that are used to calculate appropriate expense levels in relation to different revenue levels.

Variable Expenses—Expenses that fluctuate or change directly with the change in business levels and volumes. Housekeepers, bellmen, and servers are examples of variable wage positions.

Volume—The part of the revenue equation that provides the quantity of products or services consumed by the guest. Typically, rooms sold or occupied and customer counts are used to calculate total room or restaurant revenues. Volume is also used to determine the labor hours required for wage forecasting and scheduling.

Weekly Forecast—The forecast for the upcoming week that includes revenues and expenses, with a focus on wage forecasts, and provides the details by day and shift for providing the actual products and services expected by guests.

Review Questions

1. Name two ways that weekly forecasts are different from monthly or quarterly forecasts.

2. Why is volume so important in forecasting?

3. Define fixed and variable wage expenses and give two examples of wage positions in each category.

4. Name the seven steps in the forecasting time line.

5. What are the formulas for room revenue forecasts and restaurant forecasts?

6. What is the formula for forecasting the hourly wage expense?

7. List three important wage ratios.

8. Why are weekly forecasts so important to managing a business's profitability?

Problems

Revenue Forecasting Problem Sets

This section involves the revenue forecasting process for the rooms, restaurant, and room service departments. These forecasts are prepared weekly and are a key management tool for department managers to use in scheduling and controlling operating expenses. The process that will be used is to present the forecast from the first week to explain and demonstrate how a forecast is prepared and how it is used. Information will then be given for the second week that will include changes from the first week that increase the volume and revenue or decrease the volume and revenue. Students will prepare the second week forecast for practice. It will be reviewed and discussed in class. Students can work individually or in groups when preparing the forecast for the second week.

The third week will be presented again as an example with changes to the first week forecast, either a busier or a slower week. Students will prepare the third week forecast as a problem set and turn it in. It will be graded and is worth 25 points. Students can do this assignment individually or as a group. The fourth week forecast will be a quiz where students are expected to prepare the fourth week forecast by themselves. This process will be followed for room forecasts, restaurant forecasts, and room service forecasts.

Room Revenue Forecasts

Developing the rooms department revenue forecast involves two steps. The first is to forecast rooms sold, and the second is to forecast room revenue. The rooms sold forecast involves several variables as demonstrated in the following matrix:

	Transient Rooms	Group Rooms	Total Rooms
Confirmed reservations			
Definite groups			
Pickup reservations or tentative groups			
TOTAL ROOMS			

The forecast for each of these segments is prepared in different ways. The transient confirmed or guaranteed room reservations are generated from the Yield Management or Demand Tracking system of the hotel for each day. The Hotel Reservation Manager then projects or forecasts the number of additional reservations expected between the current date and the day of arrival, including same-day walk-ins, and adds that to the confirmed reservations to forecast the total rooms sold for the day. The group rooms forecast is generated by the group booking report, which provides the number of definite group rooms booked per day. The Director of Sales then determines the number of tentative or prospective group rooms that are in negotiations that have a high probability of becoming definites. Adding total tentatives or to-be-booked to total definites will result in the forecasted group rooms sold for the week.

When the total rooms sold forecast for the week is completed, average room rates are projected for each segment for each day. Total room revenues are then calculated by multiplying rooms sold times the average room rate for each day and each segment and then adding them together to get the total rooms revenue forecast by day for the next week. The weekly forecast will include rooms sold, occupancy percentage, average room rate, and total room revenue for each day of the week and for the total week. The hotel selling strategy team then reviews and approves the weekly forecast.

The steps to prepare a rooms forecast are as follows:

1. Identify confirmed transient reservations and definite group reservations for each day (DOA) from the yield management report and group rooms report.

2. Project the number of expected additional transient reservations and tentative group reservations for each day.

3. Calculate the daily average room rate for transient and for group rooms sold.

4. Calculate the daily room revenue for transient and group rooms by multiplying the daily number of rooms sold by the average room rate for each segment.

5. Add the daily rooms sold for each day of the week to get the total rooms sold for the week.

6. Add the total daily revenue for each day of the week to get the total room revenue for the week.

7. Calculate the average weekly room rate by dividing total room revenue for the week by total rooms sold for the week.

8. Calculate the daily and weekly occupancy percentage by dividing daily rooms sold by total hotel rooms.

9. Double-check the amounts by adding the daily rooms sold or revenue across and comparing it by adding the transient and group market segment down to get the same total rooms sold for the week and the total room revenue for the week.

Apply this process to the following weekly problem sets to calculate total weekly room revenues. Following are worksheets and weekly forecasts for students to use in preparing weekly room revenue forecasts. Week 1 will be provided as an example, and then weeks 2 and 3 will involve changes that require students to calculate and prepare the weekly room forecast for each week. A final quiz will involve preparing the weekly room forecast for the fourth week.

Rooms Sold Forecasting Worksheet

_____ Week _____ Period

MARKET SEGMENT	Offset Friday/ Saturday	Sunday	Monday	Tuesday	Wednesday	Thursday	Friday	Total
TRANSIENT ROOMS								
Reservations Booked								
Reservations Pickup								
Total Transient Reservations								
GROUP ROOMS								
Definite Groups								
Tentative/Prospective Groups								
Total Group Reservations								
TOTAL ROOM RESERVATIONS								
OCCUPANCY PERCENTAGE								
Arrivals/Check-ins								
Departures/Check-outs								

Room Revenue Forecasting Worksheet

Week _____ Period _____

MARKET SEGMENT	Friday/ Saturday	Sunday	Monday	Tuesday	Wednesday	Thursday	Friday	Total
TRANSIENT REVENUE								
Rooms Sold								
Average Rate								
Total Transient Revenue								
GROUP REVENUE								
Rooms Sold								
Average Rate								
Total Group Revenue								
TOTAL REVENUE								
Total Rooms Sold								
Occupancy Percentage								
Average Rate								
Total Room Revenue								

Rooms Sold Forecasting Worksheet—600 Rooms

___1___ Week   ___1___ Period

MARKET SEGMENT	Offset Friday/	Saturday	Sunday	Monday	Tuesday	Wednesday	Thursday	Friday	Total
TRANSIENT ROOMS									
Reservations Booked		150	120	300	400	400	350	180	1,900
Reservations Pickup		10	10	30	50	40	40	20	200
Total Transient Reservations		160	130	330	450	440	390	200	2,100
GROUP ROOMS									
Definite Groups		20	20	80	120	120	100	40	500
Tentative/Prospective Groups		10	0	10	30	20	20	10	100
Total Group Reservations		30	20	90	150	140	120	50	600
TOTAL ROOMS SOLD	300/	190	150	420	600	580	510	250	2,700
OCCUPANCY PERCENTAGE		31.7%	25.0%	70.0%	100%	96.7%	85.0%	41.7%	64.3%
Arrivals/Check-ins		50	100	320	280	120	130	90	1,090
Departures/Check-outs		160	140	50	100	140	200	350	1,140

Room Revenue Forecasting Worksheet

Week __1__ Period __1__

MARKET SEGMENT	Saturday	Sunday	Monday	Tuesday	Wednesday	Thursday	Friday	Total
TRANSIENT REVENUE								
Rooms Sold	160	130	330	450	440	390	200	2,100
Average Rate	$ 110	$ 110	$ 130	$ 145	$ 145	$ 140	$ 110	$ 133.55
Total Transient Revenue	$17,600	$14,300	$42,900	$65,250	$63,800	$54,600	$22,000	$280,450
GROUP REVENUE								
Rooms Sold	30	20	90	150	140	120	50	600
Average Rate	$ 100	$ 100	$ 120	$ 125	$ 125	$ 125	$ 100	$ 120.08
Total Group Revenue	$ 3,000	$ 2,000	$10,800	$18,750	$17,500	$15,000	$ 5,000	$ 72,050
TOTAL REVENUE								
Total Rooms Sold	190	150	420	600	580	510	250	2,700
Occupancy Percentage	31.7%	25.0%	70.0%	100%	96.7%	85.0%	41.7%	64.3%
Average Rate	$108.42	$108.67	$127.86	$140.00	$140.17	$136.47	$108.00	$ 130.56
Total Room Revenue	$20,600	$16,300	$53,700	$84,000	$81,300	$69,600	$27,000	$352,500

Problem Set 1
Week 2 of Period 1
A Busier Week

For the second week, the hotel is forecasting a busier week and more rooms sold. To prepare the second week rooms sold forecast, use the following steps:

1. Begin with the first week's rooms sold forecast. All changes will be made to those numbers.

2. Increase the second week's rooms sold forecast as follows: Weekdays are <u>Monday</u> through <u>Thursday</u>, weekends are <u>Friday</u> through <u>Sunday</u>:

   a. Increase transient weekday and weekend room reservations by 15 per day.

   b. Increase the transient reservations pickup per day by 10 on weekdays and 5 on weekends.

   c. Total the transient rooms sold by day and add up for the weekly total. Check by adding across and down.

   d. Total the group rooms sold by day by adding each group's number of rooms to get daily group rooms forecasted.

   e. Add the daily group room totals to get the weekly group room totals.

   f. Add the daily transient and group rooms to get the total daily rooms sold forecast.

   g. Add the seven days of total rooms sold to get the total weekly rooms sold.

3. Calculate the daily and weekly occupancy percentage by dividing total rooms sold by total hotel rooms (600).

4. Disregard the arrival and departure lines. They will be used to forecast and schedule wages.

5. Use the following second week forecast form for your calculations.

Check your forecast with the correct forecast that follows the blank forecast page. Be sure and prepare your forecast before checking it to the correct forecast.

To forecast the total room revenue for the second week, use the same daily room rates for transient and group as in the first week, and make the calculations on the rooms revenue forecasting worksheet. Take the daily rooms sold from the rooms sold forecasting worksheet, and enter them on the room revenue forecasting worksheet. You will find this worksheet after the rooms sold forecasting worksheet.

Rooms Sold Forecasting Worksheet

2 ___ Week   1 ___ Period

A Busier Week

MARKET SEGMENT	Offset Friday/	Saturday	Sunday	Monday	Tuesday	Wednesday	Thursday	Friday	Total
TRANSIENT ROOMS									
Reservations Booked									
+15 per day weekdays (w/d) and weekends (w/e)									
Reservations Pickup									
+10 per day w/d and +5 per day w/e									
Total Transient Reservations									
GROUP ROOM									
Definite Groups #1			20	30	30	30			110
#2			30	30	30				90
#3					40	40	40	20	140
Tentative/Prospective Groups #1							50	50	100
Total Group Reservations									
TOTAL ROOMS SOLD									
OCCUPANCY PERCENTAGE									
Arrivals/Check-ins									
Departures/Check-outs									

Rooms Sold Forecasting Worksheet
Answers
2   Week   1   Period
A Busier Week

MARKET SEGMENT	Offset Friday/ Saturday	Sunday	Monday	Tuesday	Wednesday	Thursday	Friday	Total
TRANSIENT ROOMS								
Reservations Booked +15 per day w/d and w/e	165	135	315	415	415	365	195	2,005
Reservations Pickup +10 per day w/d, +5 per day w/e	15	15	40	60	50	50	25	255
Total Transient Reservations	180	150	355	475	465	415	220	2,260
GROUP ROOMS								
Definite Groups #1		20	30	30	30			110
#2		30	30	30				90
#3				40	40	40	20	140
Tentative/Prospective Groups #1					50	50		100
Total Group Reservations	–0–	50	60	100	120	90	20	440
TOTAL ROOMS SOLD	180	200	415	575	585	505	240	2,700
OCCUPANCY PERCENTAGE	30.0%	33.3%	69.2%	95.8%	97.5%	84.2%	40.0%	64.3%
Arrivals/Check-ins								
Departures/Check-outs								

Room Revenue Forecasting Worksheet

Same Average Daily Rates as Week 1

Week __2__   Period __1__

MARKET SEGMENT	Friday/	Saturday	Sunday	Monday	Tuesday	Wednesday	Thursday	Friday	Total
TRANSIENT REVENUE									
Rooms Sold									
Average Rate									
Total Transient Revenue									
GROUP REVENUE									
Room Sold									
Average Rate									
Total Group Revenue									
TOTAL REVENUE									
Total Rooms Sold									
Occupancy Percentage									
Average Rate									
Total Room Revenue									

Room Revenue Forecasting Worksheet

Answers

__2__ Week __1__ Period

MARKET SEGMENT	Friday/ Saturday	Sunday	Monday	Tuesday	Wednesday	Thursday	Friday	Total
TRANSIENT REVENUE								
Rooms Sold	180	150	355	475	465	415	220	2,260
Average Rate	$ 110	$ 110	$ 130	$ 145	$ 145	$ 140	$ 110	$ 133.21
Total Transient Revenue	$19,800	$16,500	$46,150	$68,875	$67,425	$58,100	$24,200	$301,050
GROUP REVENUE								
Rooms Sold	–0–	50	60	100	120	90	20	440
Average Rate	–	$ 100	$ 120	$ 125	$ 125	$ 125	$ 100	$ 120.34
Total Group Revenue	$ –0–	$ 5,000	$ 7,200	$12,500	$15,000	$11,250	$ 2,000	$ 52,950
TOTAL REVENUE								
Total Rooms Sold	180	200	415	575	585	505	240	2,700
Occupancy Percentage	30.0%	33.3%	69.2%	95.8%	97.5%	84.2%	40.0%	64.3%
Average Rate	$110.00	$107.50	$128.55	$141.52	$140.90	$137.33	$109.17	$ 131.11
Total Room Revenue	$19,800	$21,500	$53,350	$81,375	$82,425	$69,350	$26,200	$354,000

Problem Set 2—25 Points
Week 3 of Period 1
Another Busy Week

This problem set is worth 25 points and can be done individually or in a group. Follow the same steps used in forecasting the second week. Following are the changes to be used in forecasting the third week:

1. Begin with the first week's rooms sold forecast. All changes will be made to those numbers.

2. Increase the third week's rooms sold forecast as follows:

   a. Increase weekday transient room reservations 30 per day.

   b. Increase weekday transient pickup reservations 15 per day.

   c. Increase weekend transient room reservations 20 per day.

   d. Increase weekend transient pickup reservations 10 per day.

3. Second week group room blocks are as follows:

		Saturday	Sunday	Monday	Tuesday	Wednesday	Thursday	Friday	Total
Definite	#1	20	40	40	40				140
group	#2		30	30	20				80
Tentative	#1				40	40	40	20	140
group	#2					70	70	40	180

4. Complete the total rooms sold forecasting worksheet.

5. Enter the Week 3 rooms sold from the rooms sold worksheet onto the Week 3 room revenue forecasting worksheet.

6. Use the same daily average rates as Week 1 for both the transient and group rooms sold.

7. Calculate the total room revenue for Week 3, and complete the Week 3 room revenue forecasting worksheet.

The 25 points will be graded on the daily and weekly totals from the room revenue forecasting worksheet. Turn both forecasting worksheets in for credit.

Rooms Sold Forecasting Worksheet
25-Point Problem Set

 __3__ Week __1__ Period

MARKET SEGMENT	Offset Friday/	Saturday	Sunday	Monday	Tuesday	Wednesday	Thursday	Friday	Total
TRANSIENT ROOMS									
Reservations Booked									
Reservations Pickup									
Total Transient Reservations									
GROUP ROOMS									
Definite Groups									
Tentative/Prospective Groups									
Total Group Reservations									
TOTAL ROOM RESERVATIONS									
OCCUPANCY PERCENTAGE									
Arrivals/Check-ins									
Departures/Check-outs									

Room Revenue Forecasting Worksheet
25-Point Problem Set
__3__ Week __1__ Period

MARKET SEGMENT	Friday/	Saturday	Sunday	Monday	Tuesday	Wednesday	Thursday	Friday	Total
TRANSIENT REVENUE									
Rooms Sold									
Average Rate									
Total Transient Revenue									
GROUP REVENUE									
Rooms Sold									
Average Rate									
Total Group Revenue									
TOTAL REVENUE									
Total Rooms Sold									
Occupancy Percentage									
Average Rate									
Total Room Revenue									

The final part of the Room Revenue Forecasting section is to prepare the fourth week forecast. This will be given as a 25-point quiz, and students are expected to do their own work on this quiz.

Restaurant and Room Service Forecasts

This section involves the revenue forecasting process for the restaurant and room service departments. The rooms sold forecast for the hotel is used by all the departments in the hotel because it is the best indicator of business activity in the hotel. We will use the same rooms sold forecasts for Period 1 that were prepared in the previous section to prepare the restaurant and room service revenue forecasts. Many of the steps in forecasting food and beverage revenues are the same as those used in forecasting room revenues.

We will follow the same format as that used for the room revenue forecasts: start with the first week forecast, prepare and discuss the second week forecast, and then prepare the third week forecast as a 25-point problem set. The fourth week forecast will be a 25-point quiz.

Notice how similar the restaurant and room service forecasting process is to the rooms forecasting process. This includes the format of the forecasting worksheets. The forecasting process includes forecasting customers and average checks to calculate restaurant and room service revenues. The weekly forecast will be prepared day by day and added up for the total weekly customers, average check, and revenues. The breakfast, lunch, and dinner meal periods will replace the transient and group market segments used in the room forecast.

Refer to the following restaurant and room service forecasting worksheets as we go over the steps to prepare each of these forecasts. We will start with the room service forecast and then move on to the restaurant forecast.

Room Service Customer Count Forecast

1. Enter the transient, group, and total rooms sold by day from the rooms sold forecast that was used in the previous rooms forecasting section.

2. Convert the rooms sold by day to hotel guest count by day by using the hotel's historical average of number of guests per room. In our forecasting examples, we will use 1.2 guests per room.

3. Identify the percentage capture rates calculated from the Room Service history for each meal period. A capture rate is the historical percentage of hotel guests that use Room Service for each meal period. In our forecasting examples, we will use capture rates of 25% for breakfast, 8% for lunch, and 15% for dinner.

4. Calculate Room Service customers by day by meal period. Round up to whole numbers.

5. Add the daily customer counts to get the weekly totals. Check by adding across the daily totals for the week and comparing them by adding down the meal period totals for the week. They should be the same.

6. Transfer Room Service customer counts to the Room Service Revenue worksheet.

Restaurant Customer Count Forecast

1. Enter the historical daily customer count average for each day for each meal period on the Restaurant forecasting worksheet. Total the week down and across.

2. Based on forecasted hotel house counts and on outside activities, enter the appropriate house count adjustment that will reflect the expected business levels for the restaurant.

3. Total the new forecasted daily customer counts for each day by adding the historical average to the house count adjustment. Total for the week and check across and down.

4. Transfer restaurant customer counts to the Restaurant Revenue worksheet.

Room Service and Restaurant Revenue Forecast

1. Double-check the customer counts for each outlet by comparing the customer counts on the customer count forecasting worksheet to the customer count forecasts entered on the revenue forecasting worksheets. They should be the same.

2. Enter daily average checks by meal period for each day. These are obtained from historical averages in the restaurant and room service.

3. Calculate the meal period revenue for each day and each meal period by multiplying customer counts by average checks.

4. Add the revenues for each day to get the total revenue for each meal period for the week.

5. Calculate the weekly average check for each meal period and the total restaurant by dividing total weekly sales by total weekly customer counts.

6. Check your weekly totals by adding daily customer counts and revenues across and comparing that result by adding down the weekly meal period totals for customers and revenues. They should be the same.

7. You will have one Restaurant and Room Service customer forecast worksheet and two separate Revenue Forecasting worksheets—one for Room Service and one for the Restaurant.

Note: Do not be concerned if your numbers are off one or two because of rounding. Focus on the formulas and the forcasting process.

Customer Count Forecasting Worksheet
Room Service and Restaurant
_____ Week _____ Period

	Saturday	Sunday	Monday	Tuesday	Wednesday	Thursday	Friday	Total
Total Rooms Sold								
Guest Count @ 1.2 per room								
Room Service Capture Rates								
Breakfast @ 25%								
Lunch @ 8%								
Dinner @ 15%								
Total Room Service Customers								
Restaurant Customer Counts								
Breakfast Daily Average								
Breakfast Customer Adjustment								
Total Breakfast Customers								
Lunch Daily Average								
Lunch Customer Adjustment								
Total Lunch Customers								
Dinner Daily Average								
Dinner Customer Adjustment								
Total Dinner Customers								
Total Restaurant Customers								

Room Service Revenue Forecasting Worksheet

Week _____   Period _____

	Saturday	Sunday	Monday	Tuesday	Wednesday	Thursday	Friday	Total
Breakfast								
Customer Counts								
Average Check								
Revenue								
Lunch								
Customer Counts								
Average Check								
Revenue								
Dinner								
Customer Counts								
Average Check								
Revenue								
Total Room Service								
Customer Counts								
Average Check								
Total Revenue								

Restaurant Revenue Forecasting Worksheet

Week _____   Period _____

	Saturday	Sunday	Monday	Tuesday	Wednesday	Thursday	Friday	Total
Breakfast								
Customer Counts								
Average Check								
Revenue								
Lunch								
Customer Counts								
Average Check								
Revenue								
Dinner								
Customer Counts								
Average Check								
Revenue								
Total Room Service								
Customer Counts								
Average Check								
Total Revenue								

Customer Count Forecasting Worksheet
Room Service and Restaurant
___1___ Week ___1___ Period

	Saturday	Sunday	Monday	Tuesday	Wednesday	Thursday	Friday	Total
Total Rooms Sold	190	150	420	600	580	510	250	2,700
Guest Count @ 1.2 per room	228	180	504	720	696	612	300	3,240
Room Service Capture Rates								
Breakfast @ 25%	57	45	126	180	174	153	75	810
Lunch @ 8%	19	15	41	58	56	49	24	262
Dinner @ 15%	35	27	76	108	105	92	45	488
Total Room Service Customers	111	87	243	346	335	294	144	1,560
Restaurant Customer Counts								
Breakfast Daily Average	100	100	75	125	150	150	125	825
Breakfast Customer Adjustment								
Total Breakfast Customers								
Lunch Daily Average	40	30	30	60	80	80	50	370
Lunch Customer Adjustment								
Total Lunch Customers								
Dinner Daily Average	60	50	100	120	140	120	80	670
Dinner Customer Adjustment								
Total Dinner Customers								
Total Restaurant Customers	200	180	205	305	370	350	255	1,865

Room Service Revenue Forecasting Worksheet

Week __1__   Period __1__

	Saturday	Sunday	Monday	Tuesday	Wednesday	Thursday	Friday	Total
Breakfast								
Customer Counts	57	45	126	180	174	153	75	810
Average Check	$ 10	$ 10	$ 12	$ 12	$ 12	$ 12	$ 10	$ 11.56
Revenue	$ 570	$ 450	$1,512	$2,160	$2,088	$1,836	$ 750	$ 9,366
Lunch								
Customer Counts	19	15	41	58	56	49	24	262
Average Check	$ 12	$ 12	$ 14	$ 15	$ 15	$ 15	$ 12	$ 14.18
Revenue	$ 228	$ 180	$ 574	$ 870	$ 840	$ 735	$ 288	$ 3,715
Dinner								
Customer Counts	35	27	76	108	105	92	45	488
Average Check	$14	$ 14	$ 16	$ 18	$ 18	$ 16	$ 14	$ 16.43
Revenue	$ 490	$ 378	$1,216	$1,944	$1,890	$1,472	$ 630	$ 8,020
Total Room Service								
Customer Counts	111	87	243	346	335	294	144	1,560
Average Check	$11.60	$11.59	$13.59	$14.38	$14.38	$13.75	$11.58	$ 13.53
Total Revenue	$1,288	$1,008	$3,302	$4,974	$4,818	$4,043	$1,668	$21,101

Restaurant Revenue Forecasting Worksheet

Week __1__   Period __1__

	Saturday	Sunday	Monday	Tuesday	Wednesday	Thursday	Friday	Total
Breakfast								
Customer Counts	100	100	75	125	150	150	125	825
Average Check	$ 9	$ 9	$ 10	$ 11	$ 11	$ 10	$ 9	$ 9.94
Revenue	$ 900	$ 900	$ 750	$1,375	$1,650	$1,500	$1,125	$ 8,200
Lunch								
Customer Counts	40	30	30	60	80	80	50	370
Average Check	$ 11	$ 11	$ 12	$ 13	$ 13	$ 13	$ 11	$ 12.27
Revenue	$ 440	$ 330	$ 360	$ 780	$1,040	$1,040	$ 550	$ 4,540
Dinner								
Customer Counts	60	50	100	120	140	120	80	670
Average Check	$ 13	$ 13	$ 15	$ 16	$ 16	$ 15	$ 13	$ 14.82
Revenue	$ 780	$ 650	$1,500	$1,920	$2,240	$1,800	$1,040	$ 9,930
Total Room Service								
Customer Counts	200	180	205	305	370	350	255	1,865
Average Check	$10.60	$10.44	$12.73	$13.36	$13.32	$12.40	$10.65	$ 12.16
Total Revenue	$2,120	$1,880	$2,610	$4,075	$4,930	$4,340	$2,715	$22,670

Customer Count Forecasting Worksheet
Room Service and Restaurant
Practice Week
2 __ Week __ 1 __ Period

	Saturday	Sunday	Monday	Tuesday	Wednesday	Thursday	Friday	Total
Total Rooms Sold	180	200	415	575	585	505	260	2,720
Guest Count @ 1.2 per room	216	240	498	690	702	606	312	3,264
Room Service Capture Rates								
Breakfast @ 25%	54	60	125	173	176	152	78	818
Lunch @ 8%	17	19	40	55	56	48	25	260
Dinner @ 15%	32	36	75	104	105	91	47	490
Total Room Service Customers	103	115	240	332	337	291	150	1,568
Restaurant Customer Counts								
Breakfast Daily Average								
Breakfast Customer Adjustment +10w/d								
Total Breakfast Customers								
Lunch Daily Average								
Lunch Customer Adjustment +5 All Days								
Total Lunch Customers								
Dinner Daily Average								
Dinner Customer Adjustment +15 All Days								
Total Dinner Customers								
Total Room Service Customers								

Room Service Revenue Forecasting Worksheet

2 Week   1 Period

Practice Week

	Saturday	Sunday	Monday	Tuesday	Wednesday	Thursday	Friday	Total
Breakfast								
Customer Counts								
Average Check Same								
Revenue								
Lunch								
Customer Counts								
Average Check Same								
Revenue								
Dinner								
Customer Counts								
Average Check +50 Cents All Days								
Revenue								
Total Room Service								
Counts								
Average Check								
Total Revenue								

Restaurant Revenue Forecasting Worksheet

____2____ Week ____1____ Period

Practice Week

	Saturday	Sunday	Monday	Tuesday	Wednesday	Thursday	Friday	Total
Breakfast								
Customer Counts								
Average Check +50 Cents All Days								
Revenue								
Lunch								
Customer Counts								
Average Check Same								
Revenue								
Dinner								
Customer Counts								
Average Check Same								
Revenue								
Total Room Service								
Customer Counts								
Average Check								
Total Revenue								

Customer Count Forecasting Worksheet
Room Service and Restaurant

Practice Week Answers

Week __2__   Period __1__

	Saturday	Sunday	Monday	Tuesday	Wednesday	Thursday	Friday	Total
Total Rooms Sold	180	200	415	575	585	505	260	2,720
Guest Count @ 1.2 per Room	216	240	498	690	702	606	312	3,264
Room Service Capture Rates								
Breakfast @ 25%	54	60	125	173	176	152	78	818
Lunch @ 8%	17	19	40	55	56	48	25	260
Dinner @ 15%	32	36	75	104	105	91	47	490
Total Room Service Customers	103	115	240	332	337	291	150	1,568
Restaurant Customer Counts								
Breakfast Daily Average	100	100	75	125	150	150	125	825
Breakfast Customer Adjustment +10 w/d			10	10	10	10		40
Total Breakfast Customers	100	100	85	135	160	160	125	865
Lunch Daily Average	40	30	30	60	80	80	50	370
Lunch Customer Adjustment +5 All Days	5	5	5	5	5	5	5	35
Total Lunch Customers	45	35	35	65	85	85	55	405
Dinner Daily Average	60	50	100	120	140	120	80	670
Dinner Customer Adjustment +5 All Days	15	15	15	15	15	15	15	105
Total Dinner Customers	75	65	115	135	155	135	95	775
Total Restaurant Customers	220	200	235	335	400	380	275	2,045

Room Service Revenue Forecasting Worksheet

2 Week ___ 1 ___ Period

Practice Week Answers

	Saturday	Sunday	Monday	Tuesday	Wednesday	Thursday	Friday	Total
Breakfast								
Customer Counts	54	60	125	173	176	152	78	818
Average Check Same as First Week	$ 10	$ 10	$ 12	$ 12	$ 12	$ 12	$ 10	$ 11.53
Revenue	$ 540	$ 600	$1,500	$2,076	$2,112	$1,824	$ 780	$ 9,432
Lunch								
Customer Counts	17	19	40	55	56	48	25	260
Average Check Same as First Week	$ 12	$ 12	$ 14	$ 15	$ 15	$ 15	$ 12	$ 14.14
Revenue	$ 204	$ 228	$ 560	$ 825	$ 840	$ 720	$ 300	$ 3,677
Dinner								
Customer Counts	32	36	75	104	105	91	47	490
Average Check +50 Cents	$14.50	$14.50	$16.50	$18.50	$18.50	$16.50	$14.50	$ 16.89
Revenue	$ 464	$ 522	$1,238	$1,924	$1,943	$1,502	$ 682	$ 8,275
Total Room Service								
Customer Counts	103	115	240	332	337	291	150	1,568
Average Check	$11.73	$11.74	$13.74	$14.53	$14.53	$13.90	$11.75	$ 13.64
Total Revenue	$1,208	$1,350	$3,298	$4,825	$4,895	$4,046	$1,762	$21,384

Restaurant Revenue Forecasting Worksheet

2 Week   1 Period

Practice Week Answers

	Saturday	Sunday	Monday	Tuesday	Wednesday	Thursday	Friday	Total
Breakfast								
Customer Counts	100	100	85	135	160	160	125	865
Average Check +50 Cents All Days	$ 9.50	$ 9.50	$10.50	$11.50	$11.50	$10.50	$ 9.50	$ 10.47
Revenue	$ 950	$ 950	$ 893	$1,553	$1,840	$1,680	$1,188	$ 9,054
Lunch								
Customer Counts	45	35	35	65	85	85	55	405
Average Check—Same as First Week	$ 11	$ 11	$ 12	$ 13	$ 13	$ 13	$ 11	$ 12.25
Revenue	$ 495	$ 385	$ 420	$ 845	$1,105	$1,105	$ 605	$ 4,960
Dinner								
Customer Counts	75	65	115	135	155	135	95	775
Average Check—Same as First Week	$ 13	$ 13	$ 15	$ 16	$ 16	$ 15	$ 13	$ 14.77
Revenue	$ 975	$ 845	$1,725	$2,160	$2,480	$2,025	$1,235	$11,445
Total Restaurant								
Customer Counts	220	200	235	335	400	380	275	2,045
Average Check	$11.00	$10.90	$12.93	$13.61	$13.56	$12.66	$11.01	$ 12.45
Total Revenue	$2,420	$2,180	$3,038	$4,558	$5,425	$4,810	$3,028	$25,459

Customer Count Forecasting Worksheet
Room Service and Restaurant
Problem Set—25 Points

__3__ Week __1__ Period

	Saturday	Sunday	Monday	Tuesday	Wednesday	Thursday	Friday	Total
Total Rooms Sold—from Third Week								
Rooms Forecast								
Guest Count @ 1.2 per Room								
Room Service Capture Rates								
Breakfast @ 25%								
Lunch @ 8%								
Dinner @ 15%								
Total Room Service Customers								
Restaurant Customer Counts								
Breakfast Daily Average								
Breakfast Customer Adjustment +20 w/e								
Total Breakfast Customers								
Lunch Daily Average								
Lunch Customer Adjustment +10 w/e								
Total Lunch Customers								
Dinner Daily Average								
Dinner Customer Adjustment +15 w/e								
Total Dinner Customers								
Total Restaurant Customers								

Room Service Revenue Forecasting Worksheet

3 __ Week   1 __ Period

Problem Set

	Saturday	Sunday	Monday	Tuesday	Wednesday	Thursday	Friday	Total
Breakfast								
Customer Counts								
Average Check Same as Week 1								
Revenue								
Lunch								
Customer Counts								
Average Check Same as Week 1								
Revenue								
Dinner								
Customer Counts								
Average Check +50 Cents								
Revenue								
Total Room Service								
Customer Counts								
Average Check								
Total Revenue								

Restaurant Revenue Forecasting Worksheet

___3___ Week ___1___ Period

Problem Set

	Saturday	Sunday	Monday	Tuesday	Wednesday	Thursday	Friday	Total
Breakfast								
Customer Counts								
Average Check Same as								
Week 1								
Revenue								
Lunch								
Customer Counts								
Average Check Same as								
Week 1								
Revenue								
Dinner								
Customer Counts								
Average Check Same as								
Week 1								
Revenue								
Total Room Service								
Customer Counts								
Average Check								
Total Revenue								

Customer Count Forecasting Worksheet
Room Service and Restaurant
Week _____ Period _____

	Saturday	Sunday	Monday	Tuesday	Wednesday	Thursday	Friday	Total
Total Rooms Sold								
Guest Count @ 1.2 per Room								
Room Service Capture Rates								
Breakfast @ 25%								
Lunch @ 8%								
Dinner @ 15%								
Total Room Service Customers								
Restaurant Customer Counts								
Breakfast Daily Average								
Breakfast Customer Adjustment								
Total Breakfast Customers								
Lunch Daily Average								
Lunch Customer Adjustment								
Total Lunch Customers								
Dinner Daily Average								
Dinner Customer Adjustment								
Total Dinner Customers								
Total Restaurant Customers								

Room Service Revenue Forecasting Worksheet

Week _____ Period _____

	Saturday	Sunday	Monday	Tuesday	Wednesday	Thursday	Friday	Total
Breakfast								
Customer Counts								
Average Check								
Revenue								
Lunch								
Customer Counts								
Average Check								
Revenue								
Dinner								
Customer Counts								
Average Check								
Revenue								
Total Room Service								
Customer Counts								
Average Check								
Total Revenue								

Restaurant Revenue Forecasting Worksheet

Week _____   Period _____

	Saturday	Sunday	Monday	Tuesday	Wednesday	Thursday	Friday	Total
Breakfast								
Customer Counts								
Average Check								
Revenue								
Lunch								
Customer Counts								
Average Check								
Revenue								
Dinner								
Customer Counts								
Average Check								
Revenue								
Total Room Service								
Customer Counts								
Average Check								
Total Revenue								

Wage Forecasting Problem Sets

This section involves the wage forecasting process for the Front Office and Housekeeping departments. The weekly wage forecasts are probably the most valuable tool for management in controlling expenses and ensuring that wages are scheduled in relation to the business volume expected for the week. The weekly wage schedule identifies the number of labor hours needed for the week based on changing weekly revenue forecasts.

We will use the same process to prepare weekly wage schedules as we used to prepare weekly revenue forecasts. The first week of the period will be presented, and it will show how the wage forecasts are prepared including ratios and formulas. The second week will be given as an in-class exercise. The third week will be a 25-point problem set, and the fourth week will be a 25-point quiz. We will use the weekly rooms forecasts that were prepared earlier in this section for the wage schedules.

Front desk clerks are scheduled based on the number of expected arrivals or check ins on the p.m. shift. Employees can be scheduled for full eight-hour shifts or part-time shifts of four or six hours. The weekly wage schedule will include the number of arrivals, employees necessary to check in that number of arrivals, number of labor hours needed, and the total wage cost. The steps to prepare the front desk clerk weekly wage schedule are as follows:

1. Identify the number of daily check-ins from the weekly revenue forecast.

2. Divide by the number of check-ins per shift that an employee can handle. We will use 50 check-ins per shift in our example. This will give the number of employees needed per day.

3. Multiply by eight-hour shifts to get the number of labor hours needed by day and week.

4. Multiply by the hourly rate of pay. We will use $9 in our example.

5. Calculate for each day and add for the week to get the weekly number of employees, labor hours, and wage cost.

Front desk cashiers are scheduled based on the number of expected departures or check outs on the a.m. shift. The steps are the same as those used for scheduling front desk clerks. However, there are some differences. We will use 75 check-outs per shift because many guests use express check-out and don't have to come to the front desk to check out. We will have a higher hourly rate of pay of $10 because cashiers have more responsibility with cash banks and are generally more experienced employees. The rest of the process is the same as that used for the front desk clerks.

Housekeepers are scheduled based on the number of rooms cleaned per shift per day. A key difference is that housekeepers clean the rooms from the previous day. Therefore, housekeeper daily schedules are based on the occupied rooms from the previous night.

We will refer to these as offset rooms. For example, on Saturday, the housekeepers will be cleaning the rooms that were occupied on Friday night.

1. Identify the number of occupied rooms from the previous night.

2. Divide by the number of rooms cleaned per day per housekeeper, 16 in our example.

3. Multiply by eight-hour shifts to get labor hours.

4. Multiply by the average hourly rate to get wage cost, $8 per hour in our example.

5. Calculate for each day and add to get weekly number of employees, weekly labor hours, and weekly wage cost.

The whole process of wage scheduling begins with the weekly forecasted number of rooms sold by day. This identifies how busy the hotel is and what level of employee staffing will be required to take care of the hotel guests. Each department head is responsible for preparing the weekly wage schedules. The Front Office Manager prepares two wage schedules, one for the a.m. shift and one for the p.m. shift. The Director of Housekeeping prepares one schedule because housekeepers generally work a 8:00 to 4:30 shift with a half hour for lunch.

We will now prepare the weekly forecasts for the first period. Remember that front desk clerks are scheduled based on the daily guest accounts or check-in, that the front desk cashiers are scheduled based on the daily guest departures or check-outs and that housekeepers are scheduled based on the offset rooms sold or in other words, the room occupied the previous night. In all example the typical week run from Saturday thru Friday. For housekeeper the schedule is also from Saturday thru Friday, but it is based on room sold from Friday thru Thursday – the offset rooms.

Wage Forecasting Worksheet

__1__ Week __1__ Period

	Offset Friday/	Saturday	Sunday	Monday	Tuesday	Wednesday	Thursday	Friday	Total
Departures		160	140	50	100	140	200	350	1,140
Arrivals		50	100	320	280	120	130	90	1,090
Rooms Sold	300/	190	150	420	600	580	510	250	2,700/2,750*
Occupancy Percentage		31.7%	25.0%	70.0%	100%	96.7%	85.0%	41.7%	64.3%
Desk Clerks—Arrivals									
Number of Employees @ 50 per Shift		1.0	2.0	6.4	5.6	2.4	2.6	1.8	21.8
× Eight-Hour Shift		8.0	16.0	51.2	44.8	19.2	20.8	14.4	174.4
× Hourly Rate $9		$ 72	$144	$461	$ 403	$ 173	$ 187	$ 130	$ 1,570
Cashiers—Departures									
Number of Employees @ 75 per Shift		2.1	1.9	0.7	1.3	1.9	2.7	4.7	15.3
× Eight-Hour Shift		16.8	15.2	5.6	10.4	15.2	21.6	37.6	122.4
× Hourly Rate $10		$ 168	$152	$ 56	$ 104	$ 152	$ 216	$ 376	$ 1,224
Housekeepers @ 16 Rooms per Day									
Number of Employees		18.8	11.9	9.4	26.3	37.5	36.3	31.9	172.1
× Eight-Hour Shift		150.4	95.2	75.2	210.4	300	290.4	255.2	1,377
× Hourly Rate $8		$1,203	$762	$602	$1,683	$2,400	$2,323	$2,042	$11,015

* equals offset rooms sold for Friday though Thursday

Round employees and labor hours to one decimal, wage cost to whole dollars

Wage Forecasting Worksheet
__2__ Week __1__ Period
Practice Week

Category	Offset Friday/	Saturday	Sunday	Monday	Tuesday	Wednesday	Thursday	Friday	Total
Departures		140	105	60	150	135	190	405	1,185
Arrivals		60	125	275	310	145	110	140	1,165
Rooms Sold	260/	180	200	415	575	585	505	240	2,700/2,720*
Occupancy Percentage		30.0%	33.3%	69.2%	95.8%	97.5%	84.2%	40.0%	64.3%

Desk Clerks—Arrivals
  Number of Employees @ 50 per Shift
  × Eight-Hour Shift
  × Hourly Rate $9

Cashiers—Departures
  Number of Employees @ 75 per Shift
  × Eight-Hour Shift
  × Hourly Rate $10

Housekeepers @ 16 Rooms per Day
  Number of Employees
  × Eight-Hour Shift
  × Hourly Rate $8

* equals offset rooms sold for Friday through Thursday
Round employees and labor hours to one decimal, wage cost to whole dollars

Wage Forecasting Worksheet

2 Week 1 Period
Practice Week Answers

Category	Offset Friday/	Saturday	Sunday	Monday	Tuesday	Wednesday	Thursday	Friday	Total
Departures		140	105	60	150	135	190	405	1,185
Arrivals		60	125	275	310	145	110	140	1,165
Rooms Sold	260/	180	200	415	575	585	505	240	2,700/2,720*
Occupancy Percentage		30.0%	33.3%	69.2%	95.8%	97.5%	84.2%	40.0%	64.3%
Desk Clerks—Arrivals									
Number of Employees @ 50 per Shift		1.2	2.5	5.5	6.2	2.9	2.2	2.8	23.3
× Eight-Hour Shift		9.6	20.0	44.0	49.6	23.2	17.6	22.4	186.4
× Hourly Rate $9		$86	$180	$396	$446	$209	$158	$202	$1,677
Cashiers—Departures									
Number of Employees @ 75 per Shift		1.9	1.4	0.8	2.0	1.8	2.5	5.4	15.8
× Eight-Hour Shift		15.2	11.2	6.4	16.0	14.4	20.0	43.2	126.4
× Hourly Rate $10		$152	$112	$64	$160	$144	$200	$432	$1,264
Housekeepers @ 16 Rooms per Day									
Number of Employees		16.3	11.3	12.5	25.9	35.9	36.6	31.6	170.1
× Eight-Hour Shift									
× Hourly Rate $8		$130	$90	$100	$207	$287	$293	$253	$1,360

* equals offset rooms sold Thursday through Friday

Round employees and labor hours to one decimal, wage cost to whole dollars

Wage Forecasting Worksheet

___3___ Week ___1___ Period

25-Point Problem Set

Category	Offset Friday/	Saturday	Sunday	Monday	Tuesday	Wednesday	Thursday	Friday	Total
Departures		125	200	75	70	250	225	275	1,220
Arrivals		100	100	200	225	300	200	100	1,225
Rooms Sold	360/	335	235	360	515	565	540	365	2,915/2,910*
Occupancy Percentage		55.8%	39.2%	60.0%	85.8%	94.2%	90.0%	60.8%	69.4%

Desk Clerks—Arrivals

Number of Employees @ 50 per Shift

× Eight-Hour Shift _____

× Hourly Rate _____

Cashiers—Departures

Number of Employees @ 75 per Shift

× Eight-Hour Shift _____

× Hourly Rate _____

Housekeepers @ 16 Rooms per Day

Number of Employees _____

× Eight-Hour Shift _____

× Hourly Rate _____

* equals offset rooms sold for Friday through Thursday

Round employees and labor hours to one decimal, wage cost to whole dollars

Wage Forecasting Worksheet

Week __4__   Period __1__

25-Point Quiz

Category	Offset Friday/ Saturday	Sunday	Monday	Tuesday	Wednesday	Thursday	Friday	Total
Departures								
Arrivals								
Rooms Sold								
Occupancy Percentage								
Desk Clerks—Arrivals								
Number of Employees @ 50 per Shift								
× Eight-Hour Shift								
× Hourly Rate _____								
Cashiers—Departures								
Number of Employees @ 75 per Shift								
× Eight-Hour Shift								
× Hourly Rate _____								
Housekeepers @ 16 Rooms per Day								
Number of Employees								
× Eight-Hour Shift								
× Hourly Rate _____								

Budgets

Learning Objectives

1. To understand the four types of budgets.
2. To understand the importance of the operating budget in analyzing the financial performance for a company.
3. To learn the formulas and steps used to prepare a budget.
4. To be able to prepare an operating budget.
5. To understand preopening and capital expenditure budgets.

Chapter Outline

The Use of Budgets in Business Operations

   Definition

Annual Operating Budgets

   Consolidated Hotel Budgets
   Department Budgets
   Fixed Department Budgets

Formulas and Steps in Preparing an Operating Budget

   The Goals of an Operating Budget
   Methods of Preparing Budgets
   Revenue Formulas
   Expense Formulas
   Profit Budgets

Capital Expenditure Budgets

   Definition
   Characteristics
   Preparing Capital Expenditure Budgets

Summary

Hospitality Manager Takeaways

Key Terms

Review Questions

Problems

Budgets represent an integral part of the financial management of a company. A budget is the formal business and financial plan for a business for one year. It is a plan for the future operations of a company that applies financial goals and measurements to business operations. Budgets, combined with the results from the previous year, are the key measurements of financial success to which current actual financial results are compared.

The primary budget used by department managers is the annual operating budget. It contains the specific revenue goals, the specific expense amounts, and the profit objectives that the department is expected to meet. Managers use the budgeted amounts to operate their departments. They are expected to achieve the revenue budget and spend no more than the expense budgets to achieve budgeted profits.

There are three other types of budgets. The **construction budget** establishes the cost to physically contruct the hotel. It includes architectural drawings, design and decor engineering and all actual construction costs such as permits and fees, code compliance, materials and labor. The **preopening budget** establishes amounts that are expected to be spent by management to open a new hotel or restaurant. It is the dollar amount needed to cover all expenses before the hotel or restaurant opens and starts to record revenues. It is separate from the construction budget. The **capital expenditure budget** identifies expenditures that are necessary to replace long-term assets, renovate, or to expand the business. It is a form of capitalization.

Operating managers must be knowledgeable about their department operating budget as they manage their daily operations. The budget is both a management tool and a way to measure financial performance. They must also understand the capital expenditure budget to plan for and obtain long term assets for their operation.

The Use of Budgets in Business Operations

The purpose of budgets is to provide a financial plan for a business for the next fiscal year. The annual budget generally includes an operating budget and a capital expenditure budget. Annual budgets are prepared based on the actual financial results for the previous year. Because a fundamental concept of business operations is that a business will grow from year to year, the annual budget will plan for growth and improvement

J.W. Marriott Starr Pass Resort & Spa
Tucson, Arizona

The J.W. Marriott Starr Pass Resort and Spa opened in January 2005 and is the newest resort in Arizona. It is located adjacent to the Tucson Mountain Park preserve and offers award winning views in every direction. It offers 575 guest rooms and over 88,000 square feet of meeting space. Resort recreational activities feature a 27 hole Arnold Palmer signature golf course, 20,000 square foot Hashani Spa, and expanded water recreation. It definitely provides the ambiance of the southwest desert.

over the last year's financial results. These goals are included in the annual operating budget.

What do you think the challenges are in opening a new resort or hotel, especially of this size? The owners and managers need to work with three budgets. First is the construction budget that includes all the costs to build the resort. Second is the pre-opening budget that includes all of the costs to get ready to open the resort such as sales and marketing, employee hiring and training, and the cost to furnish the resort with operating supplies. Third is the operating budget that includes all the expected revenues and expenses to operate the resort in the first year. This first-year budget is also called the Pro Forma.

Definition

The annual operating budget is the formal business and financial plan for a business for one year. The operating budget contains the details of department operations including revenue goals that the business or department is expected to achieve and the necessary expense amounts that the business will require to achieve the budgeted revenue for the next year.

The annual operating budget (also refined to as the **department budget**) contains the details and specifics of the financial operations of a business or department for one year. Characteristics of annual operating budgets are as follows:

1. They are a plan for the next year; therefore they plan future operations.

2. They are for one fiscal year.

3. They are based on the previous year's actual financial results.

4. They include growth and financial improvements over the previous year.

5. They include dollar amounts, percentages, and units or statistics.

6. The budget column is included on monthly profit and loss statements and provides a comparison for actual financial results.

7. It includes the hotel's current marketing plan.

Operating budgets are prepared for each department in a hotel. They are prepared monthly or by accounting period. If a business operates on monthly Profit and Loss (P&L) Statements, it will prepare a budget for each month of the year. Adding the department budgets for the 12 months will result in the annual operating budget for the business. If a business operates on accounting period P&L Statements, it will prepare a budget for each week of the four-week accounting period. Adding the department budgets for the 13 accounting periods will result in the annual operating budget for the business.

The Director of Finance for a hotel has the main responsibility for preparing the annual operating budget. This is because he or she is the financial expert for the hotel and not only prepares the monthly financial reports but also analyzes and critiques them with the operations managers. Each year when the budget process starts, the Director of Finance will work with each Executive Committee member and the department managers to prepare the budget for next year. The budget is then submitted to the General Manager for approval and then is forwarded to the corporate office for final approval.

All of the department annual operating budgets are added together to make the **consolidated hotel budget**. This budget summarizes all the revenues and profits for the revenue departments and total department costs for the expense departments.

For a company with a fiscal year ending December 31, the budgeting process will generally start in October and be completed in November. Final approval should be received in December so that the budget is in place when the new fiscal year starts January 1. Once the annual operating budget is approved, it is not changed. It represents the formal and final operating plan for the year. Weekly or monthly forecasts are used to update the budget. As business conditions change, a forecast is developed to reflect these changes. Forecasts can increase or decrease revenues, expenses, or profits. Therefore, actual monthly financial performance can be compared to three important measurements: last year, the budget, and the most recent forecast.

Capital expenditure budgets are also prepared annually and identify the needs for replacing long-term assets of the business, renovating the business, or expanding the business. Capital expenditure budgets generally involve projects or equipment that cost a lot of money and last longer than one year of operations. This involves capitalization and not working capital. Characteristics of capital expenditure budgets are as follows:

1. They identify purchases of specific pieces of equipment, such as a laundry machine, airport van, kitchen oven, or mechanical motor.

2. They identify projects that involve many pieces of equipment or activities, such as rooms soft-goods redo, restaurant renovation, or expansions.

3. Budget items must have a useful life of more than one year.

4. Budget items must have a minimum cost.

5. Projects must contain the details of all expenditures necessary to complete the project.

6. Expenditures have different approval levels. For example, items costing less than $5,000 can be approved by the General Manager, whereas items costing more than $5,000 need corporate approval.

7. Small expenditures can be included in one list, totaled, and approved.

8. Large expenditures are itemized and approved one by one.

Capital expenditure budgets can be funded in several ways. The first is to have owners contribute the amount necessary to purchase capital expenditure equipment or to complete capital expenditure projects. Second, the hotel contributes money from its annual operations to a capital expenditure **escrow reserve** that can be used to fund capital expenditure projects. Third, outside financing can be used, such as obtaining bank loans, utilizing a line of credit, or obtaining a lease.

Preopening budgets are established to guide a new company as it prepares to open for business. This budget identifies all the costs that will be incurred to get the business ready to open. Characteristics of a preopening budget include the following:

1. Wage expenses for all employees working before the business opens.

2. Advertising and promotional expenditures.

3. The costs of all the items necessary to furnish the hotel or restaurant, such as guest room furniture and amenities, restaurant furniture and supplies, and kitchen equipment and supplies.

4. The total cost is established for all expenses before opening.

5. The total cost is spread over or paid back over a predetermined time period.

Preopening budgets are prepared based on expected operations and expenses necessary to start up a new business. This can be tricky or difficult as there are no specifics or concrete information to base these budgets on. These budgets are true estimates, and often additional expenditures occur that need to be added to the original amount.

Construction budgets are very complicated and detailed. They include the cost of designing and planning, materials and equipment necessary to build, and all the wage cost of the labor to build a hotel or restaurant. Many specialists are involved in preparing construction budgets to identify as accurately as possible the cost of materials and labor to construct the project. These budgets generally involve the owner, the managers involved in a management contract, franchisees if appropriate, and any other parties involved in financing, developing, and building the project. Operations managers rarely get involved with these budgets.

Annual Operating Budgets

Consolidated Hotel Budgets

The consolidated hotel budget contains the summary financial information for the entire hotel. Its main purpose is to present the key financial results for all of the hotel departments. Characteristics of a consolidated budget are as follows:

1. Presents the total revenues, expenses, and total profits for operating departments in the hotel.

2. Presents the total expenses for the staff or supporting departments in the hotel.

3. Includes the hotel profit budgets for Department Profit, Total Department Profits, House Profit, Net House Profit, and Total Profit before and after Taxes.

4. Contains all of the pertinent summary financial information for the hotel.

5. Does not contain detailed budget information for line accounts.

The consolidated hotel budget is used by senior management and owners to get a quick summary of the planned financial results for a business. When the budget is prepared, reviewed, and approved, it becomes the formal operating plan for the next year. It therefore shows what the financial expectations are for the coming year. The actual financial results are compared each month to the budget to determine if the budgeted operational and financial results are achieved.

Department Budgets

The department budgets contain the detailed budget information for a specific department. Operations managers use these budget amounts as management tools in the daily operations of their departments. This budget can also be considered a roadmap of where the department operations should go and what financial results they should produce. Characteristics of a department budget are as follows:

1. Contains the detailed revenue budget for the department, including market segments, average room rates or average guest checks, and volumes such as rooms sold and customer counts.

2. Contains the budgeted amount for expenses for each line account.

3. Contains detailed wage budget guidelines including labor hours, average wage rates, and total wage costs for specific wage departments.

4. Provides detailed operating information that is used as a management tool.

5. A specific Executive Committee Member is responsible for specific department budgets.

6. A department head has the direct responsibility for meeting the department budget goals.

The department budget contains many pages compared to one page for the consolidated budget. This is because of the amount of detailed operating and financial information included in the department budget. Following are examples:

Revenue Budgets—Market Segments or Meal Periods

In the Rooms Department budget, the market segments provide average room rates, number of rooms sold, and total revenue for transient, group, and contract market segments. In the Restaurant Department budget, the meal periods include average checks, customer counts, and total revenues for breakfast, lunch, and dinner. In a typical 400-room full-service hotel, the revenue budget for the Rooms and the Food and Beverage Departments will each be several pages long.

Expense Budgets—Wage Departments

In the larger operating departments such as housekeeping and restaurants, hourly wages are separated into specific wage departments for more effective control. Each of these wage departments contains average wage rates, labor hours, and total wage cost. For example, housekeeping includes the following wage departments: housekeepers, supervisors, housemen, and public space. The wage budget includes average wage rates, labor hours, and total wage costs for each of theses wage departments. In the restaurant, the wage departments include servers, hostesses, busers, and cashiers. In the kitchen, the wage departments include station attendants, cooks, lead cooks, and expeditors.

Direct Operating Expense Accounts

These line accounts are not as detailed because they do not involve rates or volumes. Rather, they include all the purchases, inventory consumption, and transfers for a specific line account. For example, the guest supply account in the rooms department includes all of the purchases from outside vendors, issues from inventory, and transfers from other departments for guest supply items including soap, shampoo, condenser, pens, stationcry, and tissue. The total expenses for the china account, glass account, and silver account in the restaurant include all of the purchases from outside vendors, issues from inventory, and transfers from other departments during the month or accounting period.

Profit Budgets

The profit budgets do not contain any detailed information as do the revenue and expense budgets because the profit budget is calculated by subtracting total expenses from total revenues. This simple formula can involve many market segments and expense line accounts to get to the total department profit. The budgeted department profit is typically considered the most important measurement of financial performance.

Fixed Department Budgets

This budget generally includes only one department where all of the fixed expenses of operating the hotel are recorded. They are identified by single line accounts where entries are made to record the appropriate costs for the month or accounting period. For example, monthly bank loan payments are recorded in the bank loan line account, monthly insurance costs are recorded in the insurance line account, and the monthly cost of annual licenses and fees is recorded in the license line account. The most detail is contained in the depreciation account where fixed monthly depreciation costs are recorded for property, plant, and equipment.

Department managers do not get involved with managing fixed expense departments because these costs are predetermined and are not managed or changed during the month. The accounting department generally records and reviews the costs in these departments.

Formulas and Steps in Preparing a Budget

It is important for hospitality managers to be involved in the preparation of their annual department operating budget. This requires a good understanding of both daily operations and the accounting concepts and methods of financial analysis that will be used to evaluate their performance.

The Goals of an Operating Budget

These goals are used to provide a financial guideline for measuring financial performance and to provide a management tool to help achieve expected financial results. The operating budget combines last year's results with planned growth and improvements to project financial expectations for the next year. It is indeed a roadmap for operations for the next year. Actual operating results and financial performance are compared to the budget and any variations identified and explained.

When the budget is not met for a month or accounting period, operations management critiques the operations to identify problems and work on solutions to correct those problems. These budget variations identify problems and successes in operations, and management can deal with each as appropriate. By identifying problems, budget variations red-flag areas that management needs to analyze to identify problems and make corrections. By identifying successes, budget variation can reinforce positive changes that have resulted in improved financial performance or growth.

Methods of Preparing Budgets

These methods include several options that can be used depending on the goals for the budget. A business will generally use the same method from year to year to be consistent. The important point to consider in choosing a method to prepare a budget is, will it provide the necessary detail to produce the expected financial results?

Zero-Based Budgeting is a budgeting method that involves preparing each year's budget from actual needs and costs. No goals or historical information is used. It is a bottom-up budgeting approach that is very detailed and involves many specific formulas. For example, preparing a zero-based budget for guest supplies in the rooms department involves calculating the historical cost per rooms sold for each item classified in the guest supply line account. Shampoo cost per occupied room, soap cost per occupied room, and pens and stationery cost per occupied room are all multiplied by the budgeted number of rooms sold by month and for the year to establish the guest supply budget.

Historical Budgeting is a budget that is based on last year's actual expenses. Last year's actual expenses establish the base, and the budget is adjusted up or down based on changes in volumes, material costs, inflation, or operations. For example, preparing a historical budget for guest supplies in the Rooms Department involves identifying last year's actual costs and then increasing them by a certain percentage based on changes in any of the variables that are appropriate and that would apply to the next year's costs. If inflation is expected to increase 4% and rooms sold are expected to increase 1%, then the budget for guest supplies will be last year's actual expense increased by 5%.

Goal-Based Budgeting is a budget that is based on an established goal determined by the corporate office, senior management, or owners. This is a top-down budgeting approach. The corporate office gives the business a number or target, and the business fills in the budget details to meet the goals. If management wants revenues to increase 5% and profits to increase 6%, then the budget will be prepared based on last year's actual results and increased 5% in revenues and 6% in profits. Although this is an easy and quick way to prepare a budget, the danger is that it may or may not accurately reflect what is happening in the business and the current market.

Revenue Formulas

Revenue budgets are prepared by using the basic revenue formula of rate × volume for each market segment in the Rooms Department or meal period in the restaurants. Management identifies how increased revenues can be achieved by either increasing rooms sold or increasing average room rates if demand is strong. If demand is not strong, it will be difficult to increase rooms sold or average rates. Management makes the decision when and how any increases in rooms sold or average rate can be realistically achieved and put into the budget for the next year.

The Zero-Based Budgeting approach takes each day and determines the number of rooms expected to be sold for each market segment. These rooms sold are then multiplied by the average room rate budgeted for the market segment to calculate the budgeted room revenue. Adding all the market segments together will get the total room budget for the day. The days are totaled to get the weekly and monthly budgets.

The Historical Budgeting approach takes historical daily averages of rooms sold and adds the expected percentage increase to get the total rooms sold budget for a day. This can also be done for a week at a time. The weekly totals then have to be broken down into the daily budgeted rooms sold. The budgeted average rate is then multiplied by the budgeted rooms sold to get the total revenue budget for the day.

The Goal Budgeting approach involves the owner or corporate office establishing the amount of revenue increases expected for the next year's budget. The budget is then prepared by filling in the rooms sold and average room rates necessary to meet the established budget.

Expense Formulas

Expense budgets are prepared differently for the four major expense categories and involve historical averages and relationships between volume expressed as revenue or units such as rooms sold.

Cost of sales budgets can be prepared using any of the three budgeting methods. Zero-based food cost budgets are prepared by costing out each menu item and multiplying by the menu counts for that item. All the items are added to determine the food cost budget in dollars and as a percentage. Historical food cost budgets are based on the actual food costs and changed by any expected price increases or productivities to determine food cost in dollars and as a percentage. Goal-based food cost budgets are determined by the food cost percentage established by the owner or corporate office.

Wage budgets are the most complicated and detailed to prepare. The hourly employee wage cost budgets are generally prepared by a Zero-Based Budgeting approach. Formulas such as labor hours per occupied room or labor hours per customer are applied to budgeted rooms sold or customer counts. These labor hours are then multiplied by expected average wage rates to determine the wage cost budget in dollars. Wage budgets can also be prepared more quickly using the historical budgeting method by taking the average labor hours or wage cost and changing them based on inflation or any changes in volume levels. For example, if revenues increase 5%, then the historical wage cost will be increased by 5%.

Benefit budgets are relatively simple to prepare. The formula used is the historical benefit cost percentage calculated by dividing the actual benefit expense by the actual wage cost. The resulting benefit cost as a percentage of wages cost is multiplied by the new wage budget to get the new benefit budget.

Direct operating expense budgets are prepared by using many formulas that best express the relationship between expense costs and volume levels. These include the following:

1. Historical average involves taking the average cost over a specific time and using that amount for the budget. An example is if the historical average linen cost per month is $7,000, then the new budget amount will be $7,000.

2. Historical average plus inflation or cost increases involve applying expected changes to historical average cost. If the linen vendor in our previous example is increasing linen cost 5%, then we would multiply $7,000 by 5% to get our new linen budget of $7,350.

3. Percentage of sales involves using the relationship between expense costs and revenues. An example is a cleaning supplies expense of 0.3% of room's sales. This percentage is calculated by dividing the cleaning supply expense by total room sales. The new cleaning supply budget would be budgeted room sales multiplied by 0.3%.

4. Cost per occupied room or cost per customer served involves using the relationship between expense costs and rooms sold. This is similar to cost percentage but uses the relationship of expense in dollars divided by total rooms sold. An example is the guest supply expense divided by total rooms sold of $1.15 per occupied room. The guest supply budget would be calculated by multiplying the budgeted rooms sold by the $1.15 cost per occupied room.

5. Specific formulas are used to budget based on established costs. For example, the central reservation budget could be based on the formula $5 per reservation made through the central reservation office. The reservation cost budget would be calculated by multiplying the expected number of reservations by $5.

6. Allocations use formulas to spread the cost over several departments by established allocation percentages. An example is allocating laundry department costs charged

back to the rooms, restaurant, and banquet departments based on the number of items washed or the number of pounds of linen washed from each department. A typical laundry department allocation might be rooms 70%, restaurant 10%, and banquet 20%.

7. Contract budgeting involves taking the dollar amount of an annual contract and spreading the cost back to each month. For example, a $24,000 annual contract for outside window cleaning would be budgeted at $2,000 per month.

Profit Budgets

The formula for profit is revenues minus expenses. The profit budgets are therefore determined by making this calculation. Budgeted department revenues minus all the budgeted department expenses equal budgeted department profit. Compared to budgeting revenues and expenses, this is a rather basic calculation. All of the department profits are added to produce total hotel profit, or total hotel expenses are subtracted from total hotel revenues to produce total hotel profits.

Capital Expenditure Budgets

The primary concern of hospitality managers is the operating budget as it is the financial report by which their operations will be evaluated. We briefly discussed other budgets used in business that a manager should be aware of, specifically the preopening budget and the construction budget referred to earlier in the chapter. The Director of Finance at a hotel is generally responsible for these budgets.

A hospitality manager should also have a general awareness and understanding of the capital expenditure projects (CEP) budget, because this budget plans the financial needs for long-term equipment and other operating requirements.

Definition

Capital Expenditure Budgets identify the need for replacing long-term assets of the business, for renovating the business, and for expanding the business. When a business is started, the capitalization determines the amount of investment necessary to launch the business and identifies where the expenditures on **property, plant, and equipment** (PP&E) will be made. These expenditures are long term in nature, and the PP&E will last from 1 to 30 years.

Characteristics

Let's review the characteristics of capital expenditure budgets that were presented earlier in the chapter:

1. They identify purchases of specific pieces of equipment, such as a laundry machine, airport van, kitchen oven, or mechanical motor.

2. They identify projects that involve many pieces of equipment or activities, such as rooms soft-goods redo, restaurant renovation, or expansions.

3. Budget items must have a useful life of more than one year.

4. Budget items must have a minimum cost.

5. Projects must contain the details of all expenditures necessary to complete the project.

6. Expenditures have different approval levels. For example, items costing less than $5,000 can be approved by the general manager, whereas items costing more than $5,000 need corporate approval.

7. Small expenditures can be included in one list, totaled, and approved.

8. Large expenditures are itemized and approved one by one.

Because the items and equipment (PP&E) are quite different from the expenses budgeted in annual operating budgets, the CEP is prepared in a different way.

Preparing Capital Expenditure Budgets

Capital Expenditure Budgets are prepared based on the needs of the hotel or restaurant. Replacing major equipment and completing major renovations involves a great deal of operational and financial planning because the results of these budgets will last many years and will generally involve larger amounts of money.

Identifying Capital Expenditure Projects and Needs

During the year, department heads identify equipment that needs replacing or areas of the hotel that need to be upgraded or renovated. These capital needs are divided between those with small costs that are easily replaced and those with large costs that are more complicated to complete. Estimates are obtained, and all projects are reviewed by the Executive Committee Member and then submitted to the Director of Finance.

The Director of Finance accumulates all capital expenditure requests and categorizes them according to size and type of expenditure. The main categories are as follows:

1. Equipment costing less than a set amount; for example, less than $2,500

2. Equipment costing more than a set amount; for example, more than $2,500

3. Projects costing less than a set amount; in our example, less than $2,500

4. Projects costing more than a set amount; in our example, more than $2,500

All equipment and projects that cost less than the $2,500 amount will be listed one capital expenditure list as one amount and approved all together. Then it will be the hotel's responsibility to complete each project within the dollar amount budgeted for that item.

Equipment and projects that cost more than the $2,500 amount will be listed separately and contain all the necessary information describing the equipment or project and the dollar cost involved to complete the project. There can be many pieces of equipment, types of construction, and dollar costs in these project budgets. For example, a restaurant redo might include the cost to purchase several items such as new tables, chairs, point-of-sale equipment, and carpet. It also includes the cost to install the carpet, repaint the restaurant, and replace any wall coverings. A project with 15 items includes the cost for each item and the total for all items. The final project cost includes expenses such as materials and supplies, labor, permits and fees, and taxes.

Most of the time, CEP requests are more than the amount available in CEP escrow or reserve accounts. The General Manager reviews the CEP list prepared by the Director of Finance with the Executive Committee and then determines which projects to keep on the list and which projects to cancel or defer to the next year. Once the CEP budget is approved, the hotel can proceed to purchase the equipment or start the projects but must remain within the established budget. If there are cost overruns, the hotel might have to cancel other projects and use that approved budget amount to pay for the cost overruns.

Funding Capital Expenditure Projects

Funding to pay for capital expenditure projects could be obtained from outside sources such as bank loans or owner contributions. However, the main way to finance these projects is from the cash flow generated from business operations.

A company will determine what percentage of sales that it is willing to set aside in capital expenditure reserve or escrow accounts. A new hotel will not require as much additional capital investment as an older hotel that has equipment and materials that are wearing out and in need of replacement. A new hotel might set aside 3% of total sales, whereas an older hotel might set aside 5% of total sales.

Let's use an older hotel as an example. If the total annual sales for the hotel are $20 million, 5% of that amount, or $1 million, will be set aside in the CEP escrow or reserve account. That means that the hotel will have $1 million to allocate and spend on CEP projects for the year. Each month, the Director of Finance will make an accounting entry and transfer funds from the cash account to the CEP escrow or reserve account. When equipment is purchased or projects completed, a check will be drawn from the CEP account to make payments.

Operating managers do not generally get involved with CEP accounting, as that is done by the Director of Finance. However, they will be very involved in choosing the equipment to ensure that it meets requirements and stays within the budgeted costs and overseeing projects to ensure that the work is completed as planned and also stays within the CEP budget. It can become very competitive among departments to obtain approval and funding for equipment and projects that they need. A Hospitality Manager's ability to clearly explain and justify any CEP projects will be an important factor in securing approval for those projects.

Summary

Budgets play a critical role in the success of any business. Budgets connect actual operations with financial needs and results. They are the annual formal financial plan for the next year of operations. Management's actual performance is evaluated against the budget to determine if expected results have been achieved.

Annual operating budgets are used to plan for the next year and to evaluate actual financial performance from month to month and for the year. Hospitality managers are involved with the preparation of their department budgets and will use that budget in planning their department operations. Operating budgets include the detailed financial plans for revenues, expenses, and profits.

Several other budgets are used in business besides the annual operating budget. The capital expenditure budget plans for the long-term needs of the business and has an impact on many years of business operations. Hospitality managers need to understand and be involved in the preparation of capital expenditure budgets to be able to secure additional investments and capital expenditures. Other budgets include preopening and construction budgets administered by the Director of Finance. Hospitality managers are generally not involved with these budgets.

Hospitality Manager Takeaways

1. Operations managers must have a complete understanding of their operating budgets and be able to use them in their daily operations. Budgets are a key management tool.

2. Operations managers must have the ability to prepare their budgets and be actively involved in the budget approval process.

3. Hospitality managers must understand and be able to use appropriate budgeting formulas for revenues, wages, and other operating expenses.

4. Actual department financial results will be compared to the budget and to last year to evaluate the success of operating results.

5. Capital expenditure budgets are very important and provide the long-term equipment needs and plan for renovation projects that are essential in department operations.

Key Terms

Annual Operating Budget—The formal business and financial plan for a business for one year.

Consolidated Hotel Budget—The summary budget for the entire hotel including revenues, expenses, and profits.

Department Budget—The specific and detailed budget for an individual department that provides all of the financial specifics for revenues and expenses.

Capital Expenditure Budget—The formal budget that identifies the need for replacing long-term assets of the business, for renovating the business, and for expanding the business.

Construction Budget—The budget that identifies the costs needed to construct and build a hotel or restaurant.

Escrow—An account established to collect money to be used at a later date. Same as reserve account.

Preopening Budget—The budget established to guide a new business as it prepares to open for business.

Property, Plant, and Equipment (PP&E)—The term used to identify the long-term investments that will serve the business for more than one year.

Reserve—An account established to collect money to be used at a later date. Same as an escrow account.

Review Questions

1. Why is the annual operating budget one of the most important financial reports for a hospitality manager to know, understand, and use?

2. Name five characteristics of an annual operating budget.

3. Why is a capital expenditure budget important, and how do hospitality managers use it in operating their departments?

4. Name five characteristics of a capital expenditure budget.

5. What is the difference between a consolidated hotel budget and a department budget?

6. Name five ways to budget direct operating expenses.

7. Name and describe the three main ways to prepare an operating budget.

8. How is a budget used to evaluate actual financial performance?

 # Problems

There are two budget problems to complete. The first is to calculate amounts to use in budgeting based on actual information and formulas. The second is to prepare an annual budget based on that information. Following is information for the Rooms Department for the 600 room Flagstaff Hotel for the first six periods of the year:

Room Revenue			$8,713,000
Transient Rooms Sold	83,730		
Group Rooms Sold	16,270		
Total Rooms Sold	100,000		
Operating Expenses			
Linen		$ 31,100	
Cleaning Supplies		24,000	
Guest Supplies		104,800	
Outside Services		24,000	
Laundry		80,500	
Concierge Expense		60,000	
Office Supplies		19,200	
Reservation Expense			
Reservation Department	$150,000		
Fixed Reservation Center Cost	180,000		
Variable Reservation Center Cost	251,400		
Total Reservation Expense		581,400	
All Other Expense		120,000	
Total Operating Expenses			$1,045,000
Total Operating Expenses Percentage			12.0%

Problem 1

Use the following formulas to calculate each one of the line items. They will be used to prepare the annual budget for next year. Round the average cost per period to whole dollars, round the cost per occupied room to whole cents, and round the percentage of sales to four decimals. Use the laundry and reservation information as supplied.

1. Linen—Calculate the average cost per period.

2. Cleaning Supplies—Calculate the average cost per occupied room.

3. Guest Supplies—Calculate the average cost per occupied room.

4. Outside Services—Calculate the average cost per period.

5. Laundry—Calculate at 70% of total laundry department expense per period; laundry department expense at $115,000 for six periods.

6. Concierge Level Expense—Calculate as a percentage of total room sales.

7. Office Supplies—Calculate as a percentage of total room sales.

8. Reservation Cost

   a. Reservation department cost at $25,000 per period.

   b. Fixed expense at $50 per total number of rooms in hotel per period.

   c. Variable expense at $6 per reservation. Calculate the reservations as 50% for transient rooms sold.

9. All other expense at $20,000 per period.

Answers Problem 1

Use the following formulas to calculate each one of the line items: They will be used to prepare the annual budget for next year. Round the average cost per period to whole dollars, round the cost per occupied room to whole cents, and round the percentage of sales to four decimals. Use the laundry and reservation information as supplied.

1. Linen—Calculate the average cost per period:

   $5,183 per period

2. Cleaning Supplies—Calculate the average cost per occupied room:

   $0.24 per occupied room

3. Guest Supplies—Calculate the average cost per occupied room:

   $1.05 per occupied room

4. Outside Services—Calculate the average cost per period:

   $2,000 per period

5. Laundry—Calculate at 70% of total laundry department expense per period; laundry department expense at $115,000 for six periods:

   $13,416 or $115,000 × 70%/6 periods

6. Concierge Level Expense—Calculate as a percentage of total room sales:

   0.69% of sales

7. Office Supplies—Calculate as a percentage of total room sales:

   0.22% of sales

8. Reservation Cost per period:

   a. Reservation department cost at $25,000 per period:

      $25,000 per period

   b. Fixed expense at $50 per total number of rooms in hotel per period:

      $30,000 or 600 rooms × $50

   c. Variable expense at $6 per reservation. Calculate the reservations as 50% of transient rooms sold:

      $251,190 or 83,730 × 50% × $6

9. All other expense at $20,000 per period:

   $20,000 per period

Problem 2

Prepare the annual operating expense budget for the next year using the formulas from Problem 1 and the following assumptions. Remember there are 13 accounting periods in a fiscal year, each with four weeks and 28 days.

Room Revenue		$19,184,000
Transient Rooms Sold	184,000	
Group Rooms Sold	34,000	
Total Rooms Sold	218,000	
Operating Expense Annual Budget		
Linen		
Cleaning Supplies		
Guest Supplies		
Laundry		
Concierge Expense		
Office Supplies		
Reservation Expense		
Reservation Department Cost		
Fixed Reservation Center Cost		
Variable Reservation Center Cost		
Total Reservation Expense		
All Other Expense		
Total Operating Expenses in Dollars		
Total Operating Expenses as a Percentage		

Answers Problem 2

Prepare the annual operating expense budget for the next year using the formulas from problem 2 and the following assumptions. Remember there are 13 accounting periods in a fiscal year, each with four weeks and 28 days.

Room Revenue		$19,184,000
Transient Rooms Sold	184,000	
Group Rooms Sold	34,000	
Total Rooms Sold	218,000	
Operating Expense Annual Budget		
Linen $5,183 × 13 Periods		$ 67,379
Cleaning Supplies .24 Cents × 218,000		$ 52,320
Rooms Sold		
Guest Supplies $1.05 × 218,000		$228,900
Laundry $250,000 × 70%		$175,000
Annual Laundry Department Budget		
$250,000		
Concierge Expense .69% × $19,184,000		$132,370
Office Supplies .22% × $19,184,000		$ 42,211
Reservation Expense		
Reservation Department Cost		
$25,000 × 13 Periods	$325,000	
Fixed Reservation Center Cost		
600 Rooms × 13 Periods × $50	$390,000	
Variable Reservation Center Cost		
184,000 × 50% × $6	$552,000	
Total Reservation Expense		$1,267,000
All Other Expense $20,000 × 13 periods		$ 260,000
Total Operating Expenses in Dollars		$2,225,180
Total Operating Expense as a Percentage		11.6%

Corporate Annual Reports

Learning Objectives

1. To understand the purposes of Corporate Annual Reports.

2. To understand the Message to Shareholders section of Corporate Annual Reports.

3. To understand the content of Corporate Annual Reports.

4. To be able to interpret and analyze the information contained in Corporate Annual Reports.

Chapter Outline

The Purpose of Corporate Annual Reports

    Definition

    Regulations and Independent Auditors

    Public Relations

    Uses of Corporate Annual Reports

The Message to Shareholders

    Performance for the Year

    Company Culture

    Strategies for the Future

The Content of the Corporate Annual Report

    Operating and Financial Results by Brand, Concept, or Division

    Other Corporate Themes and Information

Financial Results for the Year

    Independent Auditor's Report and Management Responsibilities Report

    The Three Main Financial Statements

    Notes to Consolidated Financial Statements

Summary

Hospitality Manager Takeaways

Key Terms

Review Questions

A Corporate Annual Report is the formal documentation of a company's operating and financial performance for a fiscal year. It contains a range of information that individual and institutional investors can read to understand the company's performance for the recent year. Although annual reports record historical operating results, they are also used to discuss operating strategies and expected financial performance in the future.

One of the reasons that the Corporate Annual Report is so valuable to investors is that it is governed by strict accounting reporting requirements. Each company must have the financial information in its annual report audited for compliance by an independent accounting company. These **Certified Public Accounting** (CPAs) companies audit and review all the financial information contained in a company's annual report and **attest** that the information is correct and accurate. The required auditor's opinion is intended to give investors confidence that the financial information presented is accurate and conforms to Generally Accepted Accounting Principles (GAAP).

Originally, Corporate Annual Reports contained primarily financial information about the corporation's operating performance. Over the years, annual reports have grown to include more information about the different operating divisions as well as about the entire corporation's financial performance. They also present the culture and core values of the corporation, the strategies for growth for the future, and a good amount of public relations that highlight the strengths and successes of the corporation.

Corporate Annual Reports are also available on company websites. The company home page will generally have a link for "company information" and a link on that page for the Corporate Annual Report. A note of caution: Do not download the annual report on your computer as most hotel companies have many color pictures and it will take a long time. If you have a fast computer, the download will be faster. Following are some websites for major hotel and restaurant companies. Go to at least two of them and scroll through to see what annual reports look like and what information they contain. It is much easier to read and browse the annual reports on your computer than it is to download or print them out because of their length.

www.fourseasons.com

www.hyatt.com

www.marriott.com

www.darden.com

www.ge.com

The Purpose of Corporate Annual Reports

Definition

A company's Corporate Annual Report is the formal document that reports the company's operating and financial results for the most recent **fiscal year**. A fiscal year is one year of business operations. Fiscal years generally end December 31, the same time as the calendar year, but can also end at other times, specifically the end of any quarter. Smaller, more concise quarterly operating reports can be issued to cover operations for the first quarter, March 31; the second quarter, June 30; the third quarter, September 30; and the fourth quarter, December 31. A company can choose when its fiscal year will end, but for convenience and consistency, most fiscal years end at the same time as the calendar year, December 31. Regardless of the fiscal year ending date, the annual reports will cover business operations for 365 days.

Shareholders elect a **Board of Directors** to represent them in overseeing the management of the company. A chairman of the Board is elected to lead the board. This is generally the most powerful position in a company's organization. The Board of Directors is also responsible for selecting the President or Chief Executive Officer (CEO) of the company. This position will have the direct responsibility for the day-to-day operations of the company.

Regulations and Independent Auditors

To ensure that all the financial information contained in a Corporate Annual Report is accurate and reliable, several key regulations and requirements have been imposed on all publicly traded companies and the Corporate Annual Reports that they publish.

First, any company that is publicly traded on a stock exchange must meet the requirements established by the **Securities and Exchange Commission (SEC)**. The SEC is the government agency responsible for regulating the operations of companies publicly traded on major stock exchanges like the New York Stock Exchange or the NASDAQ. These regulations require consistency and reliability to the numbers contained in Corporate Annual Reports.

If a company is privately owned and has not issued any form of company stock, there is no need to issue an annual report. This is because there are no outside investors, therefore no financial information is made available to the public. Privately held companies are not subject to regulations of the SEC because they have no common stock and are not traded on any stock exchange.

Second, standards for the accurate and consistent collecting and reporting of company financial information must meet the standards and requirements established by the Accounting Standards Board. They have issued GAAP. These are policies and guidelines that companies use in preparing their financial statements. This review ensures that the financial information is proper, consistent, and conforms to accounting policies and regulations.

Third, the **Independent Audit Report** provides an "audit opinion" of an outside, independent accounting firm. This opinion verifies that the financial information is correct and accurate and that any reader can rely on the financial information to make an investment decision regarding the company. Most opinions are favorable, but an audit opinion can also be "qualified," meaning that there are a few issues and some of the financial information might be questionable. The qualified opinion alerts the reader to those questionable issues. On some occasions, the audit opinion will be unfavorable, and the accounting firm will not endorse or support the financial information in the annual report. This is a warning to readers that the financial information is not reliable and does not conform to GAAP or SEC standards.

Following is an example of an audit opinion contained in the Marriott International 2003 Corporate Annual Report given by Ernst & Young, the independent audit company for Marriott International:

> In our opinion, the financial statements referred to above present fairly, in all material respects, the consolidated financial position of Marriott International, Inc., as of January 2, 2004, and January 3, 2003, and the consolidated results of its operations and its cash flows for each of the three fiscal years in the period ended January 2, 2004, in conformity with accounting principles generally accepted in the United States.

Public Relations

The Corporate Annual Report offers a great opportunity for a company to highlight achievements and results of the previous years. There are many pictures of "trophy" or new hotels, smiling employees with new products and happy customers, and lists of company achievements and recognition.

The report also provides an opportunity for the company to highlight significant achievements and results. Important operating results might be the acquisition of a company, the development of a new product or process, or exceeding an important company goal. Important financial results might include the highest revenue or profit levels that the company has ever achieved, the largest percentage increase in revenues or profits, or a large increase in the stock price or earnings per share.

Public relations focuses on the positive achievements of a company and makes sure that these achievements and results are made known to potential investors and others interested in the company. The Corporate Annual Report is the highlight, and it features an opportunity to present this positive information about the company.

Uses of Corporate Annual Reports

The primary use of a company's Corporate Annual Report is to present the actual and audited financial information for the most recent year. The financial information also includes three- or five-year financial summaries so readers can see the trends and, the company hopes, improvements and growth in financial performance. It enables the readers to compare results from different time periods. The focus is on the three main financial reports: the Profit and Loss (P&L) Statement, the Balance Sheet, and the Statement of Cash Flow. There is also a great deal of accompanying documentation that provides more details and explanation to the key financial numbers. These are called Notes to Consolidated Financial Statements.

Since 2002, there has been a greater emphasis on the company senior officers signing off or attesting to the accuracy and reliability of the financial results. In addition to the independent auditor's "audit opinion," the SEC now requires that the Chief Executive Officer and the Chief Financial Officer of the company also endorse or "sign off" on the financial information contained in the annual report. This means that they know and understand the financial information and that they attest or confirm that the financial information has been prepared correctly and that the results accurately and fairly represent the operations of the company for the previous fiscal year.

Many companies have chosen to focus on the culture and core values of their company in their annual reports in addition to reporting the financial performance for the recent year. They take time to discuss the priorities and core values that the company wants to instill in its employees. They want the readers to be aware of how the company operates, where its priorities are centered, and how it expects to meet its operating and financial goals. General Electric is one organization that highlights its company culture first and then its financial performance in its annual report. Go to its website at www.ge.com to see how GE's annual report is arranged and what the company's leaders would like the reader to learn about GE.

The third use of annual reports is to provide detailed operating information about the different divisions or components of a company. Hotel companies now include revenue information by brand that includes comparisons of the recent year's average rate, occupancy percentage, and revenue per available room (REVPAR) to the previous year. This is where new acquisitions or new product development is detailed and highlights of each division are presented. It is a brief review of the opportunities, challenges, and operating results of the division, brand, or concept.

The Message to Shareholders

Performance for the Year

The Message to Shareholders is an opportunity for the senior management of a company to write a letter covering all the important aspects and achievements of the company for the year. Typically, the letter is written by the Chairman of the Board of Directors, the President of the Company, and the Chief Executive Officer of the Company. Generally there will be one person in each one of these positions, but sometimes one person holds all three titles and positions. Often the officer's picture will be included to personalize the message. It is nice to see a picture of who is in charge of the company that you have invested your money in.

The Message to Shareholders includes comments on corporate culture and operations, financial results, and goals and strategies for the future. Although most of these comments will be positive and offer a bright future, they should also address any disappointments and negative results. We will read some of these comments in the Darden Annual Report presented later in this chapter. Shareholders want to know the bad information as well as the good information. Whereas the operating and financial information highlights company performance in the past, the strategies and established goals set the path that the company expects to take in the future to overcome obstacles, meet challenges, and achieve established operating and financial goals.

It is important to address how a company is growing and improving operating and financial performance. The two main areas to examine are comparable (comp unit) performance and the growth of new units. **Comp unit** growth compares the performance of existing hotels, restaurants, or stores. This means comparing the operating and financial performance of existing hotels, restaurants, or stores from year to year. It is important to know if these existing units are improving sales and profits. The second area of growth is new unit growth. If a company is successful and customers are buying its products and services, there will be opportunities to open new units and continue to grow. A strong company will show growth in both comp units and new units. It is important for investors to understand where and how a company is growing.

Company Culture

As previously mentioned, many companies now choose to focus as much attention on their corporate culture and core values as they do on their financial results. These companies want to emphasize to the reader the strength of the company culture and core values, strong processes and favorable work environments, and all that is positive about the company. Companies value and recognize their employees in achieving superior operating and financial results. They show that good operating and financial results are achieved because of their outstanding and dedicated employees.

THE MESSAGE TO SHAREHOLDERS

Refer to www.ge.com and www.jnj.com to look at the priority placed on company culture by General Electric and Johnson & Johnson. Both companies have placed a high value on corporate culture for more than 50 years. Compare www.marriott.com and www.fourseasons.com and see the similarities that these two hospitality companies place on company culture. Both Marriott and Four Seasons make it clear that their employees are the most valuable part of their company and the main reason for the success of the company.

Strategies for the Future

The final important element of the Message to Shareholders is to comment on the future of the company. All interested stakeholders, including bankers, individual and institutional investors, employees, and customers, want to know the plans and directions the company will take in the future. This will include discussing expectations of the company, commenting on the status of the industry, addressing major positive and negative issues on the horizon, and discussing any new opportunities that the company is exploring.

Let's outline the main themes and strategies of the message to shareholders in the most recent Corporate Annual Report for Marriott International, beginning with the introductory paragraph:

> This historically challenging time in the lodging industry has truly served to demonstrate Marriott International's resilience, the strength of our business model, superior brands, strong management team, and dedicated associates.
>
> We are optimistic about a stronger business climate in 2004. And with the final disposition of our senior living and distribution services businesses in 2003, we look forward to operating as a focused lodging management, franchise and timeshare company for the first time in our 76-year history.

The rest of the message to Marriott shareholders is outlined as follows:

- 2003 Performance Summary
- What's Ahead
- The Opportunity
    Income and Revenue
    Global Expansion
    Brand Preference and Loyalty
    Leisure Segment Growth
    Timeshare Business
- Global Expansion
- Marriott's People: Our Most Important Asset
- Looking Forward

Now let's compare the Marriott comments and strategies with those of Darden Restaurants, the largest casual dining restaurant company in the world. Darden operates the Red Lobster, Olive Garden, Smokey Bones, and Bahama Breeze restaurant concepts and generates more than $4.5 billion in annual revenue:

In fiscal 2003 we faced many challenges, including a difficult business environment, management transition within our organization, and the difficulty of trying to surpass exceptional prior-year results. Though we made progress in several key areas, we were disappointed with our overall results and are focused on regaining our strong, positive momentum.

Notice that Darden addressed subpar financial performance for fiscal 2003 including a difficult economy and business environment. The focus then went to the strengths that Darden has that will help the company correct these problems and return to expected levels of financial performance.

The rest of the message to Darden shareholders is outlined as follows:

- Results by Concept
- We Are in the Right Industry at the Right Time
- We Have a Solid Foundation
- Our Strategic Framework Is Sound and Working
- We Have Focused Priorities for Fiscal 2004
- We Are Well Positioned for Growth

Finally, let's look at the General Electric Message to Shareholders:

We made GE a stronger Company in 2003. Our Businesses performed solidly despite downturns in aviation and energy, high oil prices, and slack industrial demand. We grew operating cash flow 28% and strengthened our balance sheet. We invested more than $4 billion in technology and launched dozens of leading-edge products. We grew our services revenues 10% and global revenues 14%. We reorganized our businesses around markets to simplify our operations and deepen our relationships with customers. And we committed more than $30 billion to portfolio moves to create faster growth industrial businesses and improve our returns from financial services.

Pay particular attention to the first paragraph and the key elements of financial performance that GE highlights: grew cash flow 28% (invested $4 billion in technology) and grew services revenue 10% and global revenues 14% (change, percentage increase, and comparisons to last year). The first paragraph is probably one of the most read paragraphs in an report, so companies load it with key information on company culture, direction, and performance.

The rest of the message to GE shareholders is outlined as follows:

- How Will We Grow in an Uncertain World?
- The Environment We See
- The GE Business Model
- GE's Growth Strategy

  Technical Leadership

  Services

  Customer Focus

  Globalization

  Growth Platforms

- The GE Team
- Restoring Investor Trust
- The Future

The message to shareholders is a valuable part of the annual report and provides a framework and foundation to better understand the operating and financial results of the company. By examining excerpts from the three annual reports of Marriott, Darden, and General Electric, we can see how important the core values and corporate culture are to producing outstanding products and services that result in successful operating and financial results.

The Content of the Corporate Annual Report

Operating and Financial Results by Brand, Concept, or Division

The next section of the Corporate Annual Report provides a mixture of operating results and financial results. This includes describing in more detail successes, growth, new product or service development, and any other significant operating achievements. Pictures of happy productive employees and happy satisfied customers are generally featured. There will also be financial highlights for that particular hotel **brand**, restaurant **concept**, or industrial **division**. We will again look at the organization of this section in the Marriott, Darden, and GE annual reports.

Marriott

The next section after the Message to Shareholders is Management's Discussion and Analysis of Financial Condition and Results of Operations. It is separated into a Business Overview and Consolidated Results sections including revenues and operating income. This information is divided into full-service, select-service, extended stay, and timeshare segments and compares results from 2003, 2002, and 2001.

The next major section details information on occupancy percentages, average room rates, and REVPAR results. Refer to pages 12 to 14 in the Marriott annual report. Any person interested in the details of Marriott's performance in 2003 can find a great deal of information on these pages. The pages that follow get into more detailed and complicated explanations of nonoperating activities that generally interest only accountants, financial advisors, and bankers and institutional investors. If you take the time to read and understand these pages, you will have a good understanding of Marriott's financing activities in addition to Marriott's financial performance. There is a difference between financing and financial performance. Financing activities refer to capitalization or how Marriott raises or obtains money (investments and loans). Financial performance refers to the revenues or income/profits generated by all of the operating activities of Marriott.

At this point in time, if you can understand the operating and financial results, you are doing fine. Focus on this information, because that is what the content of this book is about and it is also what you should be able to understand and use. Hospitality managers use these financial concepts in the daily operations of their hotels or restaurant. Consider all other information as above and beyond—good to know but probably hard to understand.

Darden

The next section in the Darden annual report is titled "Great Expectations—Operating Highlights." It is organized by the company's four main restaurant concepts and includes a discussion of operations, informative and basic financial graphs, and great pictures of happy people eating good food. The way Darden organizes the information is very user friendly, meaning it is easy to read and to understand in both written and graphic form. It is written this way to provide quick, useful, and concise information to the reader.

The last section is titled "New Business Opportunities." This is where Darden discusses the business opportunities and strategies that it is pursuing in the future to reach company goals and objectives. Refer to pages 12 to 16 in the online Darden Annual Report for details. This section is notably shorter than what Marriott includes, partly because Marriott is larger and has more brands and operations to discuss.

General Electric

The next section of the GE Annual Report takes a rather unique approach to the goals and strategies the company wants to pursue in the future. GE frames these goals with five questions stated as follows: "Five Questions, Five Answers, One Growth Strategy for Growing GE."

1. *How do you defeat the commodity threat?* This addresses GE's efforts to differentiate its products and services from similar products and services offered by competitors. GE does this by "investing in innovation at every point in the economic cycle."

2. *How do you make money for your customers?* This presents the strategy of providing GE products and services that will help GE customers maximize their profits. In GE's words the company is "making customers' businesses run better."

3. *What distinguishes a partner from a vendor?* This emphasizes the importance in the GE culture of "enduring relationships" with vendors and suppliers that enable both to win in the marketplace.

4. *Where do you draw your borders?* This focuses on "operating worldwide as one global team." It addresses the need to provide consistent GE culture and processes but also the need to adjust to and fit in with the different cultures of the world where GE has operations. Balance and a respect for both is the GE policy.

5. *Are you leading change or chasing it?* This emphasizes GE's ability to "swiftly evolve to seize new opportunities created by changes in technology and the economy." GE seeks to embrace and welcome change and the improvements that change will produce. This is a difficult task but one that GE is pursuing relentlessly.

Each of these five questions is discussed with examples and pictures of employees, customers, products, and services developed by GE that demonstrate how the company is addressing the five questions daily in its global operations. The GE vision and its strategies to live that vision around the globe are presented and illustrated in this section of the annual report.

These three companies provide a good range of examples of how companies report and discuss their operations and achievements. Each has its own personality and focus that is a result of its corporate culture and core values. The pictures and information provide an opportunity for readers to see and learn about company operations including the employees that produce the products and services and the customers that purchase or enjoy those products and services.

Other Corporate Themes and Information

This section of an annual report provides the opportunity for the company to present and highlight other company priorities and activities. It can be located at the beginning, middle, or end of the narrative part of the annual report, and it highlights company culture, core values, initiatives, recognitions, and progress. This information is intended to provide readers with a feel for the company—where it places its priorities, the atmosphere and work environment that it seeks to create, the expectations for performance and achievement, and examples of projects and activities the company participates in to give back to the community and its members.

Marriott highlights its leadership and the power of its brands in the opening foldout of its annual report. Marriott's vision: To be the number one lodging company in the world. The goal of its brands: "It's the Marriott Way is our promise that guests can be assured of a consistent, tailored, quality hospitality experience at any Marriott International brand in the world." Marriott also has separate highlighted sections that present "Our Diverse Workplace," which lists the achievements and awards Marriott has received for having a quality workplace. "Our Communities" is a list that shows the involvement of Marriott employees in the communities where they are located and work. Corporate responsibility and community support are the key themes in this section.

Darden frames its culture and corporate vision with a series of comments that demonstrate "Great Expectations." "Every time guests walk through our doors, we aspire to greatness." For example:

- ambiance that makes it more than just a night out . . .
- service that presents food at just the right moment . . .
- attentiveness that anticipates a need before it becomes one . . .
- knowledge that can teach even a wine connoisseur something new . . .
- friendliness that's on a first-name basis whenever you come in . . .
- cleanliness that is measured by spotlessness, every hour of the day . . .

Another section in the annual report presents the Darden Core Purpose and Core Values:

Core Purpose—To nourish and delight everyone we serve.

Core Values—1) Integrity and fairness, 2) Respect and caring, 3) Diversity, 4) Always learning/Always teaching, 5) Being "of service," 6) Teamwork, 7) Excellence.

General Electric consistently mentions its corporate culture and core values throughout its annual report, so it only covers two other aspects of operations. The first is placing a high priority on corporate governance. "There is no question about governance." GE is a big company and therefore is the focus of many accusations and complaints. There is often controversy surrounding some of its activities. Therefore, the company makes it a point to emphasize how important integrity, honesty, and professionalism are to GE operations. In this section, GE provides pictures of the different committees of the Board of Directors and their specific responsibilities to ensure readers that GE complies with all rules and regulations. The second aspect of operations discusses GE's view that "A great company must also be a good company." This focuses on all of GE's activities to be good corporate citizens in the communities where GE operates.

Financial Results for the Year

This final section of the annual report contains all of the financial numbers including specific financial activities or results and the explanations of these activities.

Independent Auditor's Report and Management Responsibilities Report

This is perhaps the most important part of any Corporate Annual Report. The fact that an independent public accounting firm has examined all of the financial reports and procedures of the company and then confirms that they conform to GAAP and SEC guidelines is intended to give credibility to the numbers and confidence to the reader that the numbers can be used to accurately analyze company operations.

As stated earlier, recently senior management has been required to "attest" or verify the correctness of the numbers and the procedures and processes that produced those numbers. The CEO (Chief Exective Officer) or Chairman of the Board now must also sign off to show that he or she concurs that all the operating activities and the financial position of the company as reported in the financial results are accurate and correctly represent both the capitalization of the company and the operating results of the company for the year.

The Three Main Financial Statements

Generally, the first section of the financial results contains the official and audited Profit and Loss Statement, the Statement of Cash Flows for the year and the Balance Sheet as of the last day of the fiscal year.

The P&L Statement includes the current year's financial results compared to last year's results. Companies may also include three- or five-year comparisons so that the reader can see the trends and changes in financial performance from year to year. The P&L is a summary of the company's financial results that includes the totals of the main revenue and expense accounts and the different profit accounts. The P&L section can also include supporting documentation that breaks down some of the P&L results into more detail or by division, brand, or concepts.

The Balance Sheet includes the current year's balances and those of the previous year. This enables the reader to identify and compare the changes in assets, liabilities, and owner equity. The changes in the current accounts—assets and liabilities—represent how working capital was used during the year in the company's operations that produce products and services. The changes in the long-term accounts—assets, liabilities, and owner equity—represent how the company obtained capital via bank loans or raising equity and how it was used in the purchase of long-term assets. The Balance Sheet provides many numbers that are used in calculating important ratios used in financial analysis.

The Statement of Cash Flow shows how cash was generated and used in company operations for the year. It starts with cash flow generated from the operations for the year, and that amount is adjusted by operating activities that increase or decrease the operating cash flow. The result is net operating cash flow. The next two sections are cash flows that resulted from investing and cash flows that resulted from financing activities. The final section compares cash at the beginning of the year to cash at the end of the year. These changes are identified and show how cash is generated and used in company operations.

Notes to Consolidated Financial Statements

This is the section of the annual report that explains and details important financial activities of the company for the year. There are many complicated transactions and activities, and the notes are expected to clearly explain the details of these complicated transactions. The idea is to explain each of the transactions and to ensure that they are legitimate and conform to required and accepted accounting policies and procedures.

Summary

The Corporate Annual Report is the most important report or publication that a company makes available to all individual or institutional investors. It is published each year and includes detailed operating and financial information for the past year. This includes the three main financial statements: Profit and Loss Statement, Balance Sheet, and Statement of Cash Flow. The annual report also includes many other supporting financial documents and notes explaining the financial transactions or account balances.

One of the most important parts of an annual report is the Audit Opinion issued by an independent accounting firm that attests or verifies that the financial information contained in the annual report was prepared according to GAAP, that the financial information is correct, and that it accurately portrays the financial condition of the company. Since 2002, the company Chairman of the Board or Chief Executive Officer also has to confirm that the financial information is accurate and correct.

The annual report also contains a Message to Shareholders where the Chairman of the Board, CEO, and President report on the activities and achievements of the company for the year. Another important section describes each operating division, brand, or concept and provides a brief discussion of the operations and achievements of the past year.

Companies take advantage of the annual report to make it an important public relations document. It offers an opportunity for the company to feature and recognize dedicated employees, satisfied customers, new products or services, and any awards and achievements that the company has received. The Corporate Annual Report is a thorough document, and companies make a great effort to ensure that it is complete and detailed.

Hospitality Manager Takeaways

1. A Corporate Annual Report is the formal yearly report of a company's operating and financial results for the most recent fiscal year.

2. The financial results include the consolidated results of all the divisions, brands, and concepts of the company.

3. The Corporate Annual Report must include an audit opinion of the correctness and accuracy of the financial information presented by an independent Certified Public Accounting firm.

4. The Message to Shareholders is a key component of the annual report; it provides the Chairman of the Board or Chief Executive Officer of the company an opportunity to present and discuss the company's performance and plans for the future.

Key Terms

Attest—To confirm or verify the accuracy of operating and financial information.

Board of Directors—The group that is responsible for overseeing all operational aspects of a company. The Chief Executive Officer of a company reports to the Board of Directors and is also a member of the Board of Directors.

Brand—The lodging term that identifies different types of hospitality properties that serve specific hospitality market segments.

Certified Public Accountant—An independent accounting firm that is responsible for examining and verifying the correctness and accuracy of a company's financial information. It issues an audit opinion stating that the company meets or does not meet established reporting and accounting guidelines.

Comp Unit—Stores, units, hotels, or restaurants in a company that have been operating for more than two years.

Concept—The restaurant term that identifies different types of restaurant operations that provide specific dining experiences and serve specific market segments.

Division—The manufacturing term that identifies the different types of products produced by a company, including the markets that it serves.

Fiscal Year—The financial year for reporting a company's financial results. It can be the same as or different from the calendar year ending December 31.

Independent Audit Report—The section of the Corporate Annual Report that contains the audit opinion presented by an independent and certified public accounting company.

Management Responsibility Report—The section of the Corporate Annual Report that contains the senior management opinion that the operating and financial information contained in the annual report is accurate and correctly portrays the financial condition of the company.

Notes to Consolidated Financial Statements—The detailed financial explanation of accounting and financial information contained in the annual report.

Public Relations—Information and news releases prepared by the company.

Securities and Exchange Commission—The government agency responsible for regulating the public stock exchanges (New York Stock Exchange, NASDAQ, and several other exchanges).

Review Questions

1. Name two types of agencies or organizations that monitor the financial information contained in Corporate Annual Reports.

2. The company financial information is verified by an internal body and an external body. Name them.

3. Define division, brand, and concept, and explain why they are important in discussing company operations.

4. Why is a company's core values and culture important to mention in its annual report?

5. What is the current P&L information for the year compared to?

6. What is the Balance Sheet information for the year compared to?

7. What is the Statement of Cash Flow information compared to?

8. Why are notes to the consolidated financial statements important?

Personal Financial Literacy

Learning Objectives

1. To understand important concepts of personal finance.

2. To be able to apply business accounting concepts to personal finance.

3. To learn about the different ways to use assets to produce income and create personal equity and net worth.

4. To understand risk and return in evaluating investment opportunities.

5. To be able to develop a personal financial plan.

Chapter Outline

Personal Financial Literacy

    Definition
    Personal Income Statement
    Personal Cash Flow
    Personal Balance Sheet

Managing Personal Finances

    The Rat Race
    Evaluating Your Personal Financial Position
    Taking Control
    Overcoming Obstacles
    Getting Started

Evaluating Assets and Sources of Income

    Company Programs
    Ownership
    Retirement

Summary

Hospitality Manager Takeaways

Key Terms

Review Questions

Many of the business accounting concepts and methods of financial analysis that we have discussed in this book can be used in managing an individual's personal finances. This chapter discusses how these concepts can help individuals to manage their personal finances. It is often the case that parents cannot or do not teach their children about managing money effectively. Also, schools do not teach students about the fundamentals of earning and managing money. The result is that often young adults start their careers with little or no knowledge of effectively earning and managing their money.

Financial literacy is the ability to understand money—how you get it and how you use it. Unfortunately, most people don't take the time or have the opportunity to learn about managing their own money. Managing money takes financial knowledge, discipline, and a plan. Anyone can improve his or her financial position by obtaining the necessary knowledge and tools. It is important to start when young to develop and apply fundamental money management principles to enable individuals to create equity and net worth.

This chapter includes information from prominent authors and corporate programs on money management and investing. This information focuses on understanding the fundamental concepts of managing and investing money and how to develop your own personal financial plan. Two important goals are, first, to generate enough monthly income or cash flow to live as you would like and, second, to develop the knowledge and establish goals to increase your own equity or net worth. An excellent source for this information is the book *Rich Dad, Poor Dad: What the Rich Teach Their Kids about Money That the Poor and Middle Class Do Not* by Robert Kiyosaki (1997, Warner Business Books).

Personal Financial Literacy

Definition

Personal **financial literacy** is the ability to know and understand the management of money to achieve personal financial and investment goals. Financial literacy is not just for the rich or people who are able to make large investments, but also for the average person who may only be able to invest in small amounts. The knowledge and principles are the same in each situation and can lead to very beneficial results.

Kiyosaki offers one rule regarding financial literacy: "You must know the difference between an asset and a liability, and buy assets. If you want to be rich, this is all you need to know. It is rule #1. It is the only rule" (p. 58). This may sound absurdly simple, but most people have no idea how profound this rule is. Most people struggle financially because they do not know the difference between an asset and a liability.

Most adults work to receive a paycheck. This paycheck generally comes every two weeks on Friday. Retired people and some other workers get their paycheck once a month on the first day of the month. What they do with that paycheck is directly related to their understanding of fundamental money management principles.

Personal Income Statement

We have already discussed company P&Ls for separate departments in a hotel, Consolidated P&L Statements for the total hotel, and Consolidated P&Ls for an entire company. The P&L measures the ability of a company to maximize revenues and minimize expenses. The result is maximum profits.

These same accounting concepts apply to personal finance and money management for an individual. Maximizing revenues in companies is the same as maximizing income for individuals. Unfortunately, most individuals relate their income only to the company paycheck that they receive every other Friday. These individuals completely miss the point by relying on this paycheck as their only source of income. Financially literate individuals find ways to have *additional* sources of income and do not rely only on their company paycheck. They maximize their income by developing additional sources of income other than their paycheck.

Controlling expenses is as important to individuals as it is to companies in order to maximize profitability. For individuals, it is building **equity** or **net worth** instead of maximizing profits. This means having money left over after paying expenses. In today's society, it is too easy for individuals to spend money that they do not have. Kiyosaki points out that often individuals spend all of their paychecks on expenses or liabilities. Then it gets worse. They charge more expenses on credit cards. This is very bad management of their money. First, they are spending all of their income and not saving or investing any of it. Second, they are spending more than they are earning with the paycheck they receive every other Friday by charging additional expenses on credit cards. Remember our profit formula for a business: **Revenue minus expenses equal profits**. For individuals, the profit formula is income from monthly paychecks minus monthly expenses results in equity or net worth. If people spend more than they earn, they will have no equity and a negative net worth, which is similar to a company having an operating loss instead of a profit.

Today individuals not only are spending more than they are making, *but they put the excess expenditures on credit cards!* This provides them a way to live with a loss by just putting it on plastic. The result is debt that grows rather than declines. Often the monthly credit card payments only pay the interest and do not reduce the outstanding balance. Finally, the third bad thing that many individuals are doing is paying high interest rates on their credit cards. Things are out of control! Individuals spend more than they make and put excessive expenditures on several credit cards with high interest rates. This often leads to two people working or one person working multiple jobs just to get enough income to meet monthly expenses and make the minimum monthly credit card payments. *Notice, we didn't say that people are paying off their credit cards. We said most individuals just make the monthly payments, which goes to interest. They are never able to pay off their credit cards.* This leads to what Kiyosaki calls *the rat race.*

Personal Cash Flow

Cash flow is the ability to maintain enough cash in your bank account or to increase the cash in your bank account so that you can cover all incurred living expenses. This primarily refers to an individual's checking account but will also include a savings account if there is one.

A *positive cash flow* means that an individual maintains enough money in her or his checking account to pay all monthly expenses without taking money out of savings or investment accounts. These individuals are earning more income than they are spending on expenses.

A *negative cash flow* means that an individual does not maintain enough money in his or her checking account to pay all monthly expenses. These individuals have to take money out of their savings or investment account or they put the excess expenses on a credit card just to take care of their monthly expenses. This means they are spending more money on expenses than they are earning with income. Again, notice that we did not say the excess pays off credit card balances. Generally, the monthly minimum only pays the interest expense or a partial payment of the total balance.

There are three main reasons that individuals cannot maintain a positive monthly cash flow. The first is that they only have one source of income—their paycheck every other Friday. The second is that they do not understand the difference between spending money on expenses and liabilities rather than investing in income-producing assets. Third, they do not have the discipline or financial knowledge to keep their monthly expenses lower than their monthly income.

Personal Balance Sheet

Individuals have assets, liabilities, and owner equity just like businesses do. This includes both current and long-term assets and current and long-term liabilities. Too often individuals don't look at their money and finances as a business but only look at how much money they make each paycheck and how they are going to spend it or try to make ends meet.

Kiyosaki has very basic descriptions of assets and liabilities. Remember them!

Liabilities **take money out of your pocket.**
Assets **put money into your pocket.**

We all make choices of what we are going to do with the money we earn. Unfortunately many individuals get caught up in the rat race and end up trying to spread their income around to pay the monthly rent, utilities, groceries, and gas and then make the minimum monthly credit card payments. They really don't have a financial choice because they owe everyone. They have to pay on their expenses and have no money left to save or invest.

Kiyosaki's Rule #1 is to invest in assets. This means that an individual must allocate some of her or his monthly income to savings and investments (assets). Assets earn income. For example, savings accounts pay interest daily, quarterly, or annually.

Certificates of Deposit (CDs) also pay interest quarterly or annually. Investments in the stock market generally pay dividends quarterly or annually and have the potential that the stock price will go up (appreciation). However, there is also the risk that the stock price can go down. The point is that individuals that have financial literacy discipline themselves to investing some portion, even if it is only 5% or 10% of their monthly income, into assets. This gives them the opportunity to start building equity or net worth. This means they will own more than they owe.

Let's look at two examples of a college student's balance sheet during senior year. We will use March 31 as our balance sheet date.

EXAMPLE 1
NO FINANCIAL LITERACY

Assets			Liabilities	
Cash—Checking Account	$	100	Car Loan @ 9%	$ 6,000
Cash—Savings Account		–0–	Student Loan @ 4%	10,000
Investments		–0–	Credit Card Debt @ 16%	5,000
Total Current Assets	$	100	Store Credit Cards @ 9%	2,000
			Total Liabilities	$23,000
Car		$ 8,000		
Furniture (mainly music/TV)		2,000	Equity	
Insurance Policies		–0–	Car	$ 2,000
Total Long-Term Assets		$10,000	Gifts from Grandparents (savings bonds)	1,000
			Total Equity	$ 3,000
			TOTAL LIABILITIES	
TOTAL ASSETS		$10,100	AND EQUITY	$26,000
			NEGATIVE NET WORTH	$15,900

Because total assets must equal total liabilities and equity, the difference between the total assets of $10,100 and the total liabilities and equity of $26,000 is a negative $15,900. This individual owes $15,900 more than she or he owns and therefore has a *negative net worth* or *no net equity*.

EXAMPLE 2
BASIC FINANCIAL LITERACY

Assets		Liabilities	
Cash—Checking Account	$ 500	Car Loan @ 9%	$ 1,000
Cash—Savings Account	2,000	Student Loan @ 4%	10,000
Investments	3,000	Credit Card Debt @ 12%	500
Total Current Assets	$ 5,500	Store Credit Cards @ 9%	200
		Total Liabilities	$11,700
Car	$ 5,000		
Furniture (mainly music/TV)	2,000	Equity	
Insurance Policies	10,000	Car	$ 4,000
Total Long-Term Assets	$17,000	Gifts from Grandparents	1,000
		Total Equity	$ 5,000
		TOTAL LIABILITIES	
TOTAL ASSETS	$22,500	AND EQUITY	$16,700
		POSITIVE NET WORTH	$ 5,800

Because total assets must equal total liabilities and equity, the difference between the total assets of $22,500 and total liabilities and equity of $16,700 is a positive $5,800. This individual owns more than he or she owes and therefore has a *positive net worth* or *net equity*.

Let's look at the similarities and differences in these two examples. Both students have $10,000 in student loans, $2,000 in furniture, and four different liabilities. The difference is that the financially literate student has a smaller car loan, smaller credit card balances, and smaller store credit card debt. The financially literate student bought a lower-priced car and made a larger down payment, therefore resulting in a smaller car loan and monthly payment. This student has been smarter and more disciplined and therefore has larger balances in his or her checking and savings accounts. And this student has been able to develop $3,000 in investments. *This student is investing in assets!*

These are both large and small differences, but they add up to a big difference. The student in Example 1 has a negative net worth of $15,900, and the student in Example 2 has a positive net worth of $5,800. The difference is $21,700! The student in Example 2 has incurred many of the same liabilities but due to financial literacy has managed to save and invest, spend wisely, and minimize liabilities. This student has put to use Rule #1: Invest in assets. Although these investments start small, they are a beginning and have resulted in the student having a positive rather than a negative net worth. This student's asset column is growing.

Another valuable concept in the management of assets is the importance of building **principal**. Principal is the amount of money invested in income-producing assets. It is money that is **earning** money. For example, $1,000 invested in a savings account is $1,000 of principal that can earn **interest** or **dividends**. If the interest rate is 3% per year, this principal of $1,000 will earn $30 of interest per year.

There are three primary ways that principal can grow. First, an individual can contribute her or his own money to the principal each paycheck or make monthly contributions. This demonstrates Rule #1, investing in assets. Second, a company can make matching contributions to an individual's account and therefore increase the principal. *This is the most important concept to understand in creating individual wealth and personal equity—take advantage of company contributions in addition to individual contributions to increase the principal.* Third, the principal can grow if the person reinvests interest and dividends that the principal earns. The larger the principal or higher the interest or dividend rate, the faster the principal will grow.

Managing Personal Finances

The Rat Race

Kiyosaki has described the rat race as individuals spending more money than they earn. They are not able to decide or control their money because they have continually overspent their income resulting in higher monthly expenses than their monthly income. They will then probably take on a second job to pay off their debts. But they use the additional income to continue spending rather than paying off their credit cards, which was their original intent—thus the rat race, which occurs when people do not have control of their money, continue to overspend, do not make progress in paying off debt, and are not able to invest in assets.

These individuals do not know about Kiyosaki's Rule #1 or they do not have the discipline to follow Rule #1. The first step that they must take to get out of the rat race is to realize that they are spending more than they are earning and that they must change their financial habits and how they use and manage money.

Evaluating Your Personal Financial Position

Every individual establishes a pattern for earning and spending money. Until one starts learning about managing money and developing financial literacy and discipline, the person will continue to earn and spend, totally unaware of the value of saving and unable to invest in assets. Financial literacy starts with changing this pattern to a pattern of earning, investing, and then spending. The investment part comes before the spending part. People who have financial literacy and financial discipline reduce their expenditures on expenses to the amount remaining after they have invested.

Take a look at your own pattern of managing your money. Do you spend more than you earn each month? Are you unable to save or invest? Are your debts getting larger each month rather than smaller each month? Do you continually use your credit card to buy things that you do not need or cannot afford? If your answers are yes to some or all of these questions, you are caught up in the rat race!

The most important point to understand at this time is that it is never too late to learn and to start managing your money. It doesn't matter what your age is, the amount of money you make, or the amount of debt that you have. You can always learn about managing money, the need to change your spending habits, and the importance of starting to manage your money in ways that will enable you to invest, build a principal, and to be able pay all your expenses. This is called financial freedom.

Taking Control

It is important that individuals make the effort to analyze their current financial position and then learn and apply smart money management principles. It will require discipline and a change in an individual's habits and lifestyle. But it will be worth the change as an individual regains control of her or his financial situation and has the freedom to choose how to invest and spend rather than be controlled by debt obligations. The important thing is to change, even if it is in small steps.

Kiyosaki offers six steps or lessons that will lead to financial independence and the ability to manage and control money and finances:

1. Remember that the rich don't work for money—the poor and middle class work for money, the rich have money work for them.

2. Teach financial literacy, the ability to read numbers. The rich buy assets. The poor only have expenses. The middle class buys liabilities they think are assets.

3. Mind your own business. Invest your income in assets that will earn additional income for you.

4. Learn the history of taxes and the power of the corporation.

5. Remember that the rich invent money. They understand numbers, develop investment strategies, understand the market, and understand the law.

6. Work to learn—don't work for money. Be able to manage cash flow, be able to manage systems including time, yourself, and your family, and be able to manage people.

These steps form an effective guideline for getting out of the rat race and controlling your income.

Overcoming Obstacles

Many individuals have the knowledge and resources to build equity and net worth. Yet they never make the effort to apply their financial knowledge to building their financial resources.

Once people have studied and become financially literate, they may still face roadblocks to becoming financially independent. There are five main reasons why financially literate people may still not develop abundant asset columns. Asset columns that could produce large sums of cash flow. Asset columns that could free them to live the life they dream of, instead of working full time just to pay bills (p. 147).

Kiyosaki's five obstacles for individuals in managing their finances are the following:

1. Fear
2. Cynicism
3. Laziness
4. Bad habits
5. Arrogance

Does any of these apply to you? What are you going to do to overcome these obstacles and start to effectively manage your money?

Getting Started

Following are Kiyosaki's activities to get an individual started and on the track to learning and gaining financial literacy. An individual can start these one at a time or work on many of them at the same time. What is important is to do each one thoroughly.

1. Have a reason to start. If not, there is no sense reading further. It will sound like too much work.
2. Choose daily—the power of choice.
3. Choose friends carefully—learn from them.
4. Master a formula, then learn a new one—continue to change and grow.
5. Pay yourself first—self-discipline.

6. Pay your brokers well—their advice and experience are worth it.

7. Be an "Indian Giver"—get something for nothing.

8. Use assets to buy luxuries—use the earnings from assets or principal to buy luxuries.

9. Don't forget the need for heroes—look up to someone and strive to be like your hero.

10. Teach and you shall receive—share your time, resources, and knowledge and you will be rewarded.

The point that Kiyosaki emphasizes throughout his book is to take the time to learn the basics of managing money. Once financial literacy is obtained, then an individual can intelligently manage his or her money to build wealth and obtain financial freedom. Financial literacy with discipline can get people out of the rate race and in control of their finances and their lives.

Evaluating Assets and Sources of Income

Company Programs

Many companies offer retirement plans (**401K accounts**) for their employees that include the company making matching financial **company contributions** to an employee's individual retirement account. These programs are generally based on the amount of employee contributions to the 401K plan. The company will contribute anywhere from 25 cents per $1 of employee contribution to $1 per $1 of employee contribution. This represents a return to the employee of 25% on a 25 cent company contribution and a 100% return to the employee on a $1 contribution. This is the reason that company retirement programs should be the number one priority for an employee in investing in assets, increasing principal, and creating equity and net worth. Whereas returns from interest and dividends are in the 1% to 3% range, the company contribution is generally in the 25% to 100% range.

Companies can also provide stock purchase programs where employees can purchase company stock with no commission and often at a discounted price. Contributions to these plans can be made conveniently with payroll deductions that avoid commissions and other fees. This is another way for individuals to build wealth at nominal expense.

An equally important benefit that most companies provide is employee health **benefits**. This includes providing health and dental insurance at group rates which are generally lower than individual rates. Often the company will pay a small or large part of this cost, thereby reducing the amount that employees have to pay for health insurance.

Companies also might offer life insurance, disability insurance, and salary continuation to help employees when they have emergencies or accidents that require expensive medical care. It is important to take advantage of these programs because they enable employees to participate and receive these benefits at a lower cost than they could on their own.

Understanding and enrolling in these savings and benefit programs can be a significant step in the process of building wealth and staying out of the Rat Race. They not only offer significant returns or cost savings, but they also provide a convenient and disciplined way to consistently save and invest for the future. Most large companies offer these programs, so it is up to the employee to learn about them and demonstrate the financial literacy that will enable an individual to benefit from them.

Ownership

In addition to company investment accounts, it is important for individuals to have their own investment or savings accounts. This is because company retirement programs are controlled by the company. They are good in that they provide both employee and company contributions. But they also have restrictions that are intended to ensure that the money is available for retirement. Therefore, access to company retirement accounts is restricted, and there are often penalties and fees for early withdrawal of money from these accounts. These company retirement or investment accounts offer a long-term component for investing.

An individual account is controlled by a person and is available to use or not use as appropriate. It offers the flexibility of saving and investing while continuing to have access to those funds as needed. The access to and control of these individual accounts should be an important part of any investment strategy. The individual has the control to make the principal increase with contributions or decrease with withdrawals. These individual investment accounts offer a short-term component for investment.

Retirement

Another valuable part of financial literacy is understanding the importance of planning for retirement at the beginning of an individual's career, not at the end. It is a fact that the sooner individuals start making contributions to retirement or 401K accounts, the more money they will have working for them for when they retire. Time is in favor of those who invest early in their careers. That is because these contributions steadily increase the principal and therefore the interest that the principal earns. Equally important is the time span that the principal is earning interest, dividends, and appreciating. It is common sense that money contributed by individuals and the company over a 25-year period will be larger than over a 15-year period because it represents more money working longer!

Retirement should be a key part of any individual's investment strategy. There are so many options available to assist in achieving retirement goals. An important part of financial literacy is understanding the retirement options and programs available and choosing the best ones that match your retirement strategy. A small amount of money invested over a long period of time will result in a much larger retirement account than larger amounts of money invested over a short period of time. Knowledge and discipline are the starting points to a comfortable and satisfying retirement.

Summary

Individuals can utilize many of the same business concepts to manage their personal finances. Financial literacy is the ability to understand and use numbers in financial planning. It is important because it gives individuals control over their finances and the freedom to be able to afford and be able to do what they want to do.

There are many books on managing personal finances. *Rich Dad, Poor Dad* by Robert Kiyosaki is one book that clearly presents the fundamentals of personal financial management. It is important that individuals take the time to learn these money management fundamentals at an early age so that they can have their money work for them rather than having them work for their money.

A key point of financial literacy is understanding the importance of investing in assets. Assets put money in your pocket. Investment assets involve building a principal amount in dollars that earns interest or dividends and contributes these earning to increasing the principal. Liabilities and expenses take money out of your pocket and are typically what most individuals do with the money they earn from their paycheck. They lack the financial knowledge and personal discipline to invest some amount in assets before paying off liabilities and expenses.

Individuals can invest in both company and their own investment accounts. Company investment accounts such as 401Ks and retirement accounts offer the advantage of having a company contribute money to these accounts. However, they are for the long term and contain restrictions and penalties for early withdrawal before retirement. Individual investment accounts offer the advantage of ownership, flexibility, and control. They are more short term in nature and the money in these accounts is available to use when needed without penalties. A financially literate individual will take advantage of both of these types of investment accounts.

Hospitality Manager Takeaways

1. It is important for hospitality managers to understand the management of money so that they can take advantage of company programs and individual accounts that can help them create equity and build net worth.

2. Assets put money in your pocket; liabilities take money out of your pocket.

3. Equity is the amount of assets, primarily investments and real estate, that an individual accumulates and is not encumbered by liabilities or debt.

4. Financial literacy provides individuals with control over their money and the freedom to do what they would like to do because they have the financial resources necessary to pay for those activities.

5. Time and discipline are two key components of a strong investment strategy.

6. Retirement should be a part of an individual's investment strategy at the beginning of one's career and not at the end.

Key Terms

Asset (Kiyosaki)—Puts money in your pocket.

Benefits—Programs offered to employees by a company that provide savings programs to invest in and health and insurance programs at reduced costs.

Company Contribution—The dollar amount that a company contributes to an employee's retirement account or benifit expenses.

Dividend—The return on the principal invested in a company stock or mutual fund.

Earnings—Money that is produced from an asset in the form of dividends or interest.

Equity—The difference between an individual's assets and liabilities.

Financial Literacy (Kiyosaki)—The ability to understand numbers.

401K Accounts—Company long-term retirement accounts that include both employee and company contributions.

Interest—The return on the principal in a savings account.

Liability (Kiyosaki)—Takes money out of your pocket.

Net Worth—What an individual has in investments that are unencumbered with corresponding liabilities or debt. Similar to equity.

Principal—The dollar amount of money in an account that is earning interest or dividends and that has the potential to appreciate or increase as well as decrease.

Review Questions

1. Define an asset and a liability according to Kiyosaki.

2. Describe the Rat Race including how you get in it and how you get out of it.

3. Why are company 401K programs so important to employees?

4. Why are company benefit programs so important to employees?

5. Why is planning for retirement at the start of a career so important?

6. What is the difference between principal and interest?

7. Name the five obstacles to investing.

8. Choose three activities that are important to you in getting started.

Glossary

Accounting Concepts—A general understanding of the bookkeeping methods and financial transactions of a business.

Accounts Payable—Products or services received by a company but not paid for that are due within one year.

Accounts Receivable—What the company is owed for providing products and services to customers. Revenues recorded but uncollected. The process of billing and collecting accounts settled after the guest or company has checked out of the hotel.

Allocations—The portion of an expense charged to a specific hotel for services received in connection with expenses incurred at the corporate level on behalf of all the hotels or restaurants in the company.

Annual Operating Budget—The formal business and financial plan for a business for one year.

Consolidated Hotel Budget—The summary budget for the entire hotel including revenues, expenses, and profits.

Department Budget—The specific and detailed budget for an individual department that provides all the financial specifics for revenues, expenses, and profits.

Asset (Kiyosaki)—Puts money in your pocket.

Assets—The resources owned by a company that are used in the production of products and services by that company.

Current—Assets that are used or consumed during a one-year time period.

Long Term—Assets with a useful life of longer than one year.

Assistant Controller—A manager in the accounting office that reports to the Director of Finance and oversees specific functions in the accounting office—either income operations or accounts receivable—to confirm or verify the accuracy of operating and financial information.

Attest—To confirm or verify the accuracy of operating and financial information.

Balance Sheet—The financial statement that measures the value or net worth of a business as of a specific date. Also called the Asset and Liability statement (A&L).

Board of Directors—The group that is responsible for overseeing all operational aspects of a company. The Chief Executive Officer (CEO) of a company reports to the Board of Directors and is also a member of the board.

Booking Pace—The current rate at which reservations are being received for a specific Day of Arrival (DOA). The booking pace is compared to historical averages to determine if demand is stronger or weaker than historical averages.

Brand—The lodging term that identifies different types of hospitality properties that serve specific hospitality market segments.

Budget—The formal business and financial plan for a business for one year.

Capital Expenditure Budget—The formal budget that identifies the needs for replacing the long-term assets of the business, for renovating the business, and for expanding the business.

Capitalization—The source and methods of raising money to invest in and start a business.

Cash—Funds that are in the cash account and available for use in daily business operations.

Certified Public Accountant—An independent accounting firm responsible for examining and verifying the correctness and accuracy of a company's financial information. It issues an audit opinion stating that the company meets or does not meet established reporting and accounting guidelines.

Change—The difference between two numbers.

Classification of Cash Flow—Operating activities, financial activities, and investment activities.

Comp Unit—Stores, units, hotels, or restaurants in a company that have been operating for more than two years.

Company Contribution—The dollar amount that a company contributes to an employee's retirement account.

Comparison—To examine in order to note the likeness or difference.

Competitive Set—A group of five or more properties selected by individual hotel management. A competitive set enables hotel managers to compare property performance with direct competition.

Concept—The restaurant term that identifies different types of restaurant operations that provide specific dining experiences and serve specific market segments.

Construction Budget—The budget that identifies all the costs involved to design, construct and build a hotel or restaurant.

Corporate Accounting Office—A central location that provides accounting support and services for individual hotels or restaurants operated by the company.

Cost Management Index (CMI)—The formula that identifies what level of expenses and profits are expected given incremental changes in revenues. Includes flow thru and retention formulas and guidelines.

Deductions from Income—The same as expense centers. The direct expenses of staff departments that support the operating departments of a hotel in providing products and services to customers.

Department Head—A manager who is directly responsible for a specific hotel department. Department Heads report to an Executive Committee Member and have line managers and supervisors reporting to them.

Department P&L—Profit and Loss Statement for one specific department that includes all revenue and expenses in detail that are involved in operating that department.

Department Profits—The dollar amounts remaining in Revenue Centers/Profit Centers after the department recognizes all revenues and pays all expenses associated with operating that department for a specific time period.

Direct Report—The managers and positions that report directly to a senior manager.

Director of Finance—The Executive Committee Member directly responsible for all accounting operations in a hotel.

Division—The manufacturing term that identifies the different types of products produced by a company including the markets that the company serves.

Earnings—Money that is produced from an asset in the form of dividends or interest.

Equity—The difference between an individual's assets and liabilities. The ownership part of a company or the amount invested by owners or shareholders.

Escrow—An account established to collect money to be used at a later date. Same as reserve account.

Executive Committee—The members of senior management that report directly to the General Manager and are responsible for specific hotel departments. Department Heads report to an Executive Committee Member.

Expense Categories—The four major categories for collecting and reporting department expenses: cost of sales, wages, benefits, and direct operating expenses.

Expense Center—A staff department that supports the hotel operating departments: Sales and Marketing, Engineering, Human Resources, and Accounting. It has no revenues or cost of sales—just wages, benefits, and direct operating expenses.

Financial Analysis—The separation of a business's management of monetary affairs into parts for individual study.

Financial Literacy (Kiyosaki)—The ability to understand numbers.

Financial Management Cycle—The process of producing, preparing, analyzing, and applying numbers to business operations.

Fiscal Year—The financial year for reporting a company's financial results. It can be the same as or different from the calendar year ending December 31.

Fixed Expenses—Direct expenses of a hotel that are constant and do not change regardless of the volume and level of business. Secretaries in the sales department and accounting clerks in the accounting department are examples of fixed positions.

Flow Thru—Measures how much profit goes up or down as a percentage of the change in revenue.

Forecast—A financial and operational report that updates the budget.

　Weekly Forecast—The forecast for the next week that includes revenues and expenses, with a focus on wage costs, and provides the details by day and shift for providing the actual products and services expected by guests.

　Monthly Forecast—A forecast of revenues for the next month, including average rates and volumes for specific market segments, departments, or meal periods.

　Quarterly Forecast—A forecast that projects revenues over a longer time period and is completed by adding the forecasts for each month of the quarter.

Fundamental Accounting Equation—Assets = Liabilities + Owner Equity.

General Manager—The senior manager in the hotel who is responsible for all hotel operations. This person is responsible for all positions and activities.

Historical Average—Average information based on four or five years of hotel operations.

Horizontal Headings—The headings across the top of a P&L that identify the type, time, and amount of financial information.

House Profit—The profit amount that includes all revenues and expenses controlled by hotel management and measures management's ability to operate the hotel profitably. It is calculated by subtracting Total Expense Center Costs from Total Department Profits.

Income Accounting—The section of the accounting office that is involved with recording income, paying expenses, and assisting other hotel managers.

Income Statement—Measures the operating success and profitability of a business.

Incremental—An increase, something gained or added. In financial analysis it describes additional revenues, expenses, or profits beyond what was expected.

Independent Audit Report—The section of the Corporate Annual Report that contains the audit opinion presented by an independent and certified public accounting company.

Inventory—Assets in the form of materials and supplies that the company has purchased but not yet used in the production of products and services.

Investment Factors—Another term for hotel fixed expenses that are constant regardless of the volume levels of the hotel and include expenses such as bank loans, lease payments, certificates and licenses, depreciation, and insurance expenses.

Last Year—The official financial performance of the previous year or month.

Liabilities—Obligations owed by a company.

Current—Obligations that are due within one year.

Long Term—Obligations that are due at a date beyond one year.

Liability (Kiyosaki)—Takes money out of your pocket.

Line Manager—The entry-level management position that has face-to-face interaction with the customers and is responsible for operating the different shifts of a hotel department.

Liquidity—The amount of cash or cash equivalents that a business has to cover its daily operating expenses.

Management Responsibility Report—The section of the Corporate Annual Report that contains the senior management opinion that the operating and financial information contained in the annual report is accurate and correctly portrays the financial condition of the company.

Market Capitalization—A measure of the value of a company that includes the number of individual and institutional investors times the current stock price of the company.

Market Segment—Customer groups defined by expectations, preferences, buying patterns, and behavior patterns.

Market Share—Total room supply, room demand, or room revenue as a percentage of some larger group.

Net Worth—What an individual has in investments that are unencumbered with corresponding liabilities or debt. Similar to equity.

Notes to Consolidated Financial Statements—The detailed financial explanation of accounting and financial information contained in the annual report.

Operating Department—A hotel department that records revenues and produces a profit by providing products and services to the guests.

Organization Chart—Describes the reporting relationships, responsibilities, and operating activities for a department or business unit.

Owner Equity—The amount invested in a company by owners or investors including Paid-in Capital, Common Stock, and Retained Earnings.

Percentages—A share or proportion in relation to the whole; part.

    Change—Measures the difference between two numbers in percentage.

    Cost—Measures the dollar cost or expense as a part of total applicable revenue.

    Mix—Measures dollars or units as a part of a whole.

    Profit—Measures the dollar profit as a part of total applicable revenues.

Point of Sale System (POS)—The equipment that records the customer transaction including identifying the method of payment and reporting the type of transaction.

Preopening Budget—The budget established to guide a new business as it prepares to open for business.

Principal—The dollar amount of money that is in an account that is earning interest or dividends and that has the potential to appreciate or increase as well as decrease.

Profit—The amount of revenues left over after all expenses have been paid.

Profit and Loss (P&L) Statement—Measure the operating success and profitability of a business over a specific period of time.

Profit after Taxes—The amount of profit remaining after corporate taxes are paid that is divided among owners, management companies, and any other entities that have an interest in the hotel.

Profit before Taxes—The same as net house profit. The profit amount remaining after all hotel operating expenses have been paid.

Profit Center—An operating department that produces revenues that result in a profit by providing products and services to customers. It includes revenues, expenses, and profits and is a term that is interchangeable with Revenue Center.

Pro Forma—The projected first year of operations prepared before actual operations begin.

Property, Plant, and Equipment (PP&E)—The term used to identify the long-term investments in fixed assets that will serve the business for more than one year.

Public Relations—Information and new releases prepared by the company.

Rate—The part of the revenue equation that provides the dollar price that guests or customers are willing to pay to secure a room or meal. Typically, average room rates and average guest checks are used to calculate total room or restaurant revenues. Rates also provide the hourly rate of pay for wage forecasting and scheduling.

Rate Structure—A list of the different room rates offered by a hotel.

Ratios—Formulas that are used to calculate appropriate expense levels in relation to different revenue levels.

Reserve—An account established to collect money to be used at a later date. Same as an escrow account.

Retention—The same definition as Flow Thru.

Revenue—The monetary amount that customers pay to receive a product or service. It can be in the form of cash, checks, credit cards, or electronic transfer.

Revenue Center—An operating product that produces revenues by providing products and services directly to customers. It includes revenues, expenses, and profits.

REVPAR—Revenue per Available Room. Total room revenue divided by total rooms available or average room rate times occupancy percentage. It combines room rate and room occupancy information to measure a hotel's ability to maximize room revenues.

Secondary Competition—A group of hotels that offer competition but provide different rates, services, and amenities and therefore are not considered direct or primary competition.

Securities and Exchange Commission (SEC)—The government agency responsible for regulating the public stock exchanges (New York Stock Exchange, NASDAQ, and several other exchanges).

Selling Strategy—The actions and decisions of the senior management of a hotel in opening and closing room rates, arrival dates, and length of stay to maximize total hotel room revenues.

Source and Use of Funds Statement—A part of the Statement of Cash Flow that shows how cash is created (source) and disbursed (used) among the different accounts on the balance sheet.

Staff Department—A hotel department that provides assistance and support to the hotel operating departments.

STAR Market Report—A monthly report published by Smith Travel Research that provides a hotel with rate, occupancy, and REVPAR information for a specific hotel and its competitive set.

Statement of Cash Flow—Measures the liquidity and identifies the flow of cash in a company.

Titles—The top portion of a financial statement that tells the name of the company, type of report, and time period covered.

Total Department Profits—The summation of the individual department profits of a hotel. Provides the amount of profit resulting from the operating departments of a hotel.

Trend—A general inclination or tendency.

Variable Expenses—Expenses that fluctuate or change directly with the change in business levels and volumes. Housekeepers, bellhops, and servers are examples of variable wage positions.

Variation—Something slightly different from another of the same type. In financial analysis, variation is the difference between a planned number and an actual number.

Vertical Headings—The names of the departments, categories, and accounts that are on the side or center of a P&L that identify the type and amount of financial information recorded on the P&L.

Volume—The part of the revenue equation that provides the quantity of products or services consumed by the guests. Typically, rooms sold or occupied and customer counts are the volume variables used to calculate total room or restaurant revenues. Volume also determines labor hours required for wage forecasting and scheduling.

Working Capital—The amount of money utilized in the daily operations of a business, including using the assets and liabilities as well as cash to produce a product or service.

Yield Management—The computer reservation tracking system that combines current reservation booking information with historical reservation booking information. It is used to implement selling strategies that will maximize total hotel room revenue.

Index

A

Accounting concept
  Definition 3
  Key term 3
  Using in operations 24
Accounting department
  Discussion 51
  Organization chart 52
Accounting period
  Discussion 61
Accounts payable
  Definition 53, 92
  Discussion 53
  Key term 65, 108
Accounts receivable
  Definition 54, 91
  Discussion 54
  Key term 65, 108
Accrued liabilities
  Definition 93
Activity ratio
  Definition 163
  Examples 163
Adjusted gross operating profit
  Discussion 22
  Formula 22
Advance deposits
  Definition 92
Ageing
  Managing 54

Allocations
  Departments 84
  Discussion 71
  Key term 87
Annual operating budget
  Characteristics 232
  Definition 230, 232
  Discussion 231
  Key term 244
Asset
  Current 12
  Definition 93
  Fundamental Accounting Equation 11
  Key term 108, 277
  Kiyosaki definition 268
  Liquid 103
  Long term 12
  Non liquid 103
Assistant Controller
  Discussion 53
  Key term 65
  Organization chart 52
  Responsibilities 53
Attest
  In Corporate Annual Reports 250
  Key term 263
  Senior officers 253
Audit opinion
  Discussion 251
  Key term 262

Department profit
 Discussion 74
 Key term 87
Depreciation
 Definition 92
Director of Finance
 Definition 51
 Key term 65
 Organization chart 46, 52
 Responsibilities 53
Director of Revenue Management
 Discussion 147
 Responsibilities 144
Direct report
 Discussion 48
 Key term 65
Discount room rates
 Examples 142
Dividends
 Key term 277
 Personal 271
Division
 In Corporate Annual Reports
  257
 Key term 263
DOA—Day of arrival
 Discussion 143
 Key term 151

E
Earnings
 Key term 277
Equity
 Key term 255
 Personal 267
Escrow
 Key term 244
 Reserve 233
Executive Committee
 Discussion 50
 Key term 65
 Organization chart 46

Expense categories
 Department P&L 83
 Four major categories 82
 Key terms 87
Expense center
 Discussion 21, 71
 Examples 21
 Key terms 87

F
401K accounts
 Definition 274
 Key term 277
Financial analysis
 Definition 3
 Key term 24
 Measuring financial performance 29
 Using in operations 2
Financial literacy (Kiyosaki)
 Definition 266
 Key term 277
Financial Management Cycle
 Discussion 29–30
 Key term 42
Fiscal year
 Corporate Annual Report 251
 Definition 251
 Key term 264
Fixed expense
 Definition 22, 128
 Key term 87, 132, 186
 Examples 85, 129
 Consolidated P&L 73
Flow thru
 Definition 128
 Examples 129
 Key term 132
Forecast
 Definition 31, 174
 Discussion 31, 174
 Forecasting timeline 176
 Formulas 182

Key term 42, 186

Revenue forecasts 179

Steps in preparing 183

Wage forecasts or schedules 184

Volume, the key to forecasting
182

Weekly

Discussion 177

Key term 187

Monthly/Period

Discussion 178

Key term 186

Quarterly

Key term 186

Restaurant forecasts

Examples 202, 204

Problem sets 207, 209

Steps in preparing 203

Rooms forecasts

Examples 190

Problem set 199

Steps in preparing 188

Room service forecasts

Examples 202, 204

Problem sets 207, 208

Steps in preparing 202

Wage forecasts

Examples 224

Problem sets 227

Steps in preparing 222

Fundamental Accounting Equation

Definition 11

Discussion 93

Formula 91

G

GAAP—Generally Accepted Accounting
Principles

Corporate Annual Reports 251

Discussion 94

General Cashier

Discussion 58

Key term 66

Position 53

General Manager

Discussion 50

Key term 66

Gross Operating Profit

Discussion 21, 74

Formula 22

Four Seasons 21

Hyatt 21

Group market segment

Definition 19

Examples 19

H

Historical average

Discussion 143

Key term 151

Yield Management 143

Hotel management reports

Daily reports 113

Definition 112

Discussion 112

Types and uses 113

Horizontal headings

Discussion 77

Key term 87

House profit

Discussion 21

Formula 22

Key term 87

Management bonus

Marriott 21

I

Income accounting

Key term 66

Income journal

Definition 53

Discussion 53

Income Statement

See P&L Statement

Incremental
  Discussion 128
  Key term 132
Independent Audit Report
  Audit opinion example 252
  In Corporate Annual Report 252
  Key term 264
Interest
  Key term 277
  On personal investments 27
Inventory
  Definition 92
  Key term 109
Investment factors
  Definition 73
  Key term 87

L
Last year
  Key term 42
Lease
  Definition 93
Liabilities
  Definition 93
  Key term 109
  Kiyosaki's definition 268
  Current
    Definition 92
    Key term 109
  Long-term
    Definition 103
    Key term 109
Liability(Kiyosaki)
  Definition 268
  Key term 277
Line manager
  Definition 51
  Key term 66
Line of credit
  Definition 93
Liquidity
  Definition 13, 97
  Discussion 97, 102

  Statement of cash flow 13
  Key term 24
Liquidity ratios
  Definition 163
  Examples 163
Long term asset
  Definition 92
  Key term 108
  Non liquid 103
Long term liability
  Definition 93
  Key term 109

M
Management Responsibility Report
  Discussion 261
  Key term 264
Management tool
  Numbers used as 29
Manhours
  Discussion 123
  Formulas 123
  Labor productivity reports 123
Market capitalization
  Definition 3
  Formula 25
  Key term 24
Market segment
  Definition 8, 18
  Examples 19
    Contract 19
    Group 19
    Transient 19
  Key term 24
Market share
  Key term 171
Message to shareholders
  Discussion 254

N
Net house profit
  Discussion 22, 75
  Formula 22

Key term 87

Management tool 29

Measuring financial performance 29

Net worth

Key term 278

Individual or personal 267

Night Audit

Discussion 54

Key term 66

Responsibilities 54

Notes to consolidated financial statements

Key term 264

Numbers

Financial language 23

To measure financial performance 23

Management tool 23

Comparing to give them meaning 159

O

Occupancy percentage

Discussion 164

Formula 25

Offset rooms

Housekeeping wage schedules
222

Operating department

Definition 50

Key term 66

Operating ratios

Definition 162

Examples 162

Organization chart

Accounting department 52

Definition 48

Hotel 49

Key term 66

Owner equity

Definition 93

Key term 109

P

Paid in capital

Definition 93

Percentage

Department profit 156

Discussion 34, 159

Formula 43

Key term 42

Four types used in financial analysis 35–38

Change

Discussion 37

Formula 38, 43

Key term 42

Cost

Discussion 35

Formula 35, 43

Key term 42

Mix

Discussion 36

Examples 36, 37

Formula 36, 43

Key term 42

Profit

Discussion 20, 36

Formula 5, 36, 43

Key term 42

Point of sale system (POS)

Key term 25

Recording sales 13

Reports 17

Sales transactions 15

Pre-opening budget

Characteristics 233

Definition 230

Discussion 233

Key term 244

Pre-paid expense

Definition 92

Primary competition

Key term 171

Principle

Importance of in personal finance 271

Key term 278

Productivities

Labor 123

Profit 123

Profit
  Best measure of financial performance 155
  Definition 20, 154
  Department 21, 74, 156
  Examples 156
  Hotel 155
  Formula 5, 17, 25, 43, 155
  Key term 25
  Profitability discussion 155
  Retention and flow thru 127
Profit and Loss Statement
  Characteristics 10
  Critiques
  Definition 10
  Differences to Balance Sheet 100
  Horizontal headings 77
  Key term 25
  Personal 267
  Similarities with Balance Sheet 101
  Title 75
  Vertical headings 77
Profit after taxes
  Discussion 75
  Key term 87
Profit before taxes
  Discussion 75
  Key term 88
Profit center
  Discussion 69
  Examples 21
  Key term 88
Profitability ratios
  Definition 163
  Examples 163
Pro forma
  Discussion 31
  Key term 42
Property
  Key term 25
Property, plant and equipment (PPE)
  Capitalization 240
  Definition 92
  Key term 244

Public relations
  In Corporate Annual Report 252
  Key term 264

R
Rat race
  Kiyosaki's definition 271
Rate
  Definition 16
  Key term 25
  Rack rate 141
Rate structure
  Discussion 141
  Establishing 141
  Examples 142
  Key term 151
  Market segments 141
Ratios
  Activity ratios 162
  Analyzing revenues 163
  Discussion 162
  Key term 171, 186
  Liquidity ratios 163
  Operating ratios 162
  Profitability ratios 163
  Solvency ratios 163
  Used in forecasting 184
Reserve
  Key term 244
Retained earnings
  Definition 93
Retention
  Discussion 127
  Examples 129
  Key term 133
  Same as flow thru
Retirement accounts
  Company 401K 274
  Company contributions 274
Retirement planning
  Planning for 275
Revenue
  Beginning of financial performance 15

Calculating room revenue 16

Calculating restaurant revenue 16

Discussion 15–16

Key term 25

Variation analysis 164

Revenue management systems

Definition 143

Revenue center

Discussion 69

Examples 21

Key term 88

REVPAR

Characteristics 137

Definition 15, 136

Examples 137

Formula 16, 18, 25, 136

Importance of 138

Key term 25, 151, 171

To measure room revenue performance 18

Uses 139

Rich Dad, Poor Dad

Six lessons for financial freedom 272

Room rate structure

Example 19

Rooms sold

Room revenue analysis 164

S

Sales

See revenue

Secondary competition

Key term 171

Securities and Exchange Commission (SEC)

Discussion 251

Key term 264

Selling strategy

Committee 147

Definition 147

Discussion 147

Examples 147

Key term 151

Yield Management 144

Solvency ratios

Definition 163

Examples 163

Source and Use of Funds Statement

As part of Statement of Cash Flows

Definition 13

Discussion 105

Key term 109, 151

Special corporate rate

Definition 142

STAR Market Report

Discussion 167

Example 168

Key term 171

Staff department

Definition 50

Key term 66

Statement of Cash Flows

Characteristics 13, 101

Definition 13, 101

Discussion 101

Key term 25, 109

T

Taxes payable

Definition 92

Titles

Key term 88

P&L Statement 75

Total department profit

Key term 88

Transient market segment

Examples 19

Trends

And variation analysis 160

Company and industry 40

Discussion 39

General economic 40

Key term 42

Revenue, expense and profits 40

Short and long term 39

V

Variable
  Definition 161
  Examples 162
Variable expense
  Definition 128
  Example 129
  Key term 133, 186
  Wages as a variable expense 179
Variation
  Definition 128
  Key term 133
Variation analysis
  Discussion 159, 161
  Examples of room revenue variation 165
  Expense variation analysis 166
  Formulas 162
  Profit variation analysis 165
  Ratios 162
  Using Foundations of Financial Analysis 159
Vertical headings
  Discussion 77
  Key term 88
Volume
  Definition 15
  Key term 186
  Occupancy percentage discussion 164
  The key to forecasting 182

W

Wage cost percentage
  Discussion 124
  Formula 124

Wages payable
  Definition 92
Wage scheduling
  Discussion 222
  Examples 224
  Problem sets 227
Weekly management reports
  Discussion 125
Working capital
  Daily operations 12
  Definition 91
  Discussion 96
  Examples 104
  Formula 25
  Key term 25
  Liquiditity measures 104
  Managing 99
  Trends 104

Y

Yield Management
  Critiques 149
  Definition 136
  Discussion 143
  Examples 143
  Key term 151
  Selling strategy 144
  Using 145